The Development of Southern Public Libraries and the African American Quest for Library Access, 1898–1963

New Studies in Southern History

Series Editor: John David Smith, The University of North Carolina at Charlotte

Race and Masculinity in Southern Memory: History of Richmond, Virginia's Monument Avenue, 1948–1996
By Matthew Mace Barbee
Racial Cleansing in Arkansas, 1883–1924: Politics, Land, Labor, and Criminality
By Guy Lancaster
George Galphin and the Transformation of the George-South Carolina Backcountry
By Michael P. Morris
Race, Gender, and Film Censorship in Virginia, 1922–1965
By Melissa Ooten
Leisure, Plantations, and the Making of a New South: The Sporting Plantations of the South Carolina Lowcountry and Red Hills Region, 1900–1940
Edited by Julia Brock and Daniel Vivian
The Federal Theatre Project in the American South: The Carolina Playmakers and the Quest for American Drama
By Cecelia Moore
The Development of Southern Public Libraries and the African American Quest for Library Access, 1898–1963
By Dallas Hanbury

The Development of Southern Public Libraries and the African American Quest for Library Access, 1898–1963

Dallas Hanbury

LEXINGTON BOOKS
Lanham • Boulder • New York • London

Published by Lexington Books
An imprint of The Rowman & Littlefield Publishing Group, Inc.
4501 Forbes Boulevard, Suite 200, Lanham, Maryland 20706
www.rowman.com

6 Tinworth Street, London SE11 5AL, United Kingdom

Copyright © 2020 The Rowman & Littlefield Publishing Group, Inc.

All rights reserved. No part of this book may be reproduced in any form or by any electronic or mechanical means, including information storage and retrieval systems, without written permission from the publisher, except by a reviewer who may quote passages in a review.

British Library Cataloguing in Publication Information Available

Library of Congress Cataloging-in-Publication Data Available

Library of Congress Control Number: 2019952985
ISBN: 978-1-4985-8628-3 (cloth)
ISBN: 978-1-4985-8629-0 (electronic)

Contents

Acknowledgments — vii

Introduction — ix

1 Reconstruction, Redemption, and Rebirth: Southern Public Library Development during the New South Era — 1

2 A New Vision, a New South: Southern Public Library Development, 1890–1950 — 15

3 "Library Users Are Seekers of Knowledge": Developing African American Library Service and Educating Black Librarians — 37

4 "It Is Simply Out of the Question to Eliminate the Colorline": The Development of Black Library Service in Atlanta and the Integration of the Atlanta Public Library — 55

5 "The Library Cannot Be Opened Indiscriminately to White People and Negroes": Nashville and the Quest for Integrated Library Service — 87

6 "This We Believe": Local Black Activism, the National Civil Rights Movement, and the Integration of the Birmingham Public Library — 113

Conclusion — 137

Bibliography — 145

Index — 155

About the Author — 165

Acknowledgments

I owe a debt of gratitude to the many people that supported me while I wrote this book. First and foremost, I must thank the faculty members at Middle Tennessee State University that served on my dissertation committee, including its chair, Dr. Rebecca Conard. She carefully and patiently guided me through the steps necessary to complete the dissertation form of this book. In particular, she taught me to look beyond the obvious and dig deeper when examining sources and narratives. This book is much stronger for that. The other members of my committee, Dr. Kelly Kolar, Dr. Elizabeth Dow, and Dr. James Beeby, all spent hours reading and commenting on this text, subsequently providing suggestions and advice that greatly enriched the story I tell in the following pages. I thank them for their many contributions.

I must also thank the archivists and librarians who helped me find sources, suggested collections I had not thought of, and made the research process of this book highly enjoyable. In particular, I extend thanks to the Nashville Metro Archives staff, including its director Ken Feith and archivist Sarah Arntz, for helping me locate and access records created by and about the Nashville Public Library. These records provided much of the material for the Nashville Public Library (NPL) case study. The NPL Special Collections division also played a substantial role in the creation of this book. In particular, NPL Special Collections staff member Megan Adovasio-Jones suggested a master's thesis that wonderfully documented the events leading up to the NPL's integration and the integration itself. I must also thank staff at the Nashville-Davidson County Metropolitan government for allowing me to peruse record book upon record book of city ordinances.

I am also grateful for the assistance provided by Atlanta Public Library (APL) Special Collections staff member John Wright and director Kelly Cornwall. Both helped me work through the APL Special Collections' impressive array of records. They also suggested materials located at other institutions as I researched the APL case study. Staff at the Atlanta History Center and the Robert Woodruff Library, located at the Atlanta University Center, also provided their time and expertise by helping me locate various sources and collections that provided additional insight as I wrote the APL chapter.

While researching the Birmingham Public Library (BPL) case study, Jim Baggett, and the staff at the Birmingham Public Library Department of Archives and Manuscripts, provided an immense amount of help. They suggested collection after collection to research, as well as made available to me their own deep knowledge about the history of the BPL. Furthermore, Jim Baggett's impressive understanding of the history of Birmingham also enriched this book.

A Bart McCash Memorial Scholarship awarded by the Middle Tennessee State University (MTSU) History Department Scholarship Committee in spring 2015 made possible much of this book's research. I remain very grateful for the department's financial support.

Finally, I must thank my wife. While writing a book has its rewards, it also involves sacrifice, not so much on the part of the author, but by the family and friends of the author. I cannot thank my wife enough for her patience and love. She made the completion of this book possible.

Introduction

Largely absent from the southern physical landscape until after the Civil War, public libraries in the South first appeared on a meaningful scale during the New South and Progressive Eras. Southern leaders tasked public libraries with many jobs, among them, demonstrating that the New South economic development agenda worked. Southern society also assigned public libraries the job of observing the rules of and institutionalizing segregation. Although playing a significant role in making de jure segregation a way of life in the South until at least the 1960s, southern public libraries never practiced total segregation.

That southern public libraries practiced segregation speaks to the inherent conflict of southern progressivism. As William Link argues in *The Paradox of Southern Progressivism, 1880–1930*, progressives acquiesced to the exclusion of African Americans from Progressive Era reform efforts in the South to increase their chances of realizing their goals. In fact, some southern progressives even advocated for racial segregation, believing that doing so would reduce political corruption. The exclusionary nature of southern progressivism tremendously influenced early southern public library development, as this project's three case studies show. However, this book also demonstrates that southern librarians did not fully commit to segregation. Southern public librarians held diverse opinions regarding segregation, to the point that some served African Americans to varying degrees, even as southern public libraries officially remained segregated. Other southern public librarians actively worked to bring about the demise of racial segregation in the public library systems they worked for.

Within the context of specific cities, a number of scholars have analyzed the development of southern public libraries, how they dealt with issues of race, when and how their integrations occurred, as well as examined the institutional effects of having practiced segregation. In this regard Cheryl Knott's work on Houston comes to mind. Others have examined the history of southern public libraries at the state level, including Patterson Toby Graham in *A Right to Read: Segregation and Civil Rights in Alabama's Public Libraries, 1900–1965*. Still other researchers have taken a broad regional approach, including Mary Edna Anders with her classic "The Development of Public Library Service in the Southeastern States, 1895–1920." Most recently Wayne and Shirley Wiegand, in *The Desegregation of Public Libraries in the Jim Crow South: Civil Rights and Local Activism*, have also studied southern public libraries and their integrations at a regional level.

Other scholarship, notably that produced by Wayne and Shirley Wiegand, brings to the fore an issue that, although slightly outside of the scope of this work, emerges when studying southern public libraries and accordingly deserves mention here. Research indicates that the integration of public libraries in urban and rural communities in the South occurred at different speeds, levels of publicity, and incidents of physical conflict. A number of factors likely played a role in the divergence between the integration of public libraries in the South's urban and rural areas. In their book *The Desegregation of Public Libraries in the Jim Crow South*, the Wiegands convincingly demonstrate that the integration of public libraries in rural areas and small communities of the South could and often became protracted, sometimes violent, affairs. As this book shows, at least in the case of the public libraries of Atlanta, Birmingham, and Nashville, the integration of public libraries in the South's large, urban areas often occurred quicker, more quietly, and less violent than in small and rural southern towns. Seemingly few scholars, if any, though, have examined the topic of the development and integration of southern public libraries in a New South, comparative context. Accordingly, this book does so by studying the intersection of public libraries and race in Atlanta, Birmingham, and Nashville.

Within its New South, comparative context, this book shows that because of the social mission of libraries, and the individuality of southern public librarians, activists saw libraries as softer targets for desegregation efforts than other public institutions. This project also demonstrates that while Andrew Carnegie's philanthropy established public libraries across the South, his policy of deferring to local custom on racial matters institutionalized segregation in southern public libraries and contributed to the entrenchment of race-based segregation in the South. However, it also reveals that other philanthropic organizations, particularly the Rosenwald Fund, played a role in creating a context in which southern public library integration might occur. Among its many endeavors, the Rosenwald Fund studied the ability of countywide library systems to effectively serve library users by funding the temporary establishment of county library systems in eleven southern counties. To receive the Rosenwald Fund county library system study funds, participating counties had to agree to equally serve whites and blacks.

As it works to discover where public libraries fit in the South's complex race relations of the early and mid-twentieth century, this study also investigates how efforts to integrate southern public libraries challenges the traditional time frame of the civil rights movement, ca. 1954–1968. It does so in multiple ways, but especially by examining black efforts to obtain library access, expand library services to African Americans, and how attempts to integrate southern public libraries began well before the traditional timeframe of the civil rights movement. Indeed, the first sit-in at a southern public library took place in 1939 at the Alexandria, Virginia, Public Library. Some southern public libraries, including the Nashville Public Library, integrated before 1954.[1]

A growing number of historians, among them Jacquelyn Dowd Hall, have challenged the traditional timeframe of the civil rights movement. Hall argues that the beginning of the movement lay in 1930s alliances between unionists and civil rights advocates.[2] However, some historians have pushed back against the long movement thesis. Sundiata Keita Cha-Jua and Clarence Lang argue that the long movement thesis has many draw-backs, including erasing temporal and spatial demarcations in the overall African American struggle for equality. They argue that while the civil rights movement did not begin in the 1930s its roots originated there. Furthermore, Cha-Jua and Lang contend that the civil rights movement, and for that matter, the Black Power Movement, constituted waves in a history of continuous struggle against racial oppression.[3] The history of African Americans' efforts to achieve access to southern public libraries and their services contributes to the growing body of scholarship indicating that the once widely accepted timeframe of the civil rights movement requires at the very least continued scrutiny and perhaps even revision.

Hall, Cha-Jua, and Lang's stances on the timeframe of the civil rights movement point to the fact that historians continue to develop an increasingly complicated narrative that considers more than ever the fact that many localized movements made up the national movement. The efforts to integrate the Atlanta Public Library (APL), Birmingham Public Library (BPL), and Nashville Public Library (NPL) demonstrate the often intensely local nature of the black freedom movement. How activists in all three cities approached advocating for library integration, while reflecting the fact that advocates knew the national context in which they operated, shows the degree to which specific community frameworks ultimately influenced local efforts at library integration. For example, in Nashville and Houston, activists at one point used a classism approach to lobby for library integration. An activist in Nashville argued that because only the "educated class of Negroes" would use the library anyway, the city should integrate the institution.[4] While perhaps jarring to more contemporary sensibilities, such an approach sometimes resonated with whites. For example, in Houston, in 1953, Mayor Roy M. Hofheinz suggested that the Houston Public Library integrate because he felt "only serious and courteous" African Americans would use the library.[5]

When activists worked to integrate the public library in their communities also influenced what approaches they would use. Cheryl Knott argues that library integration occurred in two phases. Knott describes the first phase of library integration as the "quiet phase," during which public libraries integrated in a low-key manner. During the quiet phase, even as some libraries integrated, communities continued to construct segregated branch libraries. In Birmingham, Alabama, even after the US Supreme Court's 1954 ruling in *Brown v. Board of Education* that the policy of separate but equal violated the equal protection clause of the Fourteenth Amendment, the BPL did not integrate and constructed additional black branch libraries. The BPL's actions took place squarely in the first phase of library integration.

Knott describes the second phase of library integration as one in which whites often furiously protested library desegregation. In the case of Atlanta and Birmingham, efforts to integrate both cities' library systems met some white resistance. However, in other southern communities, particularly ones smaller than Atlanta, Birmingham, and Nashville, black efforts to integrate public libraries met intense, and sometimes violent, white resistance.[6]

Who attempted to integrate southern public libraries, as well as what the desegregation of those institutions accomplished, also deserves special consideration. At least in the three southern public libraries that this book focuses on, many activists who worked to end segregation came out of the university system. Students and faculty members played key roles in desegregation efforts, particularly in various forms of direct-action protest, an approach, Wayne and Shirley Wiegand argue, that constitutes a defining characteristic of efforts to integrate southern public libraries. Middle class and elite professional African Americans outside of the universities also made vital contributions to ending segregation policies.[7]

Once southern libraries began to integrate, activists used those victories as wedges to pursue integration in other communities. Although discussed in black freedom movement scholarship, the fight to integrate southern public libraries deserves a more central place in the literature. Activists attempting to integrate them clearly recognized that denial to libraries meant denial to information, a necessity in a democratic society. The association between libraries, information, and democracy constitutes a theme that other library scholars have referenced.

In "The Publication and Reception of the Southern Negro and the Public Library," Cheryl Knott repeatedly highlights the connection between democracy, full citizenship, and access to information. In particular, Knott argues that Eliza Atkins Gleason's book *The Southern Negro and the Public Library*, among its many contributions to the discussion regarding the provision of public library service to African Americans, is important because it advocated that public libraries actually live up to the democratic ideal of their supposedly egalitarian purpose. By practicing racial exclusion, public libraries made a mockery of their core mission.[8]

As part of telling the story of the development of southern public libraries, the battle to integrate them, and how those libraries tried to move forward after integrating, this book also traces the changing roles of black and white women in southern society. During the New South and Progressive Eras, women increasingly entered the public sphere, many by launching and taking part in the reform efforts of the time. Women's organizations proved crucial to women entering the public sphere and engaging in library work. In *Southern Ladies, New Women: Race, Region, and Clubwomen in South Carolina, 1890–1930*, Joan Marie Johnson argues that white and African American women took part in women's clubs' activities for various reasons. In addition to their work on behalf of assorted progressive causes, Johnson contends that some southern white women also took part in women's clubs to create and proselytize a particular version of southern history, one in which the Lost Cause prominently featured, and to form and refine an identity related to that interpretation of southern history. Southern black women, on the other hand, engaged in club work as a form of survival. African American women's clubs worked to address numerous issues in the black community, including poverty, lack of education, a dearth of recognition of the humanity of black people, and more. As Johnson clearly explains, "Black and white clubwomen often did similar work for different reasons."[9]

Ultimately, both black and white women's organizations played key roles in fostering the development of public libraries and cultivating a taste for reading. As this book shows, women's organizations often served as the entities in a community that advocated for funds to construct libraries, staffed and managed libraries, and acted as their continued advocates. Because the Progressive Era saw women as protectors and nurturers, society tasked them with safeguarding and uplifting the country's morals. Libraries acted as a vehicle by which to accomplish this task. However, women, white and black, did not passively wait for others to act on them. Women actively used libraries as a conduit to further the agendas and agency they displayed in their club work and related endeavors.

The fact that women exerted significant control over public library development becomes unsurprising when examining their participation in women's clubs. These clubs, as Karen J. Blair points out, acted as incubators for ideas and strategies that women could use to carve out a place in the public sphere. The ability of women to expand the definition of womanhood proved key to gaining and expanding a place in public life. Because society had charged women with serving as the moral compass for her family, and deemed her as nurturing, women *had* to step into the public sphere and "supervise the moral standards of her community." Public library work provided the avenue to do so.[10]

White women flocked to librarianship to begin careers, take part in various progressive reform initiatives, and redefine as well as expand their place in the public sphere. African American women also saw librarianship as a viable career option but were initially hindered by the lack of available jobs for black librarians and few avenues to obtain the education to become a librarian.

As the twentieth century progressed, library schools for African Americans opened and southern public library systems constructed more branch libraries intended for black use. Ironically, as Cheryl Knott points out, the establishment of black library branches as the result of segregation provided African American women with opportunities to work as librarians. Given their education and employment, black female librarians constituted a part of the African American elite in their communities. Among their many tasks, African American female librarians particularly focused on nurturing the self-worth of African American children. Cheryl Knott argues that because so few, if any, positive depictions of African Americans existed in children's books in the early twentieth century, black female librarians diligently worked to use the literature available to them to craft a positive context in which African American children could engage with printed material.[11] Francesca Morgan suggests another reason as to why black female librarians directed so much attention toward black children. Morgan points outs that African American women heavily focused on black children because creating a feeling of positive self-worth in African American youth constituted a form of racial uplift.[12]

The lack of positive depictions of African Americans in children and youth literature caused black female librarians to not only try to create a constructive context for young black people in which to consume reading material, but also caused some African American librarians, like Chicago librarian Charlamae Hill Rollins, to establish reading lists of works that depicted African Americans in a good light. Rollins constructed such a list, titled *We Build Together*. Rollins also constantly demanded that presses publish works with positive depictions of African Americans.

In addition to their efforts to build the self-worth of African American children, black female librarians, including Annie L. McPheeters in Atlanta, worked to fully utilize their library educations and training to become immersed in all facets of the library profession, as well to serve their publics as thoroughly as possible within the constraints set forth by segregation. In the case of McPheeters, among her many efforts, she worked with a number of entities, including the Julius Rosenwald Fund, the American Library Association, and the Adult Education Project, sponsored by the American Association of Adult Education, to build collections, increase African American library use, and to forge a growing bond between public libraries and African Americans. In other words, African American librarians served their communities in numerous ways.[13]

In terms of their professional actions, southern white female public librarians clearly pushed gender boundaries. However, when it came to challenging racial barriers, white women librarians had a mixed record. The careers of Anne Wallace and Tommie Dora Barker of the Carnegie Library of Atlanta, Lila May Chapman of the Carnegie Library of Nashville, and others, illustrate this point. Some pushed, to varying degrees, to improve library service to African Americans, but then retreated either when they or their boards deemed their efforts, or black attempts to secure increased library service for African Americans, too far, too much, or too fast. Only in the 1950s and early 1960s did significant breaks appear in southern librarians' acquiescence to library segregation. However, once some southern white public librarians voiced their doubts about segregation's efficacy, increasing numbers of their colleagues also expressed misgivings.

Cheryl Knott contends that the literature focusing on library history has too often cast white female librarians as heroic figures for working to provide African Americans with library service. Knott argues that by focusing too much of their attention on white female librarians, scholars have obscured African American efforts to tear down library segregation. While African American agency constituted the greatest factor in doing away with library segregation, some white women's attempts to provide even highly limited library service to blacks during segregation, particularly during the earliest part of the twentieth century, still constituted radical efforts. Although in no way do the efforts of white women to provide library access to blacks during segregation justify the widespread exclusion of African Americans from public libraries until the mid-twentieth century, and although their efforts often fell far short of approaching equal, unbiased library access, the fact that even a small number of white female librarians tried to provide library service to African Americans at all during the height of the Jim Crow Era is remarkable.[14]

Structured into three case studies focusing on the APL, BPL, and NPL, this study documents the founding, early development, provision of library service to African Americans during segregation, and integration of these institutions. It also addresses how these libraries responded to various foreseen and unforeseen consequences of having practiced segregation. These case studies show how major southern public libraries helped institutionalize segregation, and then later played a role in opening the door to desegregate other public institutions in the South.

The APL, BPL, and NPL were selected as case studies because they represent prominent public institutions in cities that were at the forefront of the civil rights movement. Although sit-ins first occurred in Greensboro, North Carolina, Nashville, students—high school and college—made this protest tactic a staple of the movement. Furthermore, Nashville activists such as Diane Nash and John Lewis helped to coordinate and launch the 1961 Freedom Rides and later form the Student Nonviolent Coordinating Committee (SNCC). Atlanta, home of Martin Luther King Jr., the Southern Christian Leadership Conference (SCLC), and SNCC, also played a prominent and visible role in the civil rights movement. Of all these cities though, Birmingham may loom the largest in the public's collective conscience. From the infamous Bull Conner, vivid scenes of police dogs biting, and fire hoses spraying children and young adult marchers, to the Sixteenth Street Baptist Church bombing, Birmingham for many serves as the image of the civil rights movement.

By studying the history of racial exclusion at the APL, BPL, and NPL, and the path by which each system integrated, this book will contribute to the discussion of how public cultural institutions come to grips with difficult aspects of their past. It demonstrates that southern public libraries represented yet another battleground of the civil rights movement, thereby further illuminating the entrenched tenacity of race-based segregation in the South. Furthermore, this project adds to the discourse of change in public cultural institutions, an important component of public historical studies.

This book begins in the late nineteenth century, when public libraries first appeared in the South on a wide scale and ends in the mid-twentieth century after most southern public libraries had integrated. Chapter 1 focuses on three time periods in the South's history: Reconstruction, the New South Era, and the Progressive Era. These contexts established the environment in which southern communities first constructed and operated public libraries. Understanding that these eras significantly shaped the climate in which most southern public libraries first existed and operated aids in comprehending their policies for serving, or not, African Americans.

Chapter 2 broadly discusses southern public library development from its beginnings in the late 1800s to the desegregation of southern public libraries in the 1950s and 1960s. It points out that while many southern cities and towns used the establishment of public libraries to prove they had economically recovered from the Civil War and were prospering, several actually relied on outside aid to build and open their library, particularly the money of Andrew Carnegie. Carnegie looms large in southern public library development, especially in Atlanta and Nashville, both of which received sizeable Carnegie library construction grants.

George S. Bobinski's *Carnegie Libraries: Their History and Impact on American Public Library Development* represents one of the earliest, if not the first, comprehensive treatment of Andrew Carnegie's library construction grant program and remains central to understanding Carnegie's library giving. Bobinsky's thesis that Andrew Carnegie, and later, the Carnegie Corporation of New York (CCNY), played a large and direct role in shaping southern public library development holds particularly true in the case of Atlanta and Nashville. However, other philanthropic entities and their aid remained crucially important to southern public library development from the late nineteenth century until well into the first half of the twentieth century. Chapter 2 argues that philanthropic organizations funding the construction of public libraries did so out of a desire to provide the public with a readily available source of education and personal uplift. Born of a belief that education could help alleviate some of the societal angst caused by massive immigration to the United States and the rapid industrialization of the American economy, many progressives also saw public libraries as social control mechanisms.

Chapter 2 also examines the role that government agencies played in southern public library development. Entities like the Tennessee Valley Authority (TVA) and Works Progress Administration (WPA) significantly influenced southern public library development by contributing library training and money to construct new, or rehabilitate existing, public libraries. WPA-funded workers provided libraries with a host of services ranging from additional staff members to working on a variety of library-related projects like book repair and cataloging. Furthermore, chapter 2 addresses a theme shared by the three case studies: the central role that women played in the early development and management of southern public libraries. During the Progressive Era, society came to regard librarianship as acceptable women's work. However, even before women enrolled in library schools and became librarians, they supported public library development through a variety of ways, particularly via women's clubs.

Chapter 3 explores the development of library education and service for African Americans in the South. It contends that philanthropic organizations, such as the General Education Board (GEB), the Board of Education for Librarianship (BEL), the Rosenwald Fund, and the CCNY, played a crucial role in developing black libraries and library education. It also argues that southern public libraries desegregated faster than other public institutions and places in the South for at least seven reasons. First, activists targeted southern public libraries for integration attempts. However, these activists and their organizations had other higher-priority desegregation targets, as well as goals, to accomplish. Second, some southern leaders and librarians saw integrating libraries as less-threatening than desegregating schools or public transportation. Third, the Supreme Court's ruling in *Brown v. Board of Education* ruled the concept of separate but equal unconstitutional, striking down the legal concept at the heart of segregation in the South. Fourth, the American Library Association (ALA) attacked segregation in the library profession in a variety of ways during the mid-twentieth century. Fifth, lower federal courts ruled in favor of those attempting to integrate southern public libraries. Sixth, some southern public librarians supported library integration for personal economic reasons. If cities closed their public library systems to prevent integration, that meant librarians were not working, and accordingly not earning money. A principled stand against library integration could cause economic hardship for library staff. Seventh, peer pressure likely factored into southern public librarians either supporting library integration, or at least doubting the efficacy of keeping southern public libraries segregated.

Chapter 4, the first case study, focuses on the Atlanta Public Library. It explores the APL's founding, development, provision of library service to African Americans, integration, the aftereffects of having practiced segregation, and how it attempted to deal with them. The APL begins this book's three case studies because multiple southern public library "firsts" occurred within the system. For instance, it received the first Carnegie library construction grant in the southeast and created the first library school for whites in the South. Accordingly, its librarians and library school graduates helped open, organize, and staff libraries across the region. It served as a model of public library operation during the earliest years of southern public library development. However, when it came to matters of race, the APL, originally known as the Carnegie Library of Atlanta (CLA), had a mixed record. James V. Carmichael's "Tommie Dora Barker and Southern Librarianship" does an especially good job of documenting the CLA's uneven approach to issues of race. Carmichael effectively demonstrates that during its early years the CLA often oscillated between working to expand library service for blacks and then reversing course.

The APL also serves as a good example of how activists used New South city leaders' emphasis on sustained economic development to integrate public libraries. Chapter 4 contends that Atlanta leaders' nearly obsessive focus on maintaining the city's reputation as an economic powerhouse played a key role in the desegregation of the city's library. Recognizing that a political coalition of white business elites and upper-class African Americans ran Atlanta politics from the late 1940s until at least the late 1960s is crucial to understanding the emphasis placed on economic vitality in Atlanta and how activists used that to their advantage. In particular, Kevin Kruse's *White Flight: Atlanta and the Making of Modern Conservatism* aptly describes the context in which Atlanta's mixed-race political coalition developed and worked, as well as the framework in which activists integrated the APL.

Chapter 5, the Nashville Public Library case study, shows that unlike Atlanta, activists in the upper-South city of Nashville exclusively used behind-the-scenes lobbying to fight for the integration of the public library.

Like Atlanta however, Nashville's leaders also had a desire to preserve the city's image. Although characterized by many as a New South city, Nashville could not match Atlanta's economic magnitude. Accordingly, it carved out a niche as a center of higher education. As such, city leaders likely did not want headlines screaming that the library prevented one group of people from using its facilities while allowing others access. Among the three case studies, the character of Nashville's race relations was the hardest to discern. Accordingly, Benjamin Houston's *The Nashville Way: Racial Etiquette and the Struggle for Social Justice in a Southern City* proved an essential building block for writing the NPL case study. Houston argues that white elite Nashvillians had long prided themselves on Nashville's "moderate" race relations. In studying the NPL's integration, it became clear that activists used the tenets of moderate racial relations to their advantage. Of all the public libraries discussed in this study, the NPL integrated the earliest when it desegregated in 1950. Its early desegregation had a profound impact on the way some Nashville African Americans thought about the library. Children's author Patricia McKissack noted that for her, as a child, the library acted as a refuge where she could find a respite from segregation.

Chapter 6, the case study of the Birmingham Public Library, follows a story different from that of the APL and BPL. A highly segregated, industrial New South city, Birmingham found itself the target of a civil rights movement campaign in 1963. As Martin Luther King Jr., Fred Shuttlesworth, Andrew Young, Wyatt Walker, and James Bevel, among others, campaigned in the city during April and May 1963, the BPL's segregation practices came under fire. For two days in early April 1963, students from Birmingham's Miles College sat-in at the library. Hoping to avoid the type of media attention the rest of the 1963 campaign received, the BPL integrated.

Ultimately, this book demonstrates that New South cities, and their public libraries, struggled with the weight of segregation. Southern public libraries could not truly become public institutions until they integrated, as well as confronted and attempted to come to terms with their segregated pasts. Segregation-influenced ideas of who southern public libraries should serve, and how, checked the growth of southern public libraries and harmed their institutional health. As this book shows, African Americans living in the South had their own ideas regarding the audiences, services, and community roles of public libraries. Their vision for southern public libraries did not include segregation. The clashing of different agendas and viewpoints regarding the public library systems of large southern cities, as studied through an examination of the histories of the APL, BPL, and NPL, demonstrates that both whites and blacks greatly valued public libraries, recognized the power they possessed, and indicated that they would remain contested spaces at the very least until seekers of knowledge were no longer excluded from them.

NOTES

1. Brenda Mitchell-Powell, "A Seat at the Reading Table: The 1939 Alexandria, Virginia, Public Library Sit-in Demonstration—A Study in Library History, 1937–1941" (PhD diss., Simmons College, 2015), 244–50.
2. Jacquelyn Dowd Hall, "The Long Civil Rights Movement and the Political Uses of the Past," *Journal of American History* 91, no. 4 (March 2005): 1245.
3. Sundiata Keita Cha-Jua and Clarence Lang, "The 'Long Movement' as Vampire: Temporal and Spatial Fallacies in Recent Black Freedom Studies," *Journal of African American History* 92, no. 2 (Spring 2007): 265, 267, 270.
4. Robert S. Alvarez, *Library Log: The Diary of a Public Library Director* (Foster City, CA: Administrator's Digest Press, 1991), 282.
5. Cheryl Knott Malone, "Unannounced and Unexpected: The Desegregation of the Houston Public Library in the Early 1950s," *Library Trends* 55, no. 3 (Winter 2007): 670–71.
6. Cheryl Knott, *Not Free, Not for All: Public Libraries in the Age of Jim Crow* (Amherst: University of Massachusetts Press, 2015), viii.
7. Wayne A. Wiegand and Shirley A. Wiegand, *The Desegregation of Public Libraries in the Jim Crow South: Civil Rights and Local Activism* (Baton Rouge: Louisiana State University Press, 2018), 13.
8. Cheryl Knott, "The Publication and Reception of *The Southern Negro and the Public Library*," in *Race, Ethnicity and Publishing in America*, ed. Cécile Cottenet (New York: Palgrave Macmillan, 2014), 73.
9. Joan Marie Johnson, *Southern Ladies, New Women: Race, Region, and Clubwomen in South Carolina, 1890–1930* (Gainesville, FL: The University Press of Florida, 2004), 4.
10. Karen J. Blair, *The Clubwoman as Feminist: True Womanhood Redefined, 1868–1914* (New York: Holmes & Meier Publishers Inc., 1980), 4, 7, 117.
11. Cheryl Knott Malone, "Quiet Pioneers: Black Women Public Librarians in the Segregated South," *Vitae Scholasticae* 19, no. 1 (2000): 59–60; Cheryl Knott Malone, "Books for Black Children: Public Library Collections in Louisville and Nashville, 1915–1925," *Library Quarterly: Information, Community, Policy* 70, no. 2 (April 2000): 193–94.
12. Francesca Morgan, *Women and Patriotism in Jim Crow America* (Chapel Hill: The University of North Carolina Press, 2005), 81–82.
13. Stephanie J. Shaw, *What a Woman Ought to Be and to Do: Black Professional Women Workers during the Jim Crow Era* (Chicago: The University of Chicago Press, 1996), 204, 206; Kerrie C. Williams, "Annie L. McPheeters (1908–1994)," *New Georgia Encyclopedia*, July 23, 2018, accessed February 3, 2019, https://www.georgiaencyclopedia.org/articles/education/annie-l-mcpheeters-1908-1994.
14. Malone, "Quiet Pioneers: Black Women Public Librarians in the Segregated South," 61.

Chapter 1

Reconstruction, Redemption, and Rebirth

Southern Public Library Development during the New South Era

When southern cities began soliciting library construction grants from Andrew Carnegie in the nineteenth century, the South had experienced significant social, political, and economic turmoil for three decades. Following the Confederacy's defeat in 1865, the South went through three phases of rebuilding—Reconstruction, the New South Era, and the Progressive Era— each of which had tremendous impacts on southern politics, society, and the region's economy.

During Reconstruction, 1863–1877, the eleven former states that made up the Confederacy fulfilled numerous conditions for readmission into the Union. The Executive Office first controlled Reconstruction as presidents Abraham Lincoln and Andrew Johnson crafted the program Confederate states had to follow to return the Union. In 1866 Congress took over. During Congressional Reconstruction, 1866 to 1877, moderate and radical northern Republicans tried to accomplish many goals. Accordingly, Congressional Reconstruction sometimes was erratic, haphazard, and reactionary as the Republican Party's two wings tried to fulfill competing goals. Nonetheless, during Reconstruction, African Americans gained the franchise and could participate in southern political life. Furthermore, various Reconstruction policies disfranchised elite white Confederates and Confederate sympathizers, and new political parties and alliances emerged.

After Republican Rutherford B. Hayes won the 1877 presidential election and ended Reconstruction, elite southern whites set out to recapture the social, political, and economic power they lost during the Civil War and Reconstruction. In an effort to do so, they disfranchised African Americans and expelled them from southern politics. However, white elite southerners also wanted to achieve other objectives during the New South Era, 1877–1914, particularly growing and diversifying the South's economy. After the Civil War, southern elites found themselves confronted by a shattered, undiversified economy. To fully recover from the conflict and thoroughly participate in the nation's economy, they believed the South's economy had to expand, especially its small industrial sector. However, the New South Era did not just constitute an economic development program conceived by southern leaders; it also served as an attempt to clear away the stigma of defeat in the Civil War and the humiliation of Reconstruction. In Henry Grady, *Atlanta Constitution* part owner and editor from the mid-1870s through the 1880s, southern leaders found their spokesman. In fact, in 1874 and again in 1886, Grady used the term "New South" to describe the South's effort to grow and diversify its economy as well as articulate a new mindset about its place in the nation's economic, social, and political mainstream.[1]

During the height of the New South Era, southern cities built public libraries as a sort of capstone at the end of the long process of rebuilding and transforming the region's physical landscape, infrastructure, and economy. Libraries for many southern communities acted as trophies, evidence that the economic redevelopment program Henry Grady and other New South proponents constantly espoused could become more than words. However, by building public libraries, southern leaders did not replace an element of the South's physical landscape damaged during the Civil War; instead, they added an almost entirely new feature to it. Until the 1890s when the southern public library movement began, few libraries in the South, public or private, existed. In 1876, the US Office of Education reported that the South only had 29 libraries with at least 10,000 volumes.[2] Furthermore, the Office of Education reported the South had no public libraries in 1876, "with the exception of society libraries in Lexington and Louisville" Kentucky. Illustrating the private nature of southern libraries in the 1870s, Mary Edna Anders reported that private collections held 71 percent of all books in the South in 1870. Prior to the 1890s, subscription libraries represented the dominant library model in the South.[3]

During the New South Era, southern leaders built public libraries solely for whites. Until the beginning of the twentieth century, when public library service for blacks began to develop, African Americans had few options in terms of accessing libraries and reading materials. Using the libraries at black universities and colleges, such as Fisk University in Nashville (founded in 1865), Morehead and Spelman colleges in Atlanta (1867 and 1883), Virginia's Hampton Institute (1868), Howard University in Washington, D.C. (1867), or Tuskegee Institute in Alabama (1881), represented the primary way southern African Americans could obtain library access prior to the twentieth century.[4]

The New South Era overlapped the Progressive Era, a period that frames broader concerns associated with industrialization and capitalism, which assumed greater force in American society during the late nineteenth and early twentieth centuries. Middle-class whites became increasingly concerned about what they perceived as unbridled capitalism's numerous negative effects on the nation. Immigrants poured into Northeast and Midwest cities, like New York and Chicago, by the millions. The newcomers tested the capacity of cities to accommodate so many people, created housing shortages, and generated increased competition for low-level and menial jobs. In their quest for ever-expanding profits, corporations used child workers; produced unhealthy, contaminated, and dangerous products; and destroyed the environment. Northern and midwestern progressives wanted to end, or at least limit, child labor, as well as see the government regulate the nation's economy and curb the worst corporate excesses. Southern progressives' goals sometimes differed from those of their northern and midwestern counterparts. For instance, southern progressives wanted greater government intervention in the South's economy, not so much to regulate it, railroads as the exception, but to hasten its growth. Furthermore, southern progressives appeared to largely accept the institutionalization of de jure racism and the systematic disfranchisement of African Americans in the South during the Progressive Era. This enabled Jim Crow practices in the region to flourish. Some southern progressives believed disfranchising and removing African Americans from the political process, as well as lowering their general status in southern society, actually constituted a progressive action. These southern progressives believed that removing African Americans from meaningful positions in southern society, especially political, would reduce corruption and allow the South's white leaders to address other business.

William A. Link argues southern progressives had to work with local communities and make room for their various positions on certain topics, like race, to accomplish their goals. In the case of southern public libraries this especially holds true. Southern public librarians of a progressive bent, or otherwise, acquiesced to practices like segregation to garner support for the fledgling public libraries they worked for. To realize their objectives during the Progressive Era, which early on especially included institutional survival, southern public librarians exchanged their varying degrees of adherence to segregation for library support.[5]

The New South and Progressive eras directly and indirectly shaped the context in which southern cities asked for library building funds, constructed, and operated public libraries. Accordingly, examining each period in turn informs and sharpens the discussion and analysis of the founding, development, growth, and later, integration of public libraries in Atlanta, Nashville, and Birmingham. It also clarifies why southern communities and leaders tasked their public libraries with certain responsibilities and goals.

THE NEW SOUTH: ATLANTA, NASHVILLE, AND BIRMINGHAM

Born in Athens, Georgia, in 1850, Henry Grady became editor of Rome, Georgia's *Courier* in 1869.[6] He rose to fame when he outlined New South economic, political, and social goals, and then powerfully advocated for them. As the *Atlanta Constitution*'s editor from 1876 and part owner from 1880 to his death in 1889, Grady had a powerful platform from which to describe and push the New South agenda.[7] In 1874, Grady wrote an editorial for the *Atlanta Herald* titled "The New South." In it, he articulated the economic development plan he and other southern leaders had in mind to reintegrate the South's economy more fully into the nation's economy. In 1886 Grady delivered a speech at New York City's New England Society that captivated northerners and southerners alike. Unlike his 1874 editorial, which mostly outlined a program for southern economic development, Grady's 1886 speech strongly emphasized northern and southern reconciliation. In it, he emphasized the South's willingness to move beyond sectionalism to more fully merge into the country's social, political, and economic mainstream.[8]

Grady's position as the *Atlanta Constitution*'s editor provided him with a prominent soapbox from which to constantly extol the New South's general economic virtues and promises. However, it was Atlanta's fortuitous location as the terminus for eight railroads connecting the city to the coastal South's urban areas, the southern Black Belt, and manufacturing cities in the North and Midwest that provided it with the means to become the living embodiment of Grady's rhetoric and so many southern elites' desires.[9] James Michael Russell demonstrates that the number of railroads coming into and leaving Atlanta facilitated industrial growth, particularly textile manufacturing, by making it easy for the city's merchants to find new markets for the finished goods they produced, as well as enabling the South's agricultural producers to bring their products to market with much less frustration than ever before.[10] The *Atlanta Constitution* in 1886 boasted that Atlanta's economic dominance ranged two hundred miles out from the city. Similarly, the Atlanta Manufacturers' Association in 1889 argued that Atlanta's economic market extended from the Potomac River in Virginia to the Rio Grande in Texas. Russell also cites an August 31, 1890, *Atlanta Constitution* article noting Atlanta had taken in 270,000 bales of cotton up to that point that year. Although historians should subject both sources and their estimations of the size of Atlanta's market to close analysis, especially given the spirit of boosterism that pervaded the era, each showed that Atlanta's economic growth owed much to the many railroads leaving and entering the city.[11]

Historians can apply much of William Cronon's discussion regarding railroads' impact on Chicago's development to Atlanta. In *Nature's Metropolis*,

Cronon argues that rural areas in the Midwest suddenly found themselves sucked into Chicago's economic vortex. Rural areas, no matter how provincial they outwardly appeared, became economically tied to Chicago as railroads linked much of the Midwest to the city and vice versa. Chicago acted as a market for products produced in the countryside, and as a source from which much of the Midwest could purchase necessary and desired goods. The same occurred in relation to Atlanta. As more railroads entered and left the Gateway City, the more Atlanta and much of the rural South became closely tied. Although ports like Charleston, South Carolina, and Mobile, Alabama, continued to receive a share of the South's trade in cotton and other products, Atlanta steadily began to represent a growing market for the South's cash crops.[12]

Don Doyle advances a similar economic argument in asserting that Nashville also embodied the New South Era. Like Atlanta, Nashville experienced prolonged economic growth during the 1880s and 1890s, although not to the degree its neighbor to the east did. Doyle contended that the Union army's occupation of the city from 1862 until the summer of 1865 protected its infrastructure from destruction, and also prevented a population drain.[13] Furthermore, like Atlanta, but again not to the same extent, Nashville served as a railroad hub. However, Mary Ellen Pethel argues that Nashville's numerous higher education institutions played a greater role than economic expansion in developing Nashville into a New South city.[14] Northerners poured money into the city, helping to establish Vanderbilt University, George Peabody University (later absorbed by Vanderbilt University), Belmont & Ward Seminary (later Belmont University), Roger Williams University, Fisk University, Meharry Medical College, and David Lipscomb University, among others.[15]

W. David Lewis argues that Birmingham, founded in the 1870s, best expressed the nature of the New South. Like C. Vann Woodward in *Origins of the New South*, Lewis argues that in Birmingham's case, rural elites never lost their power after the Civil War. In fact, white elites decided to establish a city in central Alabama before the Civil War, and he contends that the conflict only delayed their plans. After the war, they reaped enormous profits when the Elyton Land Company, formed in 1870, sold land in Jones Valley, the area in central Alabama that would become Birmingham.[16] The Elyton Land Company consisted of landowners in Jefferson County (the location of Jones Valley) and members of a group of interrelated plantation owners known as the Broad River Group. Broad River planters moved to Georgia from Virginia in the 1780s, purchased land and moved into the Tennessee Valley in the 1810s, and then began moving to and buying land throughout Alabama's Black Belt region in the 1820s. According to Lewis, members of the Broad River Group were "affluent agricultural capitalists" who invested in everything from slaves and land to towns, railroads, banks, textile manufacturing plants, and more. Their economic development plan for what would become Birmingham initially centered on using slave labor to extract coal and iron ore from the rich deposits of both in central Alabama, and then refine it into various products at mills and foundries they would finance and build. Although the Civil War dashed their plans to use slave labor in the mines and mills that did spring up in Jones Valley, Birmingham elites found other ways to keep human resource costs low, including using convict-lease labor.[17]

Some historians have questioned whether they should attribute Atlanta's economic success to the machinations of the city's elites during the 1880s and 1890s, to Georgia's pre–Civil War power brokers' economic schemes for the city and region, or both. Whatever both groups' efforts to grow the city's economy, Atlanta's unparalleled railway connections were the primary economic growth driver during the New South Era. That fact aside, Russell argues that as Atlanta's postwar leaders sought ways to make Atlanta the South's premier city, they maintained connections and continuity with the city's pre–Civil War business class and their aims. In particular, Russell points to the collaboration that occurred between both groups to pass legislation regulating railroad construction and shipping rates in Georgia, which they believed would help ensure Atlanta's economic growth and place as the New South's leader for years to come.[18]

As the New South Era's exciting rhetoric and promises swept across the region, Russell contends that Old and New South business leaders sought and sometimes achieved agreement on their economic development plans.[19] However, cohesion did not always occur. Atlanta's elites eventually generated so much personal wealth that a rift opened between them and their rural counterparts. Atlanta's economic prosperity caused rural visitors to regard its conspicuous wealth and self-centeredness as different from much of the South.[20] However, William Cronon offers another perspective that helps explain why tension sometimes existed between Atlanta elites and the rural gentry. Cronon argues that as Chicago grew in regional dominance, partly due to the railroads radiating out from the city, it controlled more and more of the Midwest's economic activity. In turn, such a situation caused fear and resentment in the Midwest's nonurban areas because they had less and less control of their economic affairs. Like Chicago, Atlanta came to increasingly dominate and control the South's economy throughout the New South Era. Such a development likely caused rural southerners, including their leaders, to feel resentment toward Atlanta.[21] Still, businessmen across the region could not help but notice Atlanta's meteoric rise. Those able to reconcile their provincial and nostalgic feelings for the South's antebellum past with New South proponents' constant extolling of the virtues of a diversified economy began to emulate Atlanta business elites and Henry Grady's constant boosterism. They stood ready to explain how their communities fostered and embraced business, possessed the necessities required to take part in the

South's economic expansion, and had positioned themselves to capture business opportunities that came their way.[22]

However, Don Doyle contends that not all southern communities could or wanted to take part in the economic development plan characterizing the New South Era. Some cities like Nashville and Atlanta, through a combination of circumstances and agency, were better positioned to take advantage of New South proponents' emphasis on expanding and diversifying the southern economy. Doyle points to Mobile, Alabama, and Charleston, South Carolina, as examples of southern cities whose economic fortunes negatively changed during the New South Era as the result of circumstances outside of their control, as well as indifference to the economic development plan of the New South boosters.[23]

SOUTHERN EXPOSITIONS: FULFILLING THE NEW SOUTH VISION

Although New South boosterism took many forms, perhaps the most memorable involved the expositions that took place in Atlanta, Nashville, and other southern cities during the era. Southern economic elites and civic leaders viewed successful expositions as one way to fulfill the promises of the New South Era. However, Bruce G. Harvey argues that these festivals revealed just as much about the visions of their organizers as they did about the cities' potential to fulfill New South dreams.[24] For instance, Nashville viewed itself as a southern educational and cultural center due to its numerous universities and other higher educational institutions. City leaders went so far as to label Nashville the "Athens of the South."[25] Nashville partly used the 1897 Tennessee Centennial and International Exposition to promote and exhibit itself as a center of learning. Harvey writes, "Nashville's [civic leaders] wanted Americans to know that not all of the South, not even all southern businessmen, lusted after mammon."[26] Atlanta, on the other hand, used its 1895 Cotton States and International Exposition to proclaim its position as the New South's economic leader, and to advocate for a greater role in the national economy.[27]

Harvey contends that southern leaders desperately wanted the nation to take seriously their business acumen and the South's ability to participate in an industrial economy. This desire led southern leaders into a conundrum about how to address the South's stormy relationship with the North. Southerners especially wanted to minimize sectionalism. New South leaders employed a two-pronged strategy to accomplish reconciliation. They publicly admitted that the South once considered itself unlike the rest of the nation, had largely rejected industrialization, and embraced an agricultural economic system dependent upon slavery. While issuing that mea culpa, they also worked to convince northern industrialists and capitalists, those who could really make the New South's economic vision a reality if they chose to invest in the region, that southerners now considered themselves Americans first and southerners second. However, by extolling the New South's virtues, southern elites actually emphasized their region's distinctiveness. This in turn gives credence to Woodward's claim that using the term "New South" to describe the post-Reconstruction South actually made real the perception of the region as a separate and unique entity. However, Russell points out, specifically referring to Atlanta, that for all the city leaders' efforts to prove they could put aside sectional feelings and thereby attract northern capital, most financing raised for industrial ventures during the early years of the New South Era came from local sources.[28]

In contrast to Russell, Mary Edna Anders contends that even as the South experienced industrialization and diversified its economy, the growth did not necessarily occur in the ways southern elites wanted it to. Southern elites desired to become or remain major investors and business owners in the New South economy, but, instead, many found themselves managing northern-owned factories, banks, and other commercial interests.[29] According to Anders, while southern elites increased their wealth and welcomed to their ranks newcomers who made fortunes during the New South Era, they mostly held economic power at the local and regional level. Even then, northerners could check and exert control over the economic power southern elites did hold because they owned many companies the South's upper-crust worked for and managed.

Southern elites imbued expositions with more purposes than just convincing the country that the South could play a much more prominent role in the nation's economy. Southerners also used the festivals to assure southern whites that they remained superior to African Americans.[30] Although both the Atlanta and Nashville fairs contained African American exhibit halls displaying various black achievements, their inclusion was patronizing, not uplifting. The organizers of the fairs included African American exhibit halls and exhibits not to celebrate black success, but to demonstrate white southerners' ability to distance themselves from the past and their former attitudes toward African Americans.[31] The 1895 Atlanta and 1897 Nashville expositions did not express the true reality of race relations during the New South Era.

SOUTHERN PROGRESSIVISM, PHILANTHROPY, AND SOUTHERN PUBLIC LIBRARIES

Dewey W. Grantham argues that politics, race relations, and especially economic interests shaped the character and course of southern progressivism.

He points to the South's rapidly changing political climate in the 1880s and 1890s as a factor that influenced early southern progressivism. After the South emerged from Reconstruction, white elite southerners worked to reclaim the political control they held prior to the Civil War. However, they encountered new political parties like the Progressive Party, Virginia's Readjusters, and the Greenback-Labor Party. Furthermore, they also had to contend with the fact that African Americans could now vote and participate in the political process. As such, white southern elites often couched their various attempts to regain political power in progressive reformist language. For instance, southern elites argued that their attempts to disfranchise large segments of the South's population, including poor whites and African Americans, did not constitute efforts to recapture political control but measures to remove corruption from the electoral process and reform politics in general.[32]

Grantham further maintains that many southern progressives believed economic development represented the key to a more progressive South. Southerners' desire to see their region grow economically represents the main reason for the emergence of progressivism in the South during the late nineteenth century. Grantham writes "One of the most powerful motivating factors in the reform efforts of early twentieth century southerners was a desire to expand the regulatory functions of the state in behalf of economic opportunity. . . ."[33] Grantham's economic argument suggests significant overlap between white elite southerner's New South rhetoric and the goals of southern progressivism. Southern progressives' emphasis on economic development begs the question: did the New South Era and southern progressivism constitute two distinct, although overlapping, eras and movements? Both roughly occurred at the same time. Furthermore, supporting one movement did not preclude an individual from backing the other. Although the New South movement was wide-ranging in its goals and rhetoric, economic development was the primary goal. Conversely, economic development was just one objective of southern progressivism.

Grantham contends that southern progressivism had three broad objectives: control and regulation, social justice, and social efficiency. Control and regulation included "managing" southern race relations. As mentioned, Grantham argues that many southern progressives believed disfranchisement and other strict social controls represented progressive actions. They believed racial controls, in particular, cut down on corruption and contributed to social stability. Among other things, social justice focused on ending or limiting child labor and developing public education, whether via the state or through philanthropic organizations. Grantham's social efficiency category served as a catch-all in which southern progressives attempted to increase southern agriculture, industry, and governmental efficiency.[34]

While northern progressives expressed significant concern over massive immigration to northern and midwestern cities and the accompanying issues it brought, as well as advocated for greater governmental oversight of the economy, white southern progressives felt compelled to address southern race relations, re-assert white political control, and economically develop their region. Southern progressives also wanted government intervention in the economy. However, unlike northern progressives, southerners generally did not want government to curb corporations' predatory practices and cease exploiting the environment, workers, and society in general—with the exception of railroad freight rates. They wanted southern governments to facilitate southern economic growth. Like Grantham, Mary Ellen Pethel argues that while southern progressives sought some of the same goals as their northern counterparts, southern progressivism had its own regional distinctiveness. The ever-present concern whites had with preventing African Americans from improving themselves economically or socially, as well as from participating in southern politics, ultimately impacted southern progressivism negatively. Furthermore, she claims, white southern males remained hesitant about relinquishing any power to women.[35] However, even though white southern males did not want to accord women much of a place in the public sphere, white women still led many Progressive Era reform efforts in the South, including establishing and developing public libraries.

Although race and gender issues served as defining characteristics between northern and southern progressivism, mutual concerns caused northern and southern progressives to overlook their differences and take part in a movement to protect individual and collective morals. Reformers argued that a constantly expanding economy and growing personal and national wealth meant nothing if personal and collective morals declined as a result. Philanthropists like industrialist and financier Andrew J. Carnegie, made astronomically wealthy by the economy's rapid expansion, also worried about declining morals. Carnegie began a philanthropy program that eventually gave away millions of dollars to various causes, especially constructing public and academic libraries, purchasing organs for churches, and funding studies that in various ways analyzed librarianship. Carnegie gave away his fortune to build institutions that individuals could access and use to morally "improve" themselves, thereby helping to reverse the country's perceived moral decline.

Incorporating these long-standing themes into their work, historians Noralee Frankel and Nancy S. Dye examined the intersections between gender and the Progressive Era. They argued that Progressive Era reforms would have foundered without women participating in or initiating them. Frankel and Dye contend that the expansion of the American economy during the Progressive Era and the rapidly blurring boundary between domestic and public spheres—increasing industrialization's effect on the American economy—provided women with an entryway into public life.[36] Many women who participated in Progressive Era reform efforts worked to establish and support public libraries. Like Carnegie, these reformers viewed libraries as places where individuals could temporarily escape life's hustle and bustle, with its supposed adverse impact on their morals. Many who believed in progressivism felt public libraries represented one option among several that could help correct what they believed represented behavioral issues caused by America's rapidly growing economy and embrace of capitalism, not fundamental flaws in human nature.[37]

As Andrew Carnegie gave away millions for the construction of public libraries, southern cities and their leaders saw a prime opportunity to achieve a variety of goals while having someone else pay for it. Southerners wanted to build public libraries for many reasons. Among other things, they believed such institutions demonstrated to the North that southerners earnestly embraced public education, learning, and protecting individual and collective morals. Southern leaders also pressed hard for these funds because they could use libraries as social control mechanisms; public libraries had strong potential to shape the South's public culture, as well as enable elite whites to retain control of the region's race relations. Furthermore, constructing public libraries also outwardly demonstrated that the New South economic vision had become a reality.

Public libraries also briefly acted as sandboxes in which southern leaders could experiment with various solutions to mitigate or resolve some of the perceived problems confronting southern society. As this chapter has shown, constant conflict between maintaining tradition and embracing change characterized the South from 1866 to the early twentieth century. For a brief period of time, public libraries enabled southern leaders to experiment with different ways to manage race relations in public space—or devise new ways to segregate the races. A constant tension between retaining the old while strategically embracing the new characterized southern public library development during the New South and Progressive eras.

NOTES

1. Harold E. Davis, *Henry Grady's New South: Atlanta, A Brave and Beautiful City* (Tuscaloosa, AL: University of Alabama Press, 1990), 35, 175.

2. Mary Edna Anders, "The Development of Public Library Service in the Southeastern States, 1895–1950" (PhD diss., Columbia University, 1958), 39.

3. Anders, "The Development of Public Library Service in the Southeastern States, 1895–1950," 33, 39.

4. Rosemary Ruhig Du Mont, "Race in American Librarianship: Attitudes of the Library Profession," *Journal of Library History* 21, no. 3 (Summer 1986): 489; David M. Battles, *The History of Public Library Access for African Americans in the South: Or, Leaving behind the Plow* (Lanham, MD: The Scarecrow Press, Inc., 2009), 17.

5. William A. Link, *The Paradox of Southern Progressivism, 1880–1930* (Chapel Hill: University of North Carolina Press, 1992), xi–xii, S95.

6. Davis, *Henry Grady's New South*, 29, 32.

7. Ferald J. Bryan, *Henry Grady or Tom Watson? The Rhetorical Struggle for the New South, 1880–1890* (Macon, GA: Mercer University Press, 1994), 41–42, 59–60.

8. Davis, *Henry Grady's New South*, 34, 175–78.

9. James Michael Russell, *Atlanta, 1847–1890: City Building in the Old South and the New* (Baton Rouge: Louisiana State University Press, 1988), 243.

10. Russell, *Atlanta, 1847–1890*, 242, 246.

11. Ibid., 241.

12. William Cronon, *Nature's Metropolis: Chicago and the Great West* (New York: W. W. Norton & Company, 1991), 92.

13. Don H. Doyle, *Nashville in the New South, 1880–1930* (Knoxville: University of Tennessee Press, 1985), xiv, 15; Walter T. Durham, *Reluctant Partners: Nashville and the Union, July 1, 1863, to June 30, 1865* (Nashville: Tennessee Historical Society, 1987), 298. Durham noted that although most Union soldiers left by the summer of 1865, some remained in Nashville until the early 1870s, ostensibly to oversee Reconstruction in the city and surrounding area.

14. Mary Ellen Pethel, "Athens of the New South: College Life in Nashville, A New South City, 1987–1917" (PhD diss., Georgia State University, 2008), 46.

15. Pethel, "Athens of the New South," 8.

16. W. David Lewis, "The Emergence of Birmingham as a Case Study of Continuity Between the Antebellum Planter Class and the Industrialization in the 'New South,'" *Agricultural History* 68, no 2. (Spring 1994): 63.

17. Lewis, "The Emergence of Birmingham as a Case Study of Continuity between the Antebellum Planter Class and the Industrialization in the 'New South,'" 64–65, 67–71. For an excellent discussion of the convict-lease system, see Douglas Blackmon's *Slavery by Another Name: The Re-enslavement of Black People in America from the Civil War to WWII* (New York: Doubleday, 2008).

18. Russell, *Atlanta, 1847–1890*, 7.

19. Ibid., 5–6.

20. Ibid., 2.

21. Cronon, *Nature's Metropolis*, 92.

22. Russell, *Atlanta, 1847–1890*, 260.

23. Don H. Doyle, *New Men, New Cities, New South: Atlanta, Nashville, Charleston, Mobile, 1860–1910* (Chapel Hill: University of North Carolina Press, 1990), xv, xvi.

24. Bruce G. Harvey, *World's Fairs in a Southern Accent: Atlanta, Nashville, and Charleston, 1895–1902* (Knoxville, University of Tennessee Press, 2014), xiv, xv, xix.

25. Pethel, "Athens of the New South," 8.

26. Harvey, *World's Fairs in a Southern Accent*, xiv.
27. Ibid., xiv.
28. Russell, *Atlanta, 1847–1890*, 248.
29. Anders, "The Development of Public Library Service in the Southeastern States, 1895–1950," 15.
30. Harvey, *World's Fairs in a Southern Accent*, xxi. Donald G. Davis, Jr. and Ronald C. Stone, Jr. argue that, despite whatever they might have publicly said and done, many southerners remained conflicted about their regional identity well after the South concluded its late nineteenth-century expositions. Davis Jr. and Stone Jr. wrote, "The South of 1900 still felt the exhilaration and heartbreak of a conflict that had been resolved thirty-five years previously. After Appomattox, Southerners kept alive the memory of the Confederacy even as they struggled to make a New South. Robert Penn Warren viewed Lee's final surrender as the true birth of the Solid South, with its 'mystique of prideful 'difference,' identity, and defensiveness.'" Donald G. Davis and Ronald C. Stone Jr., "Poverty of Mind and Lack of Municipal Spirit: Rejection of Carnegie Public Library Building Grants by Seven Southern Communities," in *Carnegie Denied: Communities Rejecting Carnegie Library Construction Grants, 1898–1925*, ed. Robert Sidney Martin (Westport, CT: Greenwood Press, 1993), 137.
31. Doyle, *Nashville in the New South*, 149–52.
32. Dewey W. Grantham, *Southern Progressivism: The Reconciliation of Progress and Tradition* (Knoxville, TN: University of Tennessee Press, 1983), xv.
33. Grantham, *Southern Progressivism*, 111, xviii.
34. Ibid., xix–xxi.
35. Pethel, "Athens of the New South," 21–22.
36. Noralee Frankel and Nancy S. Dye, eds. *Gender, Class, Race, and Reform in the Progressive Era* (Lexington: The University Press of Kentucky, 1991), 2, 3.
37. Lewis W. Gould, *America in the Progressive Era, 1890–1914* (New York: Longman, 2001), 22, 39.

Chapter 2

A New Vision, a New South
Southern Public Library Development, 1890–1950

As public libraries sprang up across America, public discussion about them focused on their expected societal contributions and largely avoided deeply analyzing the complex viewpoints, objectives, and issues bound up in or associated with them. Society expected public libraries to play an instrumental role in helping to address many complicated issues confronting America at the turn of the century. In the South, public libraries developed as part of New South proponents' economic development schemes for the region. They also were an outgrowth of progressive reform efforts. However, despite whatever New South boosters might have said about the virtues of their economic programs, many southern communities needed outside help to fund the construction of public libraries.

Philanthropists and philanthropic organizations, like Andrew Carnegie and the Carnegie Corporation of New York (CCNY), and government agencies, like the Tennessee Valley Authority (TVA) and Works Progress Administration (WPA), played instrumental roles in developing the South's public libraries. However, while philanthropic organizations and government agencies played key roles in the development of southern public libraries, perhaps no entity had more of an impact on library development in the South than women and women's organizations. In many communities women raised the funds, gathered the books, applied for the Carnegie library construction grants, provided staff, and then once established, continually advocated for public libraries. Southern public library development cannot be discussed without examining women's fundamental role in the process.

SOCIETY, GENDER, AND PUBLIC LIBRARIES

Reform-minded women believed libraries occupied an important place in society. Middle- and upper-class women who viewed libraries as worthy social investments often acted through women's clubs to establish and maintain public libraries in communities across the country. Women had a tremendous commitment to and impact on southern public library development. In North Carolina and Virginia, for example, women's clubs played at least some role in establishing 90 and 80 percent, respectively, of libraries in those states.

Paula D. Watson argues that the involvement of women in the establishing, managing, and advocating of and for libraries has its origins in the Civil War. During the war women involved themselves in a variety of volunteer roles related to the war effort. With this foray into the public sphere women and women's organizations accumulated public service experience that resulted in extremely effective work on behalf of public library development, often through engagement in women's clubs, during the late nineteenth and early twentieth century. In her research, Karen J. Blair notes that beginning in the 1870s and continuing into the 1890s, during which public libraries began appearing in the southern landscape, often due to the efforts of women, women began to found literary societies. Indeed, beginning with the establishment of literary societies, women continued their extensive work pertaining to public library development to the point that the General Federation of Women's Clubs created a national program of library development. At the state level, federations of women's clubs acted as clearing houses of information that provided local groups with advice on how to apply for Carnegie library construction grants.[1]

For black women, library work did not constitute just a way to overcome gender restrictions on entering the public sphere, public libraries also acted as venues where they could counter racial stereotypes of African Americans, work on behalf of their community, and practice racial uplift. Black female librarians exerted influence, sometimes tremendously, on their professional field and its corollaries. For example, Chicago librarian Charlamae Hill Rollins constantly wrote to publishers challenging their decisions to publish works that portrayed African Americans as racist stereotypes. Rollins's advocacy pressured some publishing houses, like Thomas Y. Crowell, to hire her to review children's books. With this platform, Rollins for a time shaped American children's literature, books that African American children would read and whose messages they would absorb. When Rollins objected to various stereotypes in the book originally titled *Dark Lillibell*, the author made the suggested changes and retitled the book to *Great Day in the Morning*. When author Virginia Cunningham could not sell a biography of Paul

Laurence Dunbar, Rollins refined the text, after which Cunningham sold the manuscript.² In other words, some African American librarians, like Rollins, exerted personal agency to the point that they held a degree of power over publishers and authors of American children's literature.

Although women played a significant role in promoting and developing American public libraries, society did not immediately accept the idea that women should staff and operate them. At the end of the Victorian era, society had very definite ideas about the way women should act and move in public libraries. In her nuanced and insightful study, "The Lady and the Library Loafer: Gender and Public Space in Victorian America," Abigail A. Van Slyck introduced readers to the "ladies' reading room," a popular feature in many public libraries across the United States until the turn of the twentieth century. Van Slyck argued that ladies' reading rooms were meant to protect women from the unwanted male gaze and to serve as stages upon which to act out proper female behavior, as defined by society. These rooms varied by library. Sometimes they represented an entirely separate closed-off space. In other cases, a partially enclosed section of a library's reading room constituted the lady's reading room. Victorian society expected women to use the library in certain ways. For instance, a common opinion was that a woman using the library should only read "light literature" and control her body with what society generally agreed represented a person at ease.³

During the Progressive Era attitudes shifted regarding how women should use the library, as well as opinions about what constituted proper feminine behavior. Long regarded as nurturers and protectors, women increasingly were viewed as natural protectors of the country's morals and culture. This shift in popular conceptions regarding the nature of women and their roles in society enabled them to rapidly assume employment in libraries, which were associated with civic virtue. For instance, in 1870 men represented almost 80 percent of all librarians. By 1900 that figure flipped, with women serving as nearly 80 percent of all librarians in America.⁴

ANDREW CARNEGIE AND NATIONAL LIBRARY DEVELOPMENT

Andrew Carnegie donated millions to construct public libraries across the United States, including in the South. Born in 1835 in Dunfermline, Scotland, Andrew Carnegie became the richest man in the world, for a time, after he sold Carnegie Steel to John Pierpont (J. P.) Morgan in 1901.⁵ Even before he sold his company and realized between $300 and $400 million in gross profit, Carnegie had already commenced a library construction program, ultimately spending $41,000,000 on constructing 1,679 American public libraries. One hundred and forty-four of these were in the South. Interestingly, that number represents a figure smaller than the number of grants Carnegie and the CCNY funded in Indiana alone. Seven southern communities rejected grants after initially receiving them. Another fifty grant requests from southern communities were not funded.[6]

Carnegie divided his library giving into two distinct periods, which he termed "retail" (1886–1896) and "wholesale" (1898–1919). During the retail timeframe, Carnegie gave $1,860,869, while during the wholesale period he donated $39,172,981 to construct public libraries.[7] Until 1911, when Carnegie created the CCNY to more efficiently manage his philanthropic endeavors, including providing funds to construct public libraries, his secretary James Bertram administered the entire library giving program. Even after the CCNY's creation, Bertram continued in much the same role.

To receive a Carnegie library construction grant, before and after the CCNY's creation, communities had to fill out a grant application asking for the community's population, who would serve as the chief correspondent with Carnegie/CCNY, how much money the community was seeking, and how much the community would annually appropriate from its budget to assure library maintenance. Carnegie/the CCNY required communities to annually appropriate 10 percent of the total amount they received in grant money.[8] Until 1908, communities that had received a grant could build their libraries any way they saw fit. Many communities, at least in James Bertram's eyes, committed egregious errors when constructing their libraries by employing architectural plans that wasted space or seemed grandiose. For both offenses Nashville, Tennessee, especially caught Bertram's wrath.[9] Communities could only disagree with Bertram's architectural specifications for so long before the worst occurred: losing their grant funding. At least sixteen American communities lost their grant funding because they engaged in a protracted argument with Bertram over library design.[10]

In 1908, a fed-up Bertram demanded that communities with approved grant applications provide architectural plans for their building, which he had to approve before they received their money. By 1911, Bertram had written a pamphlet titled *Notes on Library Buildings*. The publication set forth the architectural styles Bertram and the CCNY expected communities to use when constructing libraries with CCNY funds. The pamphlet included sample architectural plans that Bertram believed maximized use of space.[11] Bertram's control over grant funds, essentially selecting the architectural styles communities employed when constructing Carnegie-funded libraries, ensured that he made a tremendous impact on American civic architecture. Scholar Abigail Van Slyck even suggested that Carnegie libraries, and especially Bertram's exacting architectural standards for them, created a distinct building style somewhere between high and vernacular architecture.[12]

Carnegie/CCNY grants usually covered only the building cost of a library. Communities awarded a grant had to obtain property on which to build the library as well as purchase books and furniture, and hire staff. Furthermore, communities awarded a grant had to agree to annually appropriate from their city's budget a sum representing 10 percent of the total grant amount received. These appropriations were to fund library maintenance and operations. However, numerous communities with Carnegie-funded public libraries did not or could not fulfill this obligation.[13]

PUBLIC LIBRARIES AND PROGRESSIVE REFORM

In keeping with the Progressive Era's emphasis on reform and the philosophy of uplift, Carnegie believed people who wanted to improve themselves and their position in life had to do so by personal initiative and hard work. However, Carnegie also believed that certain environments were more likely to foster a disposition toward self-help. He believed libraries provided an environment in which immigrants, laborers, and other people could morally, intellectually, and economically improve themselves. Wanting to and then actually attending the library to improve oneself represented the key to unlocking the public library's value to the individual and society, at least in Carnegie's mind.[14] The following quote perhaps best summarizes why Carnegie chose to fund public libraries:

> I choose free libraries as the best agencies for improving the masses of the people, because they give nothing for nothing—they only help those who help themselves—they never pauperize. They reach the aspiring, and open to these the chief treasures of the world—those steeped up in books—a taste for reading drives out lower tastes.[15]

While libraries provided the actual knowledge to achieve such goals, through books, periodicals, and other reading material, their emphasis on observing conduct codes while in the library created an environment in which people who wanted to improve themselves had to follow certain rules to do so. Not only did this keep order in the library; it also shaped library patrons' public behaviors. In other words, libraries acted as social control devices as much as knowledge centers people could use to improve their economic situation or social station.

Although Carnegie gave millions of dollars to establish public libraries across the United States, including in the South, African Americans did not immediately share in the bounty. As the Atlanta and Nashville case studies particularly show, Carnegie's library giving entrenched racial segregation in southern public libraries. Carnegie deferred to local custom when it came to matters of race. Accordingly, African Americans often found themselves prevented from using the public libraries of southern cities. While Carnegie did fund requests for money to build African American branch libraries in southern cities, including Nashville and Atlanta, the cash for these branches often came after the initial grant to build a public library in a city and for a lesser amount.

Desiring library access, African Americans took matters into their own hands. In a repeatedly occurring scenario, when southern public libraries barred African Americans from using their resources, African Americans built and staffed their own libraries. In what constitutes just one example out of many, in 1913 in Durham, North Carolina, the first black doctor in the city, Aaron McDuffie Moore, founded a library for black use in the basement of the White Rock Baptist Church. However, concerned that the library did not reach a broad spectrum of black Durham, Moore teamed up with barber John Merrick. For whatever reason, Merrick had previously purchased a lot in the heart of Durham's black community. In 1916 Merrick and Moore had a library building erected on the site. By 1918 the library received funding from the city and county. In 1969 the library became part of the Durham County Public Library System.[16]

George S. Bobinski, who wrote the first major work on Carnegie-funded public libraries, argued that American public libraries have experienced four distinct periods in their history. The first phase came in the 1850s as communities passed legislation favorable to public libraries and began to found and support them, especially in the Northeast. Carnegie's massive monetary investment in American public libraries, in terms of money for construction, constitutes the second phase. The CCNY's founding in 1911 to bring greater standardization and structure to Carnegie's philanthropy represented the third major phase. Bobinski viewed the federal government's support of public libraries from the 1960s on, particularly through favorable legislation, as the fourth phase in American library history.[17]

Mary Edna Anders argues that the first stage of southern public library development occurred between 1895 and 1920. She characterizes this stage of development as initiated by women's clubs and female leaders in the southern public library movement. The first stage of southern public library development took place squarely within the context and timeframe of the Progressive Era, as well as during Carnegie's library giving program.[18] In the North, Carnegie's philanthropy built upon a public library infrastructure already in place. In the South, Carnegie's giving helped put in place many of the region's first public libraries.

PUBLIC LIBRARIES: IMMIGRATION, CULTURE, ECONOMIC ACHIEVEMENT, AND SOCIAL CONTROL

Like Carnegie, those who supported libraries viewed them as much social control devices as tools to uplift and "improve" immigrants and the working class. Peter Mickelson argues that many middle, upper-middle, and upper-class public library proponents supported their founding and upkeep because they believed public libraries could reinforce the prevailing social and economic order. During the late nineteenth century, as European immigrants and migrants from America's small towns and countryside crowded into the cities to take part in wage work, members of the middle and upper classes feared them because they had the potential to seriously challenge the prevailing economic order. Although holding the majority of political and economic power, America's middle and upper classes recognized that immigrants and lower-class migrants outnumbered them. If the lower classes challenged the Progressive Era's so-called American values of deference to one's economic and social betters, as well as the social standards of sobriety, thrift, avoidance of sexual promiscuousness, they could undermine a system benefiting the higher levels of the American social order. According to Mickelson, this thought so alarmed the American middle and upper classes that they tasked public libraries and librarians with the job of propping up the socio-economic order by preaching the values they set while concurrently dismissing labor leaders and their ideas as worthless and untrue. Furthermore, although Andrew Carnegie may have seriously believed in the potential of libraries to morally, socially, and economically uplift, many other middle-and upper-class Americans used such rhetoric to mask their true purpose, protecting their place in the American social and economic order. Accordingly, they viewed public libraries as social control instruments and, at least initially, believed resources invested in them was money well spent.[19]

Other middle- and upper-class Americans viewed libraries as cultural producers and protectors. As Thomas Augst and Wayne Wiegand wrote, "These public libraries were not only 'instruments' of social control, but also the nineteenth century's most impressive symbols of what John Jacob Astor termed the 'general good of society,' of liberal capitalism's capacity to create civilization."[20] For this reason Robert Sidney Martin concludes that despite rhetoric about public libraries as institutions intended to protect societal morals and provide education to immigrants and the poor, they long remained middle-class establishments. Middle-class people fought to obtain the libraries, wrote applications to receive public library building grants from Carnegie and the CCNY, and then staffed and used them. Northern elites considered public libraries, many of them founded before the Civil War, as tangible evidence that their communities had committed to supporting culture.

Public libraries served as visible proof that capitalism could create and sustain culture.[21] Southern elites during the New South Era especially held these views. Vanderbilt University chancellor James H. Kirkland wrote to Andrew Carnegie pleading with him to provide funds to construct a public library building in Nashville, arguing:

> Nashville is a city of schools and colleges, the very center of educational work in the South. Students gather here in great numbers from every southern state, but there are no adequate library facilities for higher scholarly work. There does not exist in the whole South a really great library, adapted to use of students and scholars. . . . I trust therefore it will be your pleasure not merely to supply the wants of the readers of general literature, but to establish here a great library for research and scholarly work, contributing to the highest develop. [sic] of the students of this city, who will become the leaders in Southern life and Thought.[22]

By managing to build, fund, and maintain a library, southern elites could point to one physical example they believed fulfilled New South Era promises to grow the South's economy. Indeed, some southerners believed their community must possess a public library to indicate its urbane nature, economic vitality, and commitment to education and culture. Writer Ida Tarbell wrote in support of a stand-alone central library in Birmingham, Alabama, stating:

> There ought to be no question of Birmingham having a library adequately housed, centrally located and effectively operated. I am amazed that Birmingham has not before this provided itself with such a library, energetic and progressive as it has shown itself in many other ways. . . . Birmingham loses something in its industrial effectiveness, its intellectual activity and its social charm every day that it is without a great central library.[23]

Another article in the *Birmingham News* stated, "Birmingham's new public library is something that every man, woman and child can point to with infinite pride, a civic asset which means more than nearly anything else that has ever been credited to the 'Magic City of the South.'"[24] Hence, building and maintaining a public library greatly mattered to southern leaders; in many ways it validated and fulfilled their New South Era goals.

Carnegie library scholar George S. Bobinski suggested another reason why some communities seemed desperate to build a public library: to get one before the neighboring town or city did. In this respect, communities sometimes viewed libraries as civic infrastructure, in the same realm as bridges and other public works projects.[25] Indeed, especially in the South, communities intended their public libraries to serve as civic trophies. In other words, Bobinski argues, when examining the reasons why cities wanted to build and establish public libraries, scholars should not overlook the power that boosters' economic and civic development schemes had over their communities.[26]

Regardless of the reason southern leaders wanted to establish public libraries, they often had to turn to philanthropists like Andrew Carnegie to make possible that goal. Southern leaders turned to Carnegie for library construction funds for two main reasons. First, their cities' budgets legitimately did not contain enough funds to construct a library. Second, they recognized a good business opportunity. Carnegie provided the money to build the library; communities only had to agree (in an apparently non-legally binding agreement) to annually appropriate 10 percent of the total amount Carnegie gave for library construction to support ongoing operations and maintenance.[27] Before receiving the money from Carnegie, communities had to decide where to locate their libraries. This decision often turned into an intense, politicized, debate. Many reasons explain why a community selected a particular site over another: a donated and accordingly free piece of land on which to build the library, a lot selected due to price considerations, not location, and various kinds of real estate ploys. In 1915 the CCNY employed economics professor Alvin S. Johnson to study the operations of Carnegie-funded libraries. After examining 100 Carnegie libraries scattered across the United States, Johnson found that many communities had located their libraries in less than ideal locations. Johnson believed communities should build libraries in downtown locations as nearly everyone in town had to go there at one time or another. Accordingly, a centrally located library would reach as many people as possible.[28]

Abigail Van Slyck argues that where a community located its Carnegie library, as well as the architectural design it selected, conveyed who the institution would serve and denoted its social functions, as well as any other community roles and purposes it might play and fulfill.[29] Accordingly, boosters in many communities made sure to place their public library downtown. For larger towns and cities that had public library systems, those systems usually located their main branch in a community's center. Many communities wanted their public libraries located downtown not only because they believed they could reach many patrons in doing so, and show off their communities' real or imagined economic success and prosperity in the process, but also because they became swept up in a Progressive Era manifestation known as the "City Beautiful" Movement. Those who believed and invested in the City Beautiful Movement endeavored to create cohesively planned, clean, and "beautiful" downtowns.[30] As William H. Wilson argues, in addition to a concern for the condition of the urban natural environment and architectural aesthetics, the fulfillment of a cultural agenda played a part in the realization of City Beautiful Movement goals. Although many southern communities built public libraries to display economic achievement, they also built them as a way to demonstrate a commitment to supporting education and culture. In short, the construction of public libraries helped fulfill City Beautiful Movement objectives, and, in southern cities, New South planning and economic goals. According to Wilson the hallmarks of the City Beautiful Movement, particularly grand civic buildings, "are . . . important because they were the physical expression of an ideal. . . . The public buildings symbolized a coherent architecture, an ideal comprehended if not always achieved."[31]

However, public transportation became increasingly prevalent during the Progressive Era, making achievement of City Beautiful objectives harder, or perhaps in the eyes of some, unnecessary. So while cities labored to fulfill City Beautiful objectives, public transportation made it easier to ignore a plethora of urban issues, particularly those related to space, noise, pollution, and overcrowding. As public transportation became more widespread, cities could locate their cultural institutions, like libraries, in suburbs outside the downtown core. Intentional or not, this made it difficult for those of limited means to visit suburban-located libraries.[32]

Even though public transportation, and later the automobile, made it easier for communities to locate their public libraries outside the downtown core, and may have prevented lower-class and immigrant patrons from using them, libraries in general still experienced a rise in the number and variety of patrons using them. Libraries had to accommodate ever-larger numbers within their buildings. However, not all people used the library for the same reasons. While some patrons came to do "serious" research, others visited the library to read newspapers and magazines, get out of the elements, nap, and more. Accordingly, librarians began to designate certain rooms for certain uses and users. Thus, they attempted to sequester patrons in specific spaces. While this may simply seem like good librarianship, and perhaps on a certain level it did constitute that, libraries also did this as a way to manage different types of patrons. Occasionally, libraries even included separate entrances for those wishing to use children's departments, read newspapers and magazines, or loaf.[33]

Location, intended purpose, assigned or acquired responsibilities, and the diversity of patrons made public libraries complicated institutions and contested spaces. Untangling the many societal and institutional goals, competing interests, and conflicting agendas is difficult. However, as library scholar Patterson Toby Graham argues, libraries act as a societal mirror, reflecting a society's best, worst, and most complicated aspects. By looking at the context in which a community founded its library and operated it, one can start to better understand not only that they have complicated natures, but also why.[34]

SOUTHERN PUBLIC LIBRARY DEVELOPMENT

Mary Edna Anders, building on Bobinski's argument that national library development experienced four distinct periods, argues that library growth in the South can be divided into four periods: 1895–1920, 1920–1935, 1930–1943, and 1942–1950. Anders contends that during the first phase of development, women's clubs assumed the initial responsibility for founding and maintaining many southern libraries. These groups in communities across the South organized subscription libraries, traveling libraries, and other forms of library outreach and service. Also during this period, state library associations formed in southern states. After the formation of state library associations, came the establishment of state library extension agencies. Between 1897 and 1929 all southern states established state library extension agencies.

While well intentioned, and indeed laying the groundwork for the establishment of community-supported public libraries in the South, women's groups found that managing libraries and library services taxed them to their limits. Accordingly, they supported the efforts of state library associations to convince southern state legislators that supporting libraries and library service constituted a legitimate government function. Building upon the efforts of women's groups, various agencies, like state library associations, eventually took on the task of managing public libraries' growth and development.[35] Donald G. Davis Jr. and Ronald C. Stone Jr. point out that Andrew Carnegie and the CCNY also played a significant role in developing southern libraries. Carnegie provided enough funds to construct 144 southern public libraries between 1895 and 1920.[36] Bobinksi reports slightly different figures: 112 southern communities received grants from Carnegie or the CCNY to construct 135 separate buildings.[37] Despite the slight discrepancy between Bobinski's figures and those of Stone and Davis, the point remains that the South received far fewer Carnegie/CCNY grants and built significantly fewer libraries than other regions of the country (see tables 2.1 and 2.2).

Table 2.1 Carnegie Grants for Public Libraries-Regional Rank by Number of Buildings

Region	Buildings
Midwest	698
Northeast	300
Northwest	262
Far West	217
Southeast	135
Southwest	63
District of Columbia	4

Source: George S. Bobinski, *Carnegie Libraries: Their History and Impact of American Public Library Development* (Chicago: American Library Association, 1969), 20.

Table 2.2 Carnegie Grants for Public Libraries-Regional Rank by Number of Communities

Region	Buildings
Midwest	633
Northwest	252
Far West	180
Northeast	173
Southeast	112
Southwest	61
District of Columbia	1

Source: George S. Bobinski, *Carnegie Libraries: Their History and Impact of American Public Library Development* (Chicago: American Library Association, 1969), 19.

Near the end of the first development phase, according to Anders, women's clubs began transferring their control of southern public library development to state library extension agencies and state library associations.[38] However, before state library associations could begin to control public library development, southern states needed to establish legal authority. By 1895 only two southern states had created provisions in their legal codes to establish and support public libraries. Accordingly, many southern communities created their own laws providing for public libraries.[39]

Anders points to the 1920 meeting of southern librarians at Signal Mountain, Tennessee, where participants founded the Southeastern Library Association (SELA), as the event signifying the beginning of the second phase of southern public library development.[40] SELA offered many benefits to its members, including increased professionalization. While the American Library Association (ALA) had existed since 1876, it did not exclusively serve southern libraries and librarians. With the founding of SELA, southern public librarians could belong to and take part in an organization exclusively dedicated to them and their work. Furthermore, the formation of SELA allowed southern public libraries and librarians to plan and coordinate regional library development and services more cohesively and comprehensively.[41] Although SELA in many ways contributed to southern public library development, James V. Carmichael Jr. identified its 1928 statement, "Southern Library Achievement and Objectives," as especially significant because it stated that African Americans should have access to library service. Crafted by Louis Round Wilson, a former SELA president (1924–1926) and head librarian at the University of North Carolina at Chapel Hill from the early 1900s until 1932, the statement's call to provide library service to African Americans was bold. It is especially noteworthy because the ALA's "Library Work with Negroes Roundtable" disbanded in 1923 due to acrimonious debate between its northern and southern members over the most suitable methods of providing library service to African Americans.[42]

Anders attributes the relatively late and slow development of southern public libraries, when compared to New England, to the South's lack of resources. The South heavily relied on outside assistance to develop its public libraries. Anders notes that federal largess from the TVA and the WPA during the 1930s played a substantial role in library development. Although she minimizes the influence of Carnegie and the CCNY on building public libraries, Anders correctly states the impact the WPA and TVA had on the region's library development. Southern governments also played a key role by passing legislation enabling the provision of library service on a county-wide or regional level. In 1933 North Carolina was the first southern state to pass such a law. The other southern states followed suit, with Kentucky in 1944 as the last one to do so.[43]

However, until southern state governments, the federal government, and philanthropic entities became interested in developing public libraries in the South, subscription libraries represented a prevalent, if not the dominant, library model in the region. For instance, the public libraries of Atlanta, Birmingham, and Nashville started as subscription libraries. Subscription libraries remained on the southern library scene until at least the 1920s, filling the void caused by the slow and isolated development of public libraries in the region.[44] While the enduring prevalence of subscription libraries in the South speaks to the lack of support on the part of local, regional, and state governments, or the inability to provide it, it also indicates that women's clubs remained committed to providing library service to their communities and states to the best of their abilities.

Federal spending on southern public library development during the Great Depression and early years of World War II defined the third major development phase (1930–1943). Anders describes this period as unique. In a time when much of the nation suffered acute economic distress, southern public libraries grew and thrived on steady federal cash infusions, extra workers provided through Great Depression relief programs and agencies, and participation in various library expansion projects.[45]

Established in 1935 to ease unemployment caused by the Great Depression, the Works Progress Administration funded many work relief programs, including library construction, outreach services, and library work.[46] To administer library programs, the WPA created a Library Services Section in its Professional and Service Division. The Library Services Section functioned as a "clearing house for all library projects." State library extension agencies usually, but not always, sponsored library-related projects with the WPA. However, in Tennessee, the State Department of Education chose to sponsor a WPA library project. State library extension agencies proved to be valuable partners because they could reduce the distrust state library workers might have about an outside entity disrupting or coopting their work. The

WPA never attempted to undertake a library project without partnering with some state agency.[47] According to Anders, a supervisor was usually chosen to serve as the chief administrator for a state agency-sponsored, statewide WPA library project. Beneath that supervisor existed dozens of managers administering various districts within the state. Those administrators managed individual units of the project.[48]

WPA library projects usually fell into distinct categories: constructing main or branch libraries, outreach services like book mobiles, and technical services such as book repair.[49] Because the South possessed comparatively few public libraries as of 1933, the WPA often focused on developing community and especially countywide library service districts.[50] The WPA had a tremendous impact on public library development, particularly in the South. In 1930, 30,000 Americans worked as librarians and library assistants. By 1938, WPA funds had enabled the hiring of 38,324 people for library projects, which more than doubled the number of those engaged in library work in 1930. Of the library workers it funded, the WPA placed 42.1 percent of its library project managerial staff and 39.2 percent of nonmanagerial workers in the South. In 1935, 63 percent of all southerners did not have free library service. By 1947, only 30 percent did not have access to free libraries.

Although the stimulating effect the WPA had on southern public library development and service ended when the agency shut down in 1943, the WPA left a physical legacy through library building construction and renovation (see table 2.3).

The WPA also made a lasting impact on southern library development by providing southern library workers with basic librarianship training. According to Anders the state library agency, whether it was a state library extension agency, state library commission, or some other entity, committed to providing WPA-funded library workers with some level of training. For many

Table 2.3   Total Number of Libraries Built or Repaired by WPA in the South by 1941

Virginia	5
North Carolina	8
South Carolina	16
Georgia	3
Alabama	5
Mississippi	?
Louisiana	2
Arkansas	3
Tennessee	0
Kentucky	3
Florida	8
Total	71

Source: Edward Barrett Stanford, *Library Extension Under the WPA: An Appraisal of an Experiment in Federal Aid* (Chicago: University of Chicago Press, 1944), 88–89.

library workers, their only library training was that which they received when they worked on a WPA library project.[51]

The Tennessee Valley Authority also had a widespread, meaningful impact on southern public library development. Established in 1933 and still in existence, the TVA was created to bring flood control, electricity, and economic development to the Tennessee River Valley. Eight states make up the Tennessee River Valley: Tennessee, Georgia, Alabama, Mississippi, Kentucky, Arkansas, Virginia, and North Carolina. While developing the Tennessee River Valley, the TVA endeavored to provide its workers with library services.[52] In 1933 the TVA created a part-time position of library consultant. In 1946 it made the position full-time. The TVA offered library service through its technical library, located at its headquarters in Knoxville, Tennessee, and through programs originating from and managed by its Office of the Supervisor of Library Services, the title given to the library consultant when the TVA made the position full-time. The Supervisor of Library Services planned and managed TVA's various library projects. Through these library undertakings, the supervisor exercised tremendous influence over southern library development.[53]

The way the TVA provided library services evolved over time. Initially, it assumed responsibility for providing libraries at its many construction sites scattered across the Tennessee River Valley. TVA employees staffed these libraries. However, the agency eventually realized this practice duplicated local libraries and state library agencies working in the areas where the TVA operated. Accordingly, the TVA began to collaborate with local and state agencies to provide library service to its employees. Collaboration led the TVA to negotiate formal contracts with libraries and regional library associations to provide library service to TVA employees, believing it more cost-effective to do so. TVA contracts with libraries and library associations began in 1937 and ended in 1950.[54]

Because the TVA built many of its dams and other massive public works projects in mostly rural areas, the agency saw the need to construct libraries. Not only did libraries offer a form of diversion for TVA workers in largely isolated regions, they also fit into TVA's plan to transform life in the Tennessee Valley. While attempting to bring electricity, flood control, and increased economic activity to the region, the TVA also envisioned providing increased educational opportunities. Providing library service was one way to accomplish that goal. The agency also encouraged existing public libraries to form regional library associations. By forming regional library associations, libraries could secure TVA funding to pool resources and spread library services over a larger area. However, even if libraries banded together to form a regional library association, the TVA had additional qualifications for them to meet to receive funds. The library associations had to promise to establish

Table 2.4 Annual Contractual Commitments of the TVA for Library Service

Year	Dollar Amount ($)
1937	8,320
1937–1938	16,980
1938–1939	17,100
1939–1940	19,660
1940–1941	24,040
1941–1942	44,150
1942–1943	75,190
1943–1944	45,240
1944–1945	26,000
1945–1946	18,600
1946–1947	14,400
1947–1948	17,370
1948–1949	22,170
1949–1950	10,000

Source: Mary Edna Anders, "The Development of Public Library Service in the Southeastern States, 1895–1950," (PhD diss., Columbia University, 1958), 152.

a library at the TVA camp or work site in their area, provide outreach service through book mobiles and book deposit stations, and supply the staff and support necessary to provide library service to TVA employees. In some states, for instance Tennessee, the TVA's emphasis on developing regional library associations influenced statewide library growth. Many regional library associations were formed after 1937, when TVA payments to libraries started to increase substantially. These payments peaked in 1942–1943, after which point they steadily declined (see table 2.4).[55]

By 1940, the TVA's various library programs and activity had expanded to the point that an advisory board was needed. In 1940, the TVA invited partner organizations and entities, as well as those interested in its library initiatives, to send representatives to TVA headquarters in Knoxville, Tennessee. Once there, the invitees discussed ways to better coordinate and streamline the TVA's library initiatives. The idea to form an organization called the Tennessee Valley Library Council (TVLC) represented the meeting's significant outcome. The council's leadership comprised various state agency heads, including state library extension agencies and state library associations, school librarians, and other library professionals. The TVLC advised the TVA by creating committees to study specific issues. A report titled "Libraries of the Southeast: A Report of the Southeastern States Cooperative Library Survey, 1946–1947" produced by the TVLC in cooperation with the Southeastern Library Association, perhaps represents the TVLC's most lasting impact. The report attempted to measure, as comprehensively as possible, the state of southern libraries and the services provided by them. The report also recommended that the TVA and the Southeastern Library Association work together more closely to strengthen the collections of libraries in the Tennessee Valley as well as better manage resources.⁵⁶

From 1941 to 1944, when TVA funding to public libraries peaked, the TVA distributed $164,580 to public libraries in eight southern states. From 1941 to 1942 the TVA awarded libraries $44,150. In 1942–1943 it provided libraries with $75,190 in funding, and in 1943–1944 it distributed $45,240 dollars.⁵⁷ Anders notes that these payments approximated what the TVA would have spent to provide library service itself.⁵⁸ In short, Anders makes a compelling case that TVA money definitely strengthened public libraries in the short term. As TVA activity in the Tennessee River Valley slowed in the 1940s, so did its various library programs, including contracting with libraries and regional library associations. The TVA continued to partner with libraries and library associations on an as-needed basis, but for all intents and purposes, its wide-scale library funding ended in the late 1940s, and especially by 1950, as the Korean War began.⁵⁹

The WPA and TVA permanently altered the way southern libraries received their funding. The infusion of federal funds during the 1930s and 1940s required southern state governments to increase the money they spent on public libraries. By the mid-1940s, southern state governments were providing public libraries with enough funds to account for 6 percent of their budgets. This exceeded the funding other state governments provided to their public libraries, usually around 1 percent.⁶⁰ By 1950, southern public library development had greatly progressed from its late nineteenth-century origins. In 1895, the South offered no free public library service to its residents. By 1950, 76 percent of the South's population could obtain free library service. The number of southern public libraries established after 1919 provides a striking illustration of southern public libraries' late growth. Over half of southern public libraries existing in 1944–1945 were founded after 1929, and 70 percent of them came into existence after 1919. Indeed, from 1930 to 1939, the South established 188 or 34 percent of all its public libraries. Equally impressive growth took place from 1940 to 1945, as southern communities and counties founded 113, or 21 percent, of all public libraries in existence in 1945.⁶¹

As federal agencies like the WPA dissolved and the library funds that came from those entities disappeared, the fourth major phase in southern public library development began. Library construction greatly slowed as the cash and other resources from agencies like the WPA and TVA dried up. Southern library leadership also experienced a shift during this period as state library associations relinquished control over library development and management to state library extension agencies.⁶²

Southern public libraries' slow development indicated that communities across the South, as well as the southern states themselves, had few resources, or were unwilling, to establish and support public libraries with their own money. Accordingly, nongovernment entities like women's clubs played a crucial role in fostering and maintaining subscription and traveling libraries, as well as other library services, during the first stage of southern public library development. In addition to the aid women's clubs gave to the fledgling growth of southern public libraries and librarianship, philanthropic support proved crucial to the development of southern public libraries and the provision of library services. Andrew Carnegie and the CCNY's library construction grant program directly benefited the South in the form of providing funds to southern communities to build public libraries. While funding from Carnegie and the CCNY helped spur the growth of southern public libraries, the support, monetary and otherwise, provided to southern public library development by government agencies like the WPA and TVA during the Great Depression, provided a sort of "golden age" in terms of support.

The narrative of southern public library development also demonstrates their central place in the history of southern race relations, particularly their direct role in institutionalizing segregation. Most southern public libraries practiced some form of racial segregation. Indeed, even before they were built, and especially during their earliest years of operation, southern leaders pressed the public libraries in their communities to practice segregation.

As the 1950s dawned, civil rights activists increasingly tested the South's practice of segregation. African Americans, whites who opposed segregation, and the federal judiciary began to challenge the South's de jure and de facto segregation. In the end, African American efforts to establish and fund their own libraries, attempts to desegregate southern public libraries through sit-ins and other protest tactics, and the ruling of the U.S. Supreme Court in *Brown v. Board of Education* caused segregation in southern public libraries to end. What began as a question about increasing library service to African Americans evolved to demands for integrating southern public libraries. To better understand how and why southern public libraries desegregated, chapter 3 discusses African American library development, the growth of black library education, the provision of library service to African Americans, and rapidly increasing attacks in the 1950s and 1960s on the South's segregation practices.

NOTES

1. Paula D. Watson, "Carnegie Ladies, Lady Carnegies: Women and the Building of Libraries," *Libraries & Culture* 31, no. 1 (Winter, 1996): 159–61, 164; Blair, *The Clubwoman as Feminist*, 57.
2. Shaw, *What a Woman Ought to Be and to Do*, 171–72.

3. Abigail A. Van Slyck, "The Lady and the Library Loafer: Gender and Public Space in Victorian America," *Winterthur Portfolio* 31, no. 4 (Winter 1996): 239.

4. Van Slyck, "The Lady and the Library Loafer: Gender and Public Space in Victorian America," 226–27; Joanne E. Passet, "Men in a Feminized Profession: The Male Librarian, 1887–1921," *Libraries & Culture* 28, no. 4 (Fall 1993): 386.

5. David Nasaw, *Andrew Carnegie* (New York: The Penguin Press, 2006), xi, xii.

6. Nasaw, *Andrew Carnegie*, 585–86, 607. When financier Charles Schwab, acting on behalf of Wall Street magnet J. P. Morgan, informed Carnegie that Morgan wanted to buy Carnegie Steel and asked him to name a price, Carnegie stated $400 million. Morgan agreed to Carnegie's figure. However, Carnegie actually received nothing in cash and $300 million in bonds paying 5 percent interest; see George S. Bobinski, *Carnegie Libraries: Their History and Impact of American Public Library Development* (Chicago: American Library Association, 1969), 3; Davis Jr. and Stone Jr., "Poverty of Mind and Lack of Municipal Spirit: Rejection of Carnegie Public Library Building Grants by Seven Southern Communities," 139.

7. Bobinski, *Carnegie Libraries*, 13–14. The CCNY ceased awarding library construction grants on November 7, 1917, but continued to disburse funds that had previously awarded. Undoubtedly, the CCNY did so because it often took communities years to obtain a grant, hammering out the details with the CCNY along the way, before they actually received the money. Furthermore, America's entry into World War I near the end of 1917 caused many communities to put their library construction programs on hold.

8. Carnegie Corporation of New York Records, II.A.1.a, Reel 2 (Atlanta Georgia), Rare Book and Manuscript Library, Columbia University Libraries [hereafter cited as CCNY Records].

9. Carnegie Corporation of New York Records, Reel 21 (Nashville, Tennessee).

10. Bobinski, *Carnegie Libraries*, 140.

11. Ibid., 57–58, 62.

12. Abigail Van Slyck, *Free to All: Carnegie Libraries & American Culture, 1890–1920* (Chicago, University of Chicago Press, 1995), xix, xx, xxi; Theodore Jones, *Carnegie Libraries Across America: A Public Legacy* (New York, Preservation Press, 1997), makes the same argument.

13. Bobinski, *Carnegie Libraries*, 101, 102.

14. Robert Sidney Martin, "Introduction," in *Carnegie Denied: Communities Rejecting Carnegie Library Construction Grants, 1898–1925*, vii.

15. As quoted in Thomas Augst and Wayne Wiegand, *Libraries as Agencies of Culture* (Madison: University of Wisconsin Press, 2003), 11.

16. Shaw, *What a Woman Ought to Be and to Do*, 204–05.

17. Bobinski, *Carnegie Libraries*, 201.

18. Mary Edna Anders, "The Development of Public Library Service in the Southeastern States, 1895–1950," 236–38.

19. Peter Mickelson, "American Society and the Public Library in the Thought of Andrew Carnegie," *Journal of Library History* 10, no. 2 (April 1975): 129–31.

20. Augst and Wiegand, *Libraries as Agencies of Culture*, 12.

21. Ibid., 8, 12.

22. James H. Kirkland to Andrew Carnegie, letter, July 15, 1901, CCNY Records, II.A.1.a, Reel 21 (Nashville, Tennessee).

23. "Underwood O.K.'S Library Issue," May 7, 1922, *Birmingham News*.

24. Dolly Dalrymple, "'Thing of Beauty' Is Realized in Classic New Library Building," *Birmingham News*, April 10, 1927.

25. Augst and Wiegand, *Libraries as Agencies of Culture*, 10.

26. Bobinski, *Carnegie Libraries*, 101.

27. Many communities only appropriated 10 percent of the total grant they received for a few years. Some towns and cities only appropriated the agreed-upon 10 percent for a single year, and sometimes not at all. George Bobinski surmises that because city councils, city commissions, library boards, and other similar organizations so often changed, it was difficult to draw up a legal document binding a particular board, commission, council, etc., to annually appropriate 10 percent of the total grant awarded. Apparently, the law regarded the board, commission, or council as an entirely different entity each time the citizens of the community elected or appointed new members. See Bobinski, *Carnegie Libraries*, 102.

28. Bobinski, *Carnegie Libraries*, 143–44, 149–50.

29. Van Slyck, *Free to All*, xxvi.

30. Robbie D. Jones, "'What's in a Name?': Tennessee's Carnegie Libraries & Civic Reform in the New South, 1889–1919" (Master's thesis, Middle Tennessee State University, 2003), 79–80.

31. William H. Wilson, *The City Beautiful Movement* (Baltimore: The Johns Hopkins University Press, 1989), 1–2.

32. Jones, "'What's in a Name?,'" 81–82.

33. Ibid., 81–83.

34. Patterson Toby Graham, *A Right to Read: Segregation and Civil Rights in Alabama's Public Libraries, 1900–1965* (Tuscaloosa: University of Alabama Press, 2002), 4.

35. Anders, "The Development of Public Library Service in the Southeastern States, 1895–1950," abstract, 1. Anders reported that Georgia established its state library commission in 1897, Tennessee in 1902, and Alabama in 1904 (pg. 82).

36. Ibid., 1–3; Davis and Stone, "Poverty of Mind and Lack of Municipal Spirit: Rejection of Carnegie Public Library Building Grants by Seven Southern Communities," 139.

37. Bobinski, *Carnegie Libraries*, 19–20.

38. Anders, "The Development of Public Library Service in the Southeastern States, 1895–1950," 236–38.

39. Ibid., 162.

40. Ibid., 238. James V. Carmichael Jr. pointed out three of SELA's first four meetings took place at Signal Mountain, signifying the power Tennessee's librarians held during the organization's early years. James V. Carmichael Jr., "Tommie Dora Barker and Southern Librarianship" (PhD diss., Chapel Hill: University of North Carolina, 1987), 156.

41. Anders, "The Development of Public Library Service in the Southeastern States, 1895–1950," 239.

42. Carmichael Jr., "Tommie Dora Barker and Southern Librarianship," 148–49, 155–56, 270; Anders, "The Development of Public Library Service in the Southeastern States, 1895–1950," 69, 99–100; Old Chapel Hill Cemetery, "Louis Round Wilson," http://www.ibiblio.org/cemetery/university/wilson.html, accessed July 26, 2015. Wilson also served as the president of the American Library Association from 1935 to 1936. In 1932, he became dean of the University of Chicago's Library School.

43. Anders, "The Development of Public Library Service in the Southeastern States, 1895–1950," 191–92.

44. Ibid., 33–34; see also Table 1 "First incorporated subscription library in each Southeastern state, by date of incorporation" (pg. 43). The Huntsville Library Association, founded 1823, represents Alabama's first incorporated subscription library. The Savannah Library Association and the Nashville Library Company, founded respectively in 1801 and 1813, represent Georgia and Tennessee's first incorporated subscription libraries; "Big Library Started by 47 Young Men," *Atlanta Constitution*, October 11, 1959; "Mission of Pioneers Realized as New Public Library Makes Dreams True," *Birmingham News*, April 10, 1927.

45. Anders, "The Development of Public Library Service in the Southeastern States, 1895–1950," 239–40.

46. Nick Taylor, *American-Made: The Enduring Legacy of the WPA: When FDR Put the Nation to Work* (New York: Bantam Books, 2008), 523.

47. Taylor, *American-Made*, 132–34. In Alabama, the WPA partnered with the State Department of Archives and History. In Georgia the WPA teamed up with the state library commission, and in Tennessee it worked with the State Department of Education. The WPA's library project with Alabama lasted from 1939 to 1942, while its work in Georgia took place from 1936 to 1943. The WPA library project in Tennessee only lasted from 1940 to 1942.

48. Ibid., 133.

49. Ibid., 136–37, 139, 141–42.

50. Ibid., 136–37.

51. Anders, "The Development of Public Library Service in the Southeastern States, 1895–1950," 133–36, 139; Edward Barrett Stanford, *Library Extension Under the WPA: An Appraisal of an Experiment in Federal Aid* (Chicago: University of Chicago Press, 1944), 88–89.

52. Anders, "The Development of Public Library Service in the Southeastern States, 1895–1950," 145; Kenneth S. Davis, *FDR: The New Deal Years, 1933–1937* (New York: Random House, 1986), 90; Tennessee Valley Authority, "From the New Deal to a New Century," accessed August 1, 2015, http://www.tva.com/abouttva/history.htm

53. Anders, "The Development of Public Library Service in the Southeastern States, 1895–1950," 146, 148.

54. Ibid., 148, 152.

55. Ibid., 14, 150–151, 154, 160.

56. Ibid., 156–57, 158–60. Louis Round Wilson and Mary Milzewski, *Libraries of the Southeast: A Report of the Southeastern States Cooperative Library Survey, 1946–1947* (Chapel Hill: University of North Carolina Press, 1949).

57. Wilson and Milzewski, *Libraries of the Southeast*, 152.
58. Ibid., 149, 151.
59. Ibid., 159.
60. Carmichael Jr., "Tommie Dora Barker and Southern Librarianship," 409.
61. Ibid., 209–11.
62. Ibid., 241–42.

Chapter 3

"Library Users Are Seekers of Knowledge"

Developing African American Library Service and Educating Black Librarians

Southern communities founded and supported public libraries in a segregated society.[1] Thus, libraries constantly dealt with issues of race. Among the many conundrums they experienced, southern public libraries had to determine if they would serve African American patrons, and, if so, how? This chapter analyzes the responses of southern public libraries to these questions. It also addresses how African Americans and northern philanthropic aid worked to establish and support black libraries, as well as develop African American library schools.

Even with outside support and local African American backing, black library development proceeded slowly in communities across the South. Eliza Atkins Gleason argued that library service for African Americans in many ways mimicked the development of white public libraries in the South, albeit on a smaller scale and at a slower pace.[2] After 1950, however, the integration of southern public libraries occurred faster than in other public places in the region.

AFRICAN AMERICAN LIBRARY DEVELOPMENT, 1900–1941

Prior to the 1950s most southern public libraries employed various restrictions on African American use, if they allowed African Americans to use their facilities and resources at all. A branch library that exclusively served black users often represented the greatest extent of service to African Americans before integration.[3] Although many southern public libraries excluded African Americans altogether, or at best provided limited access and service to black patrons, notable exceptions did occur. The Enoch Pratt Free Library in Baltimore, Maryland, represents perhaps the best example of a public library providing full service to African Americans prior to the mass integration of southern public libraries. Founded and endowed in 1886 by industrialist, financier, and philanthropist Enoch Pratt, the Enoch Pratt Free Library reflected Pratt's belief that libraries could serve as a personal improvement and uplift tool for both whites and blacks.[4] However, even the Enoch Pratt Free Library did not remain immune from the influence of Jim Crow. Wayne Wigand pointed out that in 1934 the Enoch Pratt Free Library segregated its restrooms.[5]

Baltimore's geographic location might have had something to do with Enoch Pratt's decision to construct and fund a library that openly and freely served whites and African Americans, as well as the library board's decision to continue the policy even as some Baltimoreans publicly objected to the library's integrated status at the turn of the twentieth century. Scholars Stanley Rubinstein and Judith Farley argue that the library retained its integrated status because it had a self-perpetuating board; members did not have to worry about justifying to the public their decision to keep the library integrated. However, the fact that the leadership of the Pratt Library caved to public pressure regarding the establishment of segregated restrooms underscores the fact that no matter what side of the Mason-Dixon line libraries were on, none remained immune from the corrosive influences of segregation.[6]

Scholars have argued over whether Maryland represents a southern, northern, or border state. Of course, "The South" represents as much a construct as it does a geographical location. Accordingly, what states make up the South represents a long-standing debate. Many historians have regarded Maryland as an upper-South state, a mid-Atlantic state, as well as a state possessing "northern" and "southern" qualities, but not totally representative of either.

Access to Public Libraries: A Research Project, a 1963 report produced by the American Library Association (ALA), studied the ability of people, including African Americans, to access the South's public libraries. The report, produced by International Research Associates, identified seven characteristics that made the South a distinctive region: a large non-Caucasian population; allegiance to the Confederacy during the Civil War; a single political party dominating politics and political systems; intense legal and social discrimination toward African Americans; lower personal income levels than much of the nation; a mostly rural population; and generally lower high school graduation rates than the rest of the country. Based on the degree to which states matched the seven characteristics, International Research Associates identified three distinct sections: Deep South, Mid South, and Border South. Mississippi, South Carolina, Louisiana, Alabama, and Georgia represented deep-South states. North Carolina, Arkansas, Virginia, Florida, and Tennessee served as mid-South States. Maryland, Delaware, Texas, Oklahoma, Kentucky, West Virginia, and Washington, D.C. constituted border-South states and districts.[7]

Excepting institutions like the Enoch Pratt Free Library, most southern public libraries were averse to serving blacks in even a minimal way. In his research on library service to African Americans, Michael Fultz found it easier to point out southern public libraries that provided service to African Americans than the ones that did not. Fultz identified a 1903 partnership between Memphis, Tennessee's Cossitt Library and the LeMoyne Institute—an African American school run by the American Missionary Association—whereby the Cossitt Library provided the LeMoyne Institute with books while LeMoyne provided the actual library service, as an example of the difficulty African Americans usually had in receiving library service.[8] Fultz also pointed to Louisville, Kentucky's public library, which accommodated African American patrons at the beginning of the twentieth century, as an exception to the poor library service black patrons often received during the early years of southern public library development. In 1905 the Louisville Public Library (LPL) provided African Americans with a small branch library in a rented space. In 1908, the LPL received a Carnegie library construction grant to build a city-owned, stand-alone African American branch library.[9] Memphis and Louisville demonstrate that, at best, southern cities slowly expanded service to African Americans. According to a 1933 ALA report, only seventy-two southern public libraries provided African Americans with any public library service.[10]

Southern African Americans quickly became frustrated by their inability to receive library service. Increasingly, they took matters into their own hands, establishing libraries in black churches and schools, as well as universities and colleges.[11] Houston, Texas, provides a case study of how African Americans worked to establish their own free public libraries. After the Houston Lyceum and Carnegie Library (Houston Public Library) refused him service, African American school principal Ernest Ollington Smith and other black leaders approached Houston's white civic leaders in 1908, including Mayor H. Baldwin Rice, to inquire if the city would provide funds to establish an African American library. Rice promised Smith the city would provide $500 dollars for this purpose. However, when Houston's public library board heard about the mayor's pledged financial support, it voted to provide $100 and discarded library books to an African American library, if Houston's black community could locate a building and hire staff. Shortly thereafter, Houston's African American high school provided space for the library.[12] After securing the initial space for the library, Houston's black leaders convinced Mayor Rice and Andrew Carnegie to provide funds to establish a stand-alone library. In 1913, the Colored Carnegie Library opened and ceased receiving financial support from the Houston Public Library, thus becoming an entirely independent institution answering only to the city.

Despite the effort Houston's African American leaders expended in securing the Colored Carnegie Library, the institution did not remain on its own for long. In March 1921, the Houston Public Library's leadership requested that the city strip the Colored Carnegie Library of its independent status and return it to the public library's control. Contending that it made poor financial sense to maintain two public library systems, the library board convinced Houston's political leadership to bring the Colored Carnegie Library back into the fold of the Houston Public Library.[13]

The story of the rise and fall of Houston's Colored Carnegie Library displays the effort African Americans would expend in the quest to obtain free public library service. Furthermore, the work to establish the Colored Carnegie Library, including finding a location and funds, going to Carnegie for the money to build a stand-alone building, and having an entirely black board manage it, represented a model for other African Americans to follow as they attempted to participate as leaders in an intensely segregated and racially tense public sphere.[14] Furthermore, when studying why African Americans fought so committedly to establish their own libraries, like the Houston Colored Carnegie Library, scholars must consider the community center aspect of public libraries. African Americans perceived and used libraries as communal places where a variety of activities besides reading and checking out books occurred. Numerous examples of African Americans using libraries as a place to engage in various aspects of public life abound. In Louisville Kentucky, at the Louisville Public Library Colored Branches, a host of activities occurred, including club and organizational meetings, various classes, and more. In Atlanta, black Atlantans also took part in a range of pursuits and endeavors, such as frequenting workshops on how to register to vote, participating in classes aimed at creating an understanding of the political process, attending meetings, and more.[15]

PHILANTHROPY AND AFRICAN AMERICAN LIBRARY DEVELOPMENT

Philanthropic organizations played a significant role in establishing library service for blacks in the South. In addition to the CCNY, other important organizations included the General Education Board (GEB), founded by John D. Rockefeller Sr. in 1902 to increase educational opportunities for white and African American southerners, and the Julius S. Rosenwald Fund. Mary Edna Anders estimates that between roughly 1903 and 1950, the CCNY contributed $6,500,000, the GEB $8,200,000, and the Rosenwald Fund $800,000 to southern library development.[16]

The GEB especially supported endeavors that provided southern African Americans with educational opportunities. From 1924 to 1931 the GEB engaged in arguably its most active period, spending almost $25,000,000 on initiatives to develop African American education. The money spent during this period usually went directly to supporting black schools, colleges, and universities, although the GEB also emphasized training African American teachers. Prior to the 1924–1931 period, the GEB worked with southern state governments and school systems to develop the South's overall public education system, which it hoped would include establishing and funding African American schools. However, by working within already established educational structures and publicly supported institutions, the GEB especially spurred the development of white public education.[17]

Andrew Carnegie and the CCNY funded eleven libraries built for African Americans between 1908 and 1922. Kentucky, Georgia, Texas, Mississippi, Louisiana, North Carolina, and Tennessee all received enough funds to construct at least one African American library. Kentucky had two Carnegie-funded African American branch libraries in Louisville, the most in any southern state. Atlanta, Georgia, and Nashville, Tennessee, each had one. Birmingham, Alabama, the third city considered in this study, did not have a Carnegie-funded African American branch library.[18]

In 1912 Sears, Roebuck and Company part-owner Julius S. Rosenwald became interested in supporting African American education in the South after reading *An American Citizen*, a biography of William H. Baldwin Jr., the first GEB chairman, president of the Board of Trustees at Tuskegee Institute, and a proponent of black education. Rosenwald admired Tuskegee Institute's industrial education (vocational) curriculum and soon became friends with Booker T. Washington.[19] Washington heavily influenced Rosenwald's early giving. Until around 1920, Tuskegee and Washington managed Rosenwald's philanthropy program. In 1912 Rosenwald provided $25,000 to support schools started by Tuskegee or its graduates, as well as institutions using Tuskegee's industrial education curriculum to train African American students. Booker T. Washington managed this grant, deciding how to spend it. In 1912 Rosenwald embarked on perhaps his best-known philanthropic endeavor, constructing around 5,000 schools in the South for African Americans, a project that lasted into the 1930s.[20]

In addition to constructing African American schools across the South, the Rosenwald Fund also bankrolled experiments in select counties of specific southern states to see if countywide library systems represented the best way to effectively serve the South's spread-out, rural population. The Rosenwald Fund's county library demonstrations represent an especially important development in southern public librarianship because they covered a wide service area, generated significant collaboration with local governments, and required integrated service. As early as 1926 the Southeastern Library Association expressed interest in testing countywide library service areas as an efficacious method of bringing library service to the South's rural population. In 1929 Carl Milam, ALA executive secretary, convinced the Rosenwald Fund to finance experiments in eleven counties in seven southern states. The Rosenwald Fund agreed to provide $500,000 for the project. Counties wishing to take part in the experiment had to agree to four conditions: equally serve whites and African Americans, provide a librarian who had received library training, spend all funds provided by the Rosenwald Fund as well as money raised through additional means, and provide a library building. If a county agreed to these four conditions, the Rosenwald Fund would match money raised from other sources.[21]

In 1929 and 1930, the Rosenwald Fund picked eleven counties in the states of North Carolina, South Carolina, Tennessee, Alabama, Mississippi, Texas, and Louisiana.[22] Unfortunately, the Great Depression struck just as the project got underway. At one point the Rosenwald Fund had so little available money that the CCNY had to provide $200,000 to keep the project going. Even with this support, the county library demonstration project ended in 1932. During its short life, the Rosenwald Fund's countywide library service experiment produced, at best, mixed results. However, the project might have influenced the WPA and the TVA to use the county and regional library service model for many of their Great Depression Era library projects. At the very least, the Rosenwald Fund's experiment paved the way for the WPA and TVA library projects, which also relied on collaboration with municipal, county, and regional governments, as well as with state agencies. By working with county governments, the Rosenwald Fund perhaps made some county officials and librarians a little more comfortable working with the WPA and TVA. Additionally, with its insistence that participating counties equally serve blacks and whites, the Rosenwald Fund perhaps helped set in motion the early integration of southern public libraries, as compared to other public facilities in the South.

THE DEVELOPMENT OF AFRICAN AMERICAN LIBRARY EDUCATION IN THE SOUTH

In addition to library service, African Americans also wished to obtain education in library science and secure employment in libraries. However, library training for African Americans also developed slowly in the South. In 1911 the Louisville Public Library began a lecture series for African Americans interested in librarianship. Reverend Thomas Blue, who served as the head of Louisville Public Library's Western and Eastern Colored Branches, led this initiative. Initially, those attending the lectures had to live in Louisville. However, in 1914, the library relaxed the residency rule and invited African Americans who lived beyond Louisville to attend the training courses. The lectures at Louisville perhaps represent the earliest formal library training in the South for African Americans. Some evidence exists that these lectures soon evolved into a structured curriculum. When Houston's Colored Carnegie Library hired Bessie Osborne as its first librarian, it sent her to Louisville to participate in Blue's lecture program. Louisville Public Library director George T. Settle wrote to Julia Ideson informing her that Osborne's training had included apprenticeship work in each of the library's departments.[23]

In 1925, the CCNY's Frederick Keppel twice corresponded with Carl Milam, ALA secretary from 1920 to 1948, about establishing a library school in the South for African Americans.[24] Milam initially thought that Tuskegee Institute, located in southeast Alabama, should host any such school. To gain perspective on the issue, Milam turned to the Rosenwald Fund and the GEB.[25] Both organizations agreed that an African American higher-learning institution, located in the South, should host a library school to educate black librarians. Wickliffe Rose, GEB president, suggested Virginia's Hampton Institute, situated in southeast Virginia on the Chesapeake Bay, as a possible site.

On Milam's orders, at ALA's behest, and funded by the CCNY, Louis Round Wilson surveyed possible sites to host a southern African American library school. Sarah Bogle, Milam's assistant while he served as ALA's executive director, wanted Wilson to additionally consider Howard University in Washington, D.C., as another possible site. However, because Milam wanted the school to serve southern African American students who would then work in the South, Wilson dismissed Howard University as a location. Wilson believed that Howard University, with its upper-South location and high tuition, would not help the ALA, CCNY, Rosenwald Fund, and GEB accomplish their goals for black library education. Instead, Wilson suggested Fisk University in Nashville, Tennessee, as another potential location for the school. Between Hampton Institute and Tuskegee Institute, Wilson favored Hampton because it had white faculty members on staff. Thus, he reasoned, it would have an easier time convincing white library instructors to serve on the library school's faculty than would Tuskegee with its all African American staff. Although Wilson considered the Tuskegee Institute to be a well-managed institution, he regarded Hampton Institute as a better financed and administered school, possessing a more superb overall curriculum.[26]

His glowing observations about Hampton Institute aside, Wilson came away from his visit to Fisk University convinced it would have served as the best possible location for the school had its students not rioted and gone on strike in response to university president Fayette Avery McKenzie's heavy-handed nature in dealing with student affairs and his obsequiousness toward Nashville's white power structure. Wilson ultimately dismissed Fisk University as a possible site for the school. In addition to Wilson, the GEB and the CCNY also favored Hampton Institute as the site of the library school. In 1925 the Hampton Institute Library School opened. The CCNY not only provided the grant that made the opening of the school possible, but funded nearly its entire budget through most of its existence. Interestingly, the National Association for the Advancement of Colored People (NAACP) opposed the opening of a library school for African Americans. The NAACP believed that with the opening of a library school for blacks, library schools that did admit African Americans at the time would cease to do so. In short, it appears that the NAACP believed that opening a library school at Hampton Institute would actually intensify segregation in higher education.[27]

In 1929, Sarah Bogle met with representatives from the GEB and the Rosenwald Fund at the opening of the University of North Carolina's (UNC) new library building (Louis Round Wilson directed the UNC library at the time). After the meeting, Bogle asked the CCNY's Frederick Keppel to bring together the CCNY, GEB, Board of Education for Librarianship (BEL), Rosenwald Fund, and SELA at a 1930 meeting to better coordinate their southern library development plans and objectives. Library education for African Americans came up during the meeting. The Rosenwald Fund's Clark Foreman suggested moving Hampton Institute's library school to Atlanta, although nothing immediately happened. Deciding to survey all southern institutions providing library education represents the meeting's most important outcome. The CCNY paid for the survey and Sarah Bogle conducted it.[28]

In November 1930, the BEL discussed Bogle's survey. She reported that Hampton's library school trained its students mostly for work in college libraries. Accordingly, she recommended establishing another library school that would focus on training librarians for employment in schools and public libraries and suggested Atlanta University. Her report and its recommendations set in motion discussions about moving the Hampton Institute library school to either Fisk or Atlanta University, or creating an entirely new library school to train African American librarians.

Meanwhile, the CCNY and other organizations began to significantly downsize their financial contributions to Hampton Institute's library school. In the early 1930s the CCNY annually provided $12,500 to the Hampton library school budget, while the Rosenwald Fund contributed $5,500. Hampton Institute itself provided only $2,450 in funding to its library school. In 1937, the CCNY informed Hampton it would cut its funding to the library school to $7,500 per year for the next two years, after which it would no longer provide any money. As a result, the Hampton library school closed in

1939. That same year the BEL employed Tommie Dora Barker to undertake a survey similar to the one Bogle completed in 1930. Barker concluded that the South required a library school to train African American librarians. With funding from the CCNY and the GEB, Atlanta University's library school opened in 1941 with Eliza Atkins Gleason as its first director.[29]

THE SOUTH'S PUBLIC LIBRARIES INTEGRATE

Efforts to make library education available to African Americans proceeded alongside southern blacks' attempts to gain access to public libraries. Slowly, southern public libraries began to increase the service they provided to African Americans. By the early 1950s, southern public libraries began the process of integrating, often before other public places and facilities. Why so many southern public libraries either offered full or limited integration prior to the Supreme Court's 1954 decision in *Brown v Board of Education* remains a fascinating question. Michael Futz argues that although public libraries constituted public spaces, and thereby were subject to some variation of the South's race code, interactions between whites and blacks at the library differed from those occurring in schools, on public transportation, and in stores.

According to Fultz, the thinking went that on public transportation, in schools, and in stores, whites and African Americans would have to interact. On the other hand, social interaction between whites and blacks in public libraries remained largely voluntary, except when African American patrons had to speak to a librarian to check out books, ask for reference assistance, or attempt to use some other library service.[30]

Wayne and Shirley Wiegand offer their own take on why library integration sometimes occurred earlier than in other public places in the South. The Wiegands claim that some whites saw the integration of public libraries as the price to pay to avoid more public integration efforts like bus boycotts. In particular, the Wiegands contend, whites viewed the integration of southern public libraries, while undoubtedly a shame in the eyes of some, a far superior alternative to the ultimate fear, school integration.[31]

A 1962 study by International Research Associates, commissioned by the ALA, suggests other reasons as well. International Research Associates gathered quantitative and qualitative data, including the opinions of civic leaders and librarians, regarding racially integrated libraries. Explaining how their city had successfully integrated its public library, one civic leader stated:

> You have to realize that the class of Negroes who want to use the library is a pretty high class. Just like the whites who use the library are high class. What

made it easy was that the class who would oppose Negroes does not use the library. . . . There are two classes of people. Library users are seekers of knowledge. The rough class of either race doesn't go to the library.[32]

An earlier study conducted in 1948 also suggests that perceptions of social class influenced library desegregation. In her survey of twenty-two southern libraries' practices and policies on service to African American patrons, Emily Miller Danton, Birmingham Public Library director from 1947 to 1953, quoted one librarian as stating, "Only the more educated Negroes would be involved, and their numbers would be too small to endanger the status quo." The librarian Danton quoted also regarded communities that attempted to maintain two, racially separated public library systems to stave off integration as pursuing an ultimately unsustainable action.[33]

In 1941, only sixteen public libraries in the entire South provided library access to African Americans. Four, including those in Brady, Pecos, and El Paso, Texas, and Covington, Kentucky, provided full service to black patrons. A decade later, the situation significantly changed. In 1953, the Southern Regional Council's (SRC) Ann Holden surveyed 172 public libraries in communities across the South to gauge the extent and quality of service they provided to African Americans.[34] Holden found that fifty-nine southern communities offered full service to African Americans at their main branch, twenty-four provided limited service at the main branch, eleven library systems served both white and black patrons at their branch libraries, and three library systems had African Americans serving on their boards. In Tennessee, four library systems provided full service to blacks at their main branch, while none had branch libraries providing integrated service. African Americans in Georgia and Alabama fared worse than their Tennessee counterparts. In Alabama and Georgia, only one library system in each state provided limited service to African Americans at their main branch. None provided blacks with full service at their main branches or possessed branch libraries equally serving whites and blacks.[35] Among Atlanta, Birmingham, and Nashville, only Nashville provided full service to African American patrons at its main branch, although Birmingham started providing limited service to blacks at its main branch in 1953.[36]

The percentage of African Americans receiving library service prior to 1950 in Alabama, Georgia, and Tennessee illustrates just how few blacks could actually use southern public libraries. In 1926 only 8 percent of African Americans living in Alabama could visit a library and use its services. In 1947 this number rose to 26 percent. Nine percent of blacks living in Georgia in 1926 could access public libraries. In 1947 the figure rose to 33 percent. In 1926 28 percent of Tennessee's African Americans could use public libraries. In 1947 56 percent of blacks living in Tennessee could use public libraries.[37]

African Americans living in communities with small black populations had a slight advantage in their ability to access public libraries over blacks living in areas with large numbers of African Americans. Holden reported that public libraries located in communities with small African American populations tended to integrate more often than libraries located in areas with larger African American concentrations. Four-fifths of the fifty-nine library systems providing black patrons with full services at their main branches in 1953 were located in communities where African Americans represented 20 percent or less of the overall population.[38]

Although libraries were among the first public institutions in the South to provide services on a desegregated basis, this did not always mean full, unrestricted integration. Many southern public libraries practiced limited integration, often falling far short of total desegregation. For example, several library systems allowed African American patrons to use their main branch library's materials, but not the reading room. In other instances, libraries set aside separate reading rooms for blacks, or designated specific tables in their reading room for exclusive African American use. Sometimes, library systems would only serve African American students and professionals—doctors, lawyers, preachers, etc.—at the main branch. Through inter-library loan some library systems would let blacks borrow materials that other patrons could not.[39]

Limited integration often became outright bizarre. Three of the strangest examples occurred in Memphis, Tennessee; Danville, Virginia; and Montgomery, Alabama. In Memphis, public facilities like the zoo and library remained closed to African Americans except on "Black Thursday," when those facilities closed to whites and opened to African Americans. When the National Association for the Advancement of Colored People (NAACP) won a May 1960 court order commanding the Danville, Virginia, public library to integrate, the city closed the library. Danville reopened its library in September 1960 using a "vertical integration" plan. Whites and African Americans could use the library together. However, the library removed all tables and chairs in an attempt to prevent black and white patrons from sitting down and engaging in prolonged social interaction. Montgomery, Alabama's public library also employed the same scheme in 1962.[40]

After it reopened as an integrated institution, the Danville Public Library also implemented a new application process patrons had to follow to obtain a library card. The library required applicants to fill out a four-page application form that asked for the applicant's place and date of birth, their college degrees (if they had any), the subject matter of the books they wanted, the number of books they wished to check out, two references attesting to their character, and two work-related references. Furthermore, applicants had to pay a $2.50 application fee.[41]

Other southern cities employed similarly ludicrous and frustrating schemes. Although the courts ordered the Talladega, Alabama, public library to integrate in 1962, the library's trustees found what they thought constituted a work-around to court-mandated integration. They reasoned that the Talladega Public Library should only have to serve those living in the community. To determine who lived in the community, the trustees of the Talladega Public Library consulted the phone book. As Wayne Wiegand points out in his book *Part of Our Lives: A People's History of the American Public Library*, many African Americans in Talladega did not have phones. Accordingly, the phone book did not list many blacks who lived in the city.[42]

Stephen Cresswell argues that most efforts to integrate public libraries, as well as the greatest number of public library integrations, occurred by and largely ended in the mid-1960s. He attributes this decline to what he perceived as the civil rights movement's increasing attention on taking the battle for civil rights North. Although Cresswell overlooks a significant argument in civil rights movement scholarship—that local movements across the nation made up the overall movement—he correctly identifies the time period when most southern public libraries integrated. For instance, the Nashville Public Library integrated in 1950, the Atlanta Public Library in 1959, and the Birmingham Public Library in 1963.[43]

While sometimes exhibiting a less than totally firm stance, the ALA did ultimately oppose racial discrimination in American public libraries and the library profession. In 1936, the ALA decided not to have its annual meeting in segregated cities. It did not hold another annual meeting below the Mason-Dixon line until 1956 when it met at Miami Beach, Florida. Despite its policy not to meet in cities practicing segregation, the ALA took a step backward in 1960 by failing to oppose racial discrimination in libraries. When pressed for a response about the ALA's stance on segregated public libraries, the organization's president, Benjamin Powell, responded by stating that ALA could not interfere in what amounted to local issues. The ALA's vacillatory position on library segregation over the years did not go unnoticed by African American librarians. Atlanta Public Library (APL) black librarian Annie L. McPheeters notes that many African American librarians, already barred from state and regional library associations, felt that the ALA accepted them at best as "a silent partner." Accordingly, argues McPheeters, black librarians chose to form their own state library associations. McPheeters points to efforts by African American librarians in North Carolina, Kentucky, Georgia, and Mississippi as particularly noteworthy.[44]

In 1954, the ALA voted to accept only one chapter from each state. Previously, many southern states had two chapters, one African American, the other white. The ALA gave all states until 1956 to comply with the requirement. Alabama and Georgia did not satisfy ALA's demand by the deadline and subsequently had no ALA-recognized state chapters for some years. In 1961, ALA added an amendment to its Library Bill of Rights, stating that libraries could not deny service to a person because of their race, religion, country of birth, or political sensibilities. ALA required state chapters to adhere to the organization's constitutional requirement to remain in good standing. Furthermore, in 1962, ALA commissioned its *Access to Public Libraries* report to gauge the public's ability to gain admittance to American public libraries and use the services provided therein. Based on the report's findings, the ALA determined that southern public libraries had made commendable progress toward integration. Also in 1962, at its annual meeting, the ALA explicitly stated what constituted its members' rights. Unable to comply with these standards, the Louisiana and Mississippi state chapters withdrew from the ALA, although Louisiana rejoined in 1965.[45]

Although the Supreme Court may have had little to no discernible impact on the desegregation of southern public libraries, hearing only one case tangentially related to public library discrimination, federal district and appeals courts did. For example, in 1962 African American Robert L. Cobb tried to use Montgomery, Alabama's public library. After the library refused to serve him, Cobb sued the city in federal court and won. The court ordered Montgomery to desegregate its public library.[46] Cobb's victory illustrates that local activists had the power, backed by the authority of the federal court system, to integrate public libraries in their communities. As the case studies on Atlanta and Birmingham will show, the efforts of local activists, supported by the possibility of the federal courts becoming involved, caused those cities to desegregate their public libraries. In Atlanta's case, a threatened lawsuit, the result of a long effort to integrate the Atlanta Public Library (APL), induced that city to integrate its library. Atlanta's civic leaders believed that a federal court would look favorably upon a lawsuit to integrate the APL. Students sat-in at the Birmingham Public Library (BPL) during the Southern Christian Leadership Conference's (SCLC) 1963 campaign in the city, a time when the eyes of the nation, including its court system, were directed toward Birmingham. Thus, Atlanta, Birmingham, Montgomery, Talladega, and Danville, Virginia, as well as other examples, illustrate that the federal courts played a role of some significance—even if they did not always become directly involved—in integrating southern public libraries.

Southern public libraries desegregated for numerous reasons besides fear of a federal court order telling them to do so. Other factors influencing southern public libraries to integrate include the ALA's actions intended to tear down segregation and racism in the library profession, as well as many public librarians in the South appearing to think library segregation wrong, or, the desegregation of public libraries inevitable. As the civil rights movement reached its zenith in the mid-1960s, many public libraries wanted to avoid becoming targets for an integration attempt. Many, if not most, librarians in the South believed public libraries would eventually have to integrate, knew that most southern communities could not or did not want to maintain two public library systems, and felt that only a few African Americans would use integrated libraries anyway.

While some librarians undoubtedly felt that integrating public libraries represented the right thing to do, others probably viewed library integration as a pragmatic economic decision. If communities closed their libraries to prevent integration, as Danville, Virginia, did for part of 1960, the librarians staffing those facilities faced potential economic hardship. Communities that considered trying to maintain two library systems—one white and one African American—knew the futility of such an attempt. Two entirely equal library systems represented a financial burden most southern communities could not or did not want to bear. Furthermore, after the Supreme Court's 1954 decision in *Brown v. Board of Education*, southern communities recognized that various schemes to prevent or stall library integration, such as dual library systems, would not work. Indeed, when International Research Associates polled southern librarians on why their libraries desegregated, many librarians reported that the Supreme Court's *Brown v. Board of Education* ruling had a significant impact on their decision, more so than any ALA action against segregation.[47] Although libraries, librarians, and state library organizations could function without holding membership in or taking part in ALA activities, they could not defy the law without the real possibility of severe consequences.

Although libraries were contested sites during the civil rights movement, it appears as though activists targeted them less for integration attempts than other facilities like eating establishments, public transportation, theaters, and schools. Civil rights movement leaders and participants deemed library integration important, but less so than desegregating other public places. Civil rights movement organizations prioritized their goals when attempting to desegregate specific places and therefore very consciously selected what they would target for a desegregation attempt. Furthermore, the division between what national and local organizations wished to accomplish also played a role. For example, the NAACP worked to legally dismantle segregation especially through the court system. The SCLC, long headed by Dr. Martin Luther King Jr., focused on pressuring Congress to pass a civil rights and voting act.[48] The Student Nonviolent Coordinating Committee (SNCC) often worked in communities off the path frequently travelled by other organizations to register voters and organize African Americans for political action. In sum, organizations like the NAACP, SCLC, and SNCC, while caring about attacking segregation everywhere, did not have unlimited resources. These organizations had to selectively choose what specific political or legal objectives they planned to pursue and work to achieve at any given time.⁴⁹

During their early years, few southern public libraries provided access and services to African Americans. As Eliza Atkins Gleason argues, the development of libraries and library services for African Americans occurred on a smaller scale and at a slower pace than white library development. African Americans had to find ways to speed it up and expand its scope. They could not wait on the southern white power structure to do it for them. Besides African American efforts, northern philanthropic organizations like the CCNY, GEB, Rosenwald Fund, and BEL did the most to develop black libraries and African American library education. Although well-intentioned, these organizations' involvement sometimes seemed paternalistic. While the organizations often met among themselves to chart southern and African American public library development, they consulted black leaders only occasionally. Still, northern philanthropic organizations provided valuable funds for African American libraries and library education in the South.

Ultimately, the successful efforts to integrate the South's public libraries came from the unceasing efforts of African Americans. African Americans fought to end library segregation because it constituted a moral and legal wrong, as well as prevented them from taking rightful advantage of all their rights as American citizens. A deep love for reading, libraries, and education served a constant source of motivation for African Americans as they tirelessly worked to gain access to southern public libraries. ⁵⁰

The libraries in this book's three case studies all integrated for some of the above reasons, including the APL, the first case study. The APL's case study comes first because of the library's leadership role in southern public library development. However, despite its influence over the southern public library movement on many fronts, the APL, like most other southern public libraries, struggled with questions of race and had a somewhat messy integration experience. Indeed, for decades it worked to come to grips with its segregated past, particularly with issues of staff and race. The following chapter begins with the APL's founding and moves through its early growth up to its integration in the late 1950s. Along the way, the APL's case study illustrates how the APL played a significant role in institutionalizing segregation in southern public libraries while at the same time seeking and developing ways to provide African Americans with some form of library service during segregation. It also demonstrates that not only could the integration of southern public libraries prove intricate and confusing, but dealing with the complications of having practiced racial segregation could long cause unforeseen, complicated dilemmas and questions for southern public libraries.

NOTES

1. Dallas Hanbury, "'It is simply out of the question to eliminate the colorline': The Development of Black Library Service in Atlanta and the Integration of the Atlanta Public Library," *Libraries: Culture, History, and Society* 2, no. 1 (2018): 24–47. copyright (c) 2018, The Pennsylvania State University Press. This article is used by permission of the Pennsylvania State University Press.

2. Eliza Atkins Gleason, *The Southern Negro and the Public Library: A Study of the Government and Administration of Public Library Service to Negroes in the South* (Chicago: The University of Chicago Press, 1941), 18.

3. Gleason, *The Southern Negro and the Public Library*, 19.

4. Stanley Rubinstein and Judith Farley, "Enoch Pratt Free Library and Black Patrons: Equality in Library Services, 1882–1915," *Journal of Library History* 15, no. 4 (Fall 1980): 445–47, 450.

5. Wiegand and Wiegand, *The Desegregation of Public Libraries in the Jim Crow South*, 25.

6. Rubinstein and Farley, "Enoch Pratt Free Library and Black Patrons," 448–49.

7. International Research Associates, *Access to Public Libraries: A Research Project, Prepared for the Library Administration Division, American Library Association, International Research Associates, Inc.* (Chicago: American Library Association, 1963), 3, 4–10.

8. Michael Fultz, "Black Public Libraries in the South in the Era of De Jure Segregation," *Libraries and the Cultural Record* 41, no. 3 (Summer 2006): 339.

9. Fultz, "Black Public Libraries in the South in the Era of De Jure Segregation," 339–40.

10. American Library Association, *Books for the South* (Chicago: American Library Association, 1933), 7, accessed July 22, 2015, HathiTrust.

11. Fultz, "Black Public Libraries in the South in the Era of De Jure Segregation," 340, 342–43.

12. Cheryl Knott Malone, "Autonomy and Accommodation: Houston's Colored Carnegie Library, 1907–1922," *Libraries & Culture* 34, no. 2 (Spring 1999): 98–99.

13. Malone, "Autonomy and Accommodation," 103, 105.

14. Ibid., 96.

15. Annie L. McPheeters, interviewed by Kathryn L. Nasstrom, June 8, 1992, P1992-09, transcript, Georgia Government Documentation Project, Special Collections and Archives, Georgia State University Library, Atlanta, 8–9, 15, 32; Wayne A. Wiegand, *Part of Our Lives: A People's History of the American Public Library* (New York: Oxford University Press, 2015), 97.

16. Mary Edna Anders, "The Development of Public Library Service in the Southeastern States, 1895–1950" (Ph.D. diss., Columbia University, 1958), 116, 117–18.

17. Eric Anderson and Alfred A. Moss, Jr., *Dangerous Donations: Northern Philanthropy and Southern Black Education, 1902–1930* (Columbia: University of Missouri Press, 1999), 95, 99–101.

18. Robbie D. Jones, "'What's in a Name?': Tennessee's Carnegie Libraries & Civic Reform in the New South, 1889–1919" (master's thesis, Middle Tennessee State University, 2003), 69, 74.

19. James D. Anderson, *The Education of Blacks in the South, 1860–1935* (Chapel Hill: University of North Carolina Press, 1988), 77.

20. Anderson and Moss Jr., *Dangerous Donations*, 10, 83, 193, 195.

21. Mary Edna Anders, "The Development of Public Library Service in the Southeastern States, 1895–1950" (PhD diss., Columbia University, 1958), 121–23.

22. Edwin R. Embree, *Julius Rosenwald Fund: Review of Two Decades, 1917–1936* (Chicago: Julius Rosenwald Fund, 1936), 42.

23. Anders, "The Development of Public Library Service in the Southeastern States, 1895–1950," 23; Fultz, "Black Public Libraries in the South in the Era of De Jure Segregation," 340; Malone, "Autonomy and Accommodation," 104; See also Robert Sidney Martin and Orvin Lee Shiflett, "Hampton, Fisk, and Atlanta: The Foundations, the American Library Association, and Library Education for Blacks, 1925–1941," *Libraries & Culture* 31, no. 2 (Spring 1996): 301.

24. American Library Association, "Past Executive Directors & Secretaries," accessed July 25, 2015, http://www.ala.org/aboutala/history/past-executive-directors. In 1958 the ALA renamed the title of Secretary to Executive Director; Peggy Sullivan, *Carl H. Milam and the American Library Association* (New York: H. W. Wilson, 1976), 70–72. Carl Milam also served as the Birmingham Public Library's director from 1913 to 1919.

25. Martin and Shiflett, "Hampton, Fisk, and Atlanta," 300–1.

26. Ibid., 300–4.

27. Ibid., 302–3, 305, 317; Wiegand and Wiegand, *The Desegregation of Public Libraries in the Jim Crow South*, 186.

28. Martin and Shiflett, "Hampton, Fisk, and Atlanta," 311–12.

29. Ibid., 311–12, 317, 319.

30. International Research Associates, *Access to Public Libraries*, accessed July 27, 2015, HathiTrust.

31. Wiegand and Wiegand, *The Desegregation of Public Libraries in the Jim Crow South*, 186.

32. International Research Associates, *Access to Public Libraries*, 28–29.

33. Emily Miller Danton, "South Does Less Restricting," *Library Journal* 73, no. 13 (July 1948): 990; "Birmingham Public Library: 50th Anniversary," Subject Files (Birmingham), Birmingham Public Library.

34. Liberal whites and African Americans created the Atlanta-located Southern Regional Council in 1944 to advocate for moderately paced improvement in southern race relations. Jeff Woods, *Black Struggle, Red Scare: Segregation and Anti-Communism in the South, 1948–1968* (Baton Rouge: Louisiana State University Press, 2004), 99.

35. Ann Holden, "The Color Line in Southern Libraries: A Progress Report," *New South* 9, no. 1 (January 1954): 2.

36. Holden, "The Color Line in Southern Libraries," 3.

37. Anders, "The Development of Public Library Service in the Southeastern States, 1895–1950," 220.

38. Holden, "The Color Line in Southern Libraries," 4.

39. Ibid., 2.

40. Stephen Cresswell, "The Last Days of Jim Crow in Southern Libraries," *Libraries & Culture* 31, no. 3–4 (Summer-Fall 1996): 558–59.

41. Cresswell, "The Last Days of Jim Crow in Southern Libraries," 559, 564; Annie L. McPheeters, *Library Service in Black and White: Some Personal Recollections, 1921–1980* (Metuchen, NJ: The Scarecrow Press, 1988), 23.

42. Wiegand, *Part of Our Lives*, 173.

43. Cresswell, "The Last Days of Jim Crow in Southern Libraries," 558–59, 562, 568; Mary Ellen McCrary, "A History of Public Library Service to Negroes in Nashville, Tennessee, 1916–1958" (master's thesis, Atlanta University, 1958), 15; John Pennington, "Library Director Sees No Mix Issue: Expects Small Use of Main Branch by Negroes; Cites Reading Records," *Atlanta Constitution*, May 24, 1958; Richard Raycraft, "Negroes Ask Integration Court Order," *Birmingham Post-Herald*, December 6, 1963. Among the many works implicitly or explicitly arguing the localized nature of the civil rights movement, see Christina Greene, *Our Separate Ways: Women and the Black Freedom Movement in Durham, North Carolina* (Chapel Hill: University of North Carolina Press, 2005).

44. Du Mont, "Race in American Librarianship," 496–98, 501; McPheeters, *Library Service in Black and White*, 9–10.

45. Du Mont, "Race in American Librarianship," 498–501; Cresswell, "The Last Days of Jim Crow in Southern Libraries," 563–64, 565–66. *Brown v. Louisiana* represented the one case the Supreme Court heard related in some way to segregated southern public libraries. The case itself did not actually concern many southern public libraries' segregated nature. Instead, the Court had to decide if African American protests in three different Louisiana communities, opposing their local libraries' segregated status, constituted disturbances of the peace. In a 5–4 decision, the Court ruled in favor of the protesters.

46. Cresswell, "The Last Days of Jim Crow in Southern Libraries," 564.

47. Du Mont, "Race in American Librarianship," 504; *Brown et al. v. Board of Education of Topeka et al.*, 349 U.S. 294 (1955).

48. Congress passed the Civil Rights Act in 1964 and the Voting Rights Act in 1965.

49. William Pickens, "The American Congo-The Burning of Henry Lowry," *Nation*, March 23, 1921, 426; Wesley C. Hogan, *Many Minds, One Heart: SNCC's Dream for a New America* (Chapel Hill: University of North Carolina Press, 2007), 66–70. SNCC first went to Albany to register African Americans to vote. The project soon grew into an effort to desegregate the city. Capitalizing on its previous projects in Mississippi, and working with the closely affiliated Council of Federated Organizations (COFO), SNCC launched Freedom Summer in 1964. Registering African Americans to vote in the 1964 national election represented the project's primary goal. However, it spawned numerous other activities, including establishing "Freedom Libraries." See Woods, *Black Struggle, Red Scare*, 200–1; Donald G. Davis Jr., and Cheryl Knott Malone, "Reading for Liberation: The Role of Libraries in the 1964 Mississippi Freedom Summer Project," in *Untold Stories: Civil Rights, Libraries, and Black Librarianship*, ed. John Mark Tucker (Champaign: University of Illinois Graduate School of Library and Information Science, 1998), 110–25.

50. Wiegand, *Part of Our Lives*, 1.

Chapter 4

"It Is Simply Out of the Question to Eliminate the Colorline"

The Development of Black Library Service in Atlanta and the Integration of the Atlanta Public Library

The Atlantic Public Library (APL) was at the forefront of southern public library development. It received the first Carnegie library construction grant in the South, created the first library school in the Southeast, helped organize new public libraries across the region, and provided staff for existing ones.[1] In short, other southern public libraries compared themselves, and looked to, the APL for advice and leadership on public library growth and management.

Besides trying to influence the course of early southern library education and helping to grow other southern public libraries, the APL acted as a leader of southern public librarianship in additional ways. By employing white female librarians from its very beginning, the APL offered white women the opportunity to embark on a professional career that allowed them to professionally grow and accumulate institutional power, as well as challenge gender boundaries. The APL's early employment of white female librarians makes studying their stances on race relations, the segregation of public libraries, and the provision of library service to African Americans, fascinating to analyze, particularly when trying to answer the question: did southern white female librarians value protecting their own careers more than increasing library service to African Americans? As this case study shows, at least in the example of the APL, protecting one's own career, especially during the early years of southern public library development, while working to provide African Americans with library service, proved a tricky balancing act. In Atlanta, white female public librarians endeavored to provide African Americans with as much library service as they could without jeopardizing their careers or pushing too much against the South's ingrained institutional racism. The Atlanta case study presents white women, like Anne Wallace and Tommie Dora Barker, who used a combination of their institutional power, social status, and professional training, to simultaneously advance their own careers, work for the continued development of southern public libraries, and develop library service to African Americans as much as they could within the constraints they faced.

This case study also illustrates how the history of the APL intersects with the history of black librarianship in the South, particularly the careers of black female librarians. From the 1920s on, when the APL opened its first branch library for African American use, the system employed black female librarians. African American librarians had to overcome not only gender barriers, but racial ones as well. As the APL developed branch libraries for black use, female and eventually male African American librarians began to make their presence felt within the library system, and within the community.

APL African American librarian Annie L. McPheeters recalled that at least in the case of the APL, black female librarians worked to not only expand library access for African Americans, they also labored to increase their political involvement and defeat segregation in partnership with Atlanta's black community. McPheeters noted that while she worked as a librarian at the APL she and her staff at the Auburn Avenue and later the West Hunter Branch Library, frequently attended meetings of various political groups in Atlanta. In particular, McPheeters remembered that the library worked with the Atlanta Negro Voters League, particularly by providing members with information about various candidates.[2]

Once the APL integrated in the mid-twentieth century, racial tensions among library staff members became especially pronounced as black women challenged white privilege by attempting to climb the administrative hierarchy and make their voices more widely heard. This particular outcome of having practiced racial segregation plagued the APL well into the twenty-first century.

Although a leader in many aspects of southern public library development, the APL struggled with questions of race. Indeed, its complicated relationship with African Americans dates to before its founding. As Atlanta's leaders pursued a library construction grant from Andrew Carnegie, they insisted that the library exclude African Americans. When the APL opened, it did not provide service to blacks. The decision to institutionalize segregation in the APL resulted in the creation of an institutional culture constantly troubled by questions of race.

From the day the APL opened in March 1902, African Americans, including W. E. B. Du Bois, pushed for its integration. The repeated efforts to integrate the APL challenge the traditional timeframe of the civil rights movement. Until the library's integration, activists in Atlanta used a variety of strategies and tactics, all tailored to fit the state of the city's race relations, to constantly advocate for the library's integration. The APL's integration story demonstrates an element common to all three case studies in this book; the central role of black, and some white, individuals in the university system advocating and working to integrate southern public libraries.

This chapter explores the abovementioned themes through an examination of the APL's founding, provision of service to African American patrons during segregation, its integration, and how it dealt with the ramifications of having practiced segregation.[3] It also sets the stage for the second and third case studies because it identifies and teases out motifs common to all three.

BEGINNINGS

The APL originated as the Young Men's Library Association of Atlanta (YMLAA), which began as a subscription library in 1867 with around 300 members. Although only individuals holding membership could check out books, the YMLAA allowed all white Atlantans to patronize its reading room and use its materials on site. For example, it encouraged Atlanta's high-school students to use its facilities and materials to study and conduct research.[4] Although the YMLAA technically provided library service to Atlanta, it did not possess enough resources to adequately serve the city's rapidly growing population.

In 1897 Walter M. Kelley, Andrew Carnegie's business manager for southern affairs, joined the YMLAA Board of Directors. Soon after, Kelley began communicating with Carnegie about Atlanta's need for a public library. Largely through Kelley's efforts, Andrew Carnegie in 1898 promised Atlanta $100,000 to construct a public library. However, due to the YMLAA Board of Directors—it appears the directors of the YMLAA made up the first board of trustees of the Carnegie Library of Atlanta—and their lobbying efforts, Carnegie added another $25,000 to the grant.[5] To make sure Carnegie provided the money, Anne Wallace, former YMLAA librarian and librarian of the new Carnegie Library of Atlanta (CLA), traveled to New York in November 1899. She journeyed to the city under the cover of going to study the newest library management methods and equipment to prepare for the opening of the CLA. While in New York, Wallace secured the additional appropriation. Conveniently timed, her trip coincided with Carnegie's return to the city from Europe. While in New York, Wallace met with Carnegie face-to-face.[6] Whether Wallace and Carnegie, both in New York City at the same time, represented a fortuitous coincidence for the CLA or a shrewd maneuver by its board, Wallace obtained the $25,000. In any case, Wallace evidently intrigued and impressed Carnegie. When she married Max Howland in 1908, Carnegie gave her a $5,000 bond as a wedding present.[7]

Anne Wallace acted as a trailblazer for white female public librarians in the South. For her, simply working as a librarian was not enough. During her career, Wallace strived to, and did, take on leadership roles. In 1902, she became first vice president of the ALA. She also served as a spokesperson for southern libraries, briefing the ALA at its 1907 annual meeting on the state of southern library development. In addition to her commitment to professionalism, Wallace possessed significant social status in Atlanta, which she likely used to her advantage.

Wallace's father had served with distinction in the Confederate army during the Civil War. He later worked as Collector of Customs during President Grover Cleveland's administration. In acknowledgment of the Wallace family's social status, the *Social Register* listed the Wallaces among its pages of the South's elite families.[8]

After Atlanta received its initial Carnegie library construction grant, the YMLAA transferred its estimated $100,000 in property assets to the CLA.[9] Concurrently, the CLA Board of Trustees had to determine where to build the library. Although the YMLAA offered its property as a site, the board rejected it as too small. The board had at least four factors in mind when considering where to build the library: an adequately sized lot and close proximity to streetcar lines, to as much of the city's population as possible, and to downtown. On September 23, 1899, the board voted 10-2 to build the library at the corner of Forsyth and Church Streets in downtown Atlanta. On May 15, 1900, construction began.[10] In 1901, as construction proceeded, Walter M. Kelley wrote to Carnegie and asked for an additional $20,000. The library specifically needed the extra funds to purchase shelves and furniture. Construction had exceeded the original grant amount because the board committed to using only the highest quality materials. Kelley disclosed that with the initial $125,000 in hand, Atlanta's civic leaders saw their chance to build a public library that would inspire awe in state legislators coming to Georgia's capital city. However, such a scheme required more resources than Carnegie had originally provided.[11]

As Walter M. Kelley urged Carnegie to provide Atlanta with its initial library construction grant, he also insisted the library must practice segregation. In an October 22, 1898, letter to Carnegie, Kelley expounded why the CLA, although a public library, must not serve African Americans. White southerners, he explained, would not accept a racially integrated library. Kelley reminded Carnegie that he had lived in the South seven years, during which time he believed he had come to understand southern racial dynamics. His argument against a racially integrated CLA crested when he referenced Booker T. Washington's 1895 Atlanta Exposition speech. Later dubbed the

"Atlanta Compromise," Booker T. Washington characterized the relationship between African Americans and whites as fingers on a hand. Economically speaking, whites and African Americans needed each other, as the fingers on a hand. However, when it came to social relations, Washington argued that whites and blacks separately existed, like fingers. Kelley also pointed out that Georgia separated state funding for education: $1,020,000 for white education and $623,000 for black education.[12] Kelley referenced state funding levels for black and white education attempting to prove Georgia provided for African Americans' education; the CLA did not need to serve blacks.

Carnegie ultimately respected southern racial customs. George S. Bobinski noted that Carnegie never tried to use his library construction grants to encourage racial integration. However, while allowing communities to determine who their public libraries would serve, Carnegie, and later the Carnegie Corporation of New York (CCNY), also funded the construction of African American branch libraries in the South, including Atlanta.[13]

A lengthy letter written by Evan P. Howell, *Atlanta Constitution* owner and editor, and future mayor of Atlanta, to Kelley in either October or December 1898 reveals the concerns Atlanta elites had regarding the potential integration of the CLA. Howell stated that Atlanta would not accept Carnegie's money if the philanthropist insisted upon integrating the library. He did note, however, that the city remained open to later establishing a library for African American use.[14]

Atlanta elites' insistence that the APL open as a segregated institution, and the library administration's acceptance of it, although typical of the times, institutionalized segregation in the library and set it on a course of constant racial tension with African Americans who wanted library service, as well as the black librarians who would later work for the library. Still, when the APL first opened in 1902, it tried to put these concerns in the background. Establishing a library school administered by the CLA served as director Anne Wallace's first objective. However, problems created by the library's decision to open as a segregated institution would soon surface.

In 1905 Anne Wallace convinced Carnegie to provide $4,000 dollars a year for at least three years to establish a library school controlled by the CLA.[15] The library administered the Carnegie Library School of Atlanta (CLSA) until 1930 when more stringent standards for evaluating library schools, set by the Board of Education for Librarianship (BEL), essentially forced the library to transfer the school to Atlanta's Emory University. The CSLA, first known as the Southern Library School, represents an important component in CLA and southern public library history.[16] It served as the first library school for southern whites, educated many female southern librarians, including CLA director Tommie Dora Barker, and helped grow, as well as strengthen, several southern public library systems. Georgia public libraries especially benefited from the school. During the CLSA's earliest years, graduates who found employment in a Georgia public library worked in either the Atlanta or Savannah public library system.[17]

While leading Atlantans like Howell remained adamant that the library must exclude African Americans, blacks did try, and sometimes succeeded, in using the library. The day the CLA opened, W.E.B. DuBois, National Association for the Advancement of Colored People (NAACP) co-founder, scholar, and activist, appeared before the library's board of trustees. DuBois petitioned the board to permit African Americans to use the library. The board refused his request. However, Walter M. Kelly said the board of trustees would eventually build a library for black Atlantans.[18] According to James V. Carmichael Jr., African American preachers and teachers sometimes tried to use the library, and CLA librarians did not always turn them away. However, the librarians made the preachers and teachers use spare rooms, closets, and other similar spaces to review the materials they requested.[19]

SYSTEM GROWTH AND THE DEVELOPMENT OF BLACK LIBRARY SERVICE IN ATLANTA

In August 1904 the CLA first appealed to Carnegie for funds to construct an African American branch library. The library requested $10,000. In November 1904, Carnegie's secretary, James Bertram, wrote to CLA Board of Trustees president James R. Nutting, informing him that Carnegie agreed to fund the August request. However, seventeen years would pass before the CLA constructed an African American branch.[20]

The 1904 request languished because white and black Atlantans reached an impasse in deciding how to, and who should, pay for Atlanta's proposed African American branch library. Atlanta's white elites argued that since African Americans would use the library, they should help pay for it. Furthermore, Atlanta's leaders stated that the city could not afford to pay the operating costs of another library. Black Atlantans countered by arguing that the funds used to buy the CLA's lot, as well as support the library's annual operating costs, came from the city's general fund. Why should the money to pay for the African American library not come from the general fund as well, especially since whites *and* blacks paid the taxes going into it?[21]

In November 1910, Carnegie approved another request by Atlanta for funds to construct an African American library. This time CLA assistant librarian Tommie Dora Barker, who would later become the director of the library, made the inquiry. Barker formally asked for either $21,000 or $25,000.[22] However, Atlanta again failed to build an African American library. When Carnegie offered to provide the CLA with money to construct a black branch, African American Atlantans also asked the library board of trustees to add black representatives to their number. The board refused. Barbara M. Adkins argues that this request for black representation on the board of trustees partly caused the long delay in the CLA building a branch library for African Americans.[23]

In October 1914, CLA director Delia Foracre Sneed wrote to James Bertram explaining that H. H. Procter, an African American preacher in Atlanta, had mentioned to the CLA Board of Trustees that the CCNY had promised Atlanta $25,000 with which to build an African American library, referring to the 1910 grant offer not accepted by the city. To receive the money the city had to have a lot to build the facility on, as well as promise to annually appropriate the equivalent of 10 percent of the $25,000 for the library's upkeep. Sneed assured Bertram that the board wanted the grant but explained poor economic conditions would likely make it difficult to secure land on which to build the library. Sneed then wondered whether the CCNY sometimes made exceptions to the rule requiring a city to possess property on which to build a library before receiving a construction grant. She closed her letter asking whether Procter's inquiry had any validity. Bertram promptly replied stating that the CCNY did not make such exceptions.[24] Oddly, in December 1914 the *Library Journal* published a story stating that the CCNY had awarded Atlanta $25,000 with which to build an African American library.[25] On December 15, 1914, Bertram wrote to Sneed stating that the CCNY constantly had to write to the *Library Journal's* editor disputing false claims made regarding the CCNY and closed with a leading question: "I wonder if we could locate the informant in this case." Sneed caught the hint and quickly replied that the article had surprised her as well.[26]

No further communication took place between the CLA and CCNY until late April 1916, when the CLA's new director, Tommie Dora Barker, wrote Bertram telling him that the library would likely obtain property on which to build an African American branch library. Barker wanted to know if the CCNY would again consider providing funds to construct the library. Bertram responded by asking how many African Americans lived in Atlanta in 1910, according to the U.S. Census. Barker provided the requested figure: 51,902 African Americans.[27] Surprisingly, Bertram replied that Carnegie's offer of $10,000 in 1904 represented too small an amount, based on the 1910 African American population of Atlanta. He asked Barker how much a library adequately serving Atlanta's African American population might cost. Barker replied that the CLA Board of Trustees believed $40,000 or $50,000 represented a suitable sum. Bertram balked at the figure, believing the estimate too high. The $25,000 given to Nashville, Louisville, and New Orleans to construct their African American libraries represented the most money Carnegie and the CCNY had dispensed for such projects.[28]

On May 31, 1916, Barker presented a revised request asking for $25,000, and also stated that two African American residents had offered a lot to construct the library on. Furthermore, Barker explained that the CLA Board of Trustees originally asked for $40,000 to $50,000 because the funds would be used to build the only library serving Atlanta's entire African American population. The board believed such a sum was needed to construct a facility able to handle heavy use. By 1916, the CLA had built four branch libraries to serve white patrons: Anne Wallace (1909), Oakland City (1912), Uncle Remus (1913), and South Branch (1916).[29]

On November 9, 1916, Bertram informed Barker that the CCNY had approved the CLA's $25,000 request.[30] However, circumstances again intervened and denied Atlanta's African Americans their library. Due to America's involvement in World War I, the CLA for two years did nothing. On November 20, 1918, Barker asked Bertram if the $25,000 remained available. At the behest of the board of trustees, she also asked if the CCNY might consider adding to the $25,000.[31] Bertram said the grant remained available to the CLA for four years after the CCNY awarded it, meaning that Atlanta needed to start constructing its African American library by 1920 to receive the money. He also informed Barker that the CCNY would not add to the grant.[32]

However, the CLA's efforts to build an African American branch library experienced another delay. Around fifteen months elapsed between Barker's 1918 communication with Bertram and Atlanta Mayor James L. Key's 1920 announcement that the city would secure funds to buy land on which to build the library. On March 5, 1920, Atlanta's city clerk issued a proclamation stating Atlanta would annually appropriate $2,500 (10% of the $25,000 grant). Ten days later mayor Key issued a statement declaring that the city had secured a lot on which to build the library. On March 17, 1920, the mayor and city clerk's statements were sent to the CCNY.[33] Again Barker tried to convince Bertram that $25,000 would not build a library sufficient to provide adequate service to black Atlantans. She cited figures demonstrating that the population of Atlanta had significantly grown since the 1910 census. This time Bertram more gently rebuffed Barker. He did not know when the CCNY board would again meet and explained that it had ceased providing funds for library construction. Bertram suggested that Atlanta make do with $25,000.[34] On September 28, 1920, Barker wrote to Bertram stating that the library board had raised an additional $25,000 to supplement the CCNY grant. Atlanta and Fulton County each added $10,000, and the CLA raised the final $5,000 through public subscriptions.[35]

Although it may appear that James Bertram and the CCNY conspired to provide meager library service to African Americans in Atlanta, other factors, not some sort of agenda on the part of the CCNY to provide African Americans with poor library service, contributed to the length of time it took to receive the money to build the APL's black branch and the amount provided for it. Atlanta's dithering, foolishness in attempting to negotiate with Bertram, and circumstances beyond the control of anyone, namely World War I, contributed to the long delay. James Bertram may have had some formula for funding African American libraries he did not share with Atlanta's librarians. However, the city of Atlanta and the APL hold much, if not the majority of the blame, for delaying library service to African Americans. The city of Atlanta had to apply for the funds to build the black branch, and it long postponed doing so, partly because of black activist efforts at getting African American representation on the APL board of trustees, while the library created numerous unnecessary barriers to more quickly getting the CCNY's money.

On November 11, 1920, the CLA informed the CCNY that it had begun building the branch on a lot located in the traditional heart of Atlanta's black community.[36] Since 1910 the city's African American population had grown, increasing from 51,902 or 33.5 percent of the city's population, to 62,796, an increase of 10,894. However, presumably because of the growth of other demographics in the city, African Americans declined to 31.3% of the city's population in 1920.[37]

Atlanta barely built its African American branch library within the timeframe put forth by Bertram. In fact, Atlanta could only build their library after 1917 because they received their grant from the CCNY in 1916. When the Auburn Avenue Branch opened in 1921, the CLA joined other southern public library systems, including Louisville, Kentucky; New Orleans, Louisiana; Jacksonville, Florida; and Nashville, Tennessee, among others, to have constructed a black branch with Carnegie money.[38] During the Auburn Avenue Branch's first year of operation about 2,500 people registered as borrowers, helping the branch to circulate on average 3,000 books a month. Tommie Dora Barker hired Alice Cary as the branch's first librarian. Cary had studied librarianship under Thomas Blue at the Louisville Public Library, speaking to Blue's importance in early African American library education in the South. When Cary resigned her position in 1929, the library replaced her with Mae Z. Marshall, a Hampton Institute Library School graduate.[39]

At the CLA's January 11, 1921, board of trustees meeting, twelve African American clergyman thanked Barker for her role in obtaining funding to construct the Auburn Avenue Branch. The ministers, however, had another purpose for attending the meeting, which was to ask the trustees to select leaders from Atlanta's black community to advise the Auburn Avenue librarian on library matters. The board approved the request and, in turn, asked the clergymen to appoint twelve people to a committee. By granting the request to form an advisory committee, the CLA's Board of Trustees enabled black Atlantans to increase their stake in the Auburn Avenue Branch and expand their participation in the city's public sphere, although only momentarily. While this gesture attested to the power black ministers wielded in Atlanta's African American community, and perhaps the city overall, the advisory committee had a short existence. The Auburn Avenue Branch Library played a positive role in Atlanta's black community, but the city's racial climate limited how much the CLA could, or would, integrate the branch and its librarian into the library system's operations and culture. Carmichael points out that during Barker's tenure as CLA director, the Auburn Avenue Branch librarian never received an invitation to attend a board of trustees or staff meeting. Furthermore, when the Auburn Avenue Branch Library Advisory Committee did not confine its activities to providing advice, Barker shut it down. According to Carmichael, "Barker confessed that the black advisory committee was dissolved shortly after it was formed" in 1921. Cheryl Knott notes that the APL board of trustees acquiesced to the creation of the committee because they had failed to set aside money to purchase books for the Auburn Avenue Branch. Knott argues that the APL board wanted the committee to raise money to fund the creation of the book collection.[40]

It remains hard to discern if Barker shut down the advisory committee entirely on her own volition or because the library board pressured her to do so. While Barker fought hard to get the Auburn Avenue Branch established, and clearly supported the development of some library service to Atlanta African Americans, she still worked as a librarian within the context of the segregated South. Although Barker did work to extend a then-significant measure of library service to blacks in Atlanta, she surely did not remain totally immune from the pressure of the South's restrictive racial codes. Additionally, Barker likely did not want to jeopardize her career. As a female librarian in the early twentieth century, Barker undoubtedly recognized that librarianship represented a career in which women could advance and gain institutional power. In fact, Barker's career as a librarian tracked upward until her retirement in the 1950s. From 1915 to 1930 she served as the CLA's director, and from 1930 to 1936 she worked as the ALA's southern field agent, touring the South's public libraries and reporting her findings to the ALA. Beginning in 1936 and until 1948, she worked as the dean of Emory University's library school, and from 1948 until 1954 she served as the library school's director.[41]

Despite the setback posed by the advisory committee's dissolution, the Auburn Avenue Branch quickly became more than a library. Because it offered many services, the library assumed a community-center role in black Atlanta. APL librarian Annie L. McPheeters described the Auburn Avenue

Branch as "the community's cultural and intellectual center."[42] It even possessed a 250-seat auditorium, providing a place to hold community events. It provided blind African American patrons with library service, managed three book deposit stations in the city, and administered school libraries for three African American schools. To advertise its services, in 1948 the Auburn Avenue Branch began publishing a column titled "The Bookshelf," in the *Atlanta Daily World*.[43]

The Auburn Avenue Branch also fostered the intellectual growth of some of America's most influential and well-known black leaders, including Martin Luther King Jr., and the first African American mayor of Atlanta, Maynard Jackson.[44] In an oral history recorded in the early 1990s, Annie L. McPheeters stated that she and King would frequently engage in various forms of word play when he visited the library as a child. For example, McPheeters recalled that King would often stand by her desk and wait for her to engage him in conversation. As they talked, King repeatedly used a certain word. McPheeters recollected that King had apparently learned a new word that week and wished to demonstrate to her his intellectual prowess, and to firmly imbed the term in his vocabulary. In another game, King would begin to recite a verse of poetry and McPheeters would finish it. While a user of the Auburn Avenue library, King became familiar with the works of Mahatma Gandhi. McPheeters remembered that because the library classified the books as adult, King had to check them out under his father's library card.[45]

McPheeters also recalled three-time mayor of Atlanta Maynard Jackson's use of the library. McPheeters noted that Jackson, an avid user of the library, liked to eat while he read. One time as Jackson used the library, McPheeters heard the rustling of a paper bag. When she investigated, she found that the bag contained Jackson's lunch and that he had chosen to read and eat at the same time. When McPheeters told him that the library did not allow eating, Maynard Jackson politely said "Yes, Miss Watters [McPheeters' maiden name]" and closed his lunch bag. Not long after, McPheeters again heard the bag open, she remembered "Maynard loved to eat while he was reading."[46]

Much of the success of the Auburn Avenue Branch, in terms of serving Atlanta African Americans as a library and a community center, frequently traces back to the work of Annie L. McPheeters. The career of McPheeters serves as an amazing example of the accomplishments black female librarians achieved as they labored in the shadow of Jim Crow. Born in Floyd County, Georgia, in 1908, as Annie L. Watters, McPheeters graduated Clark University (now Clark Atlanta University) in 1929, the Hampton Institute School of Library Service in 1933, and earned an M.S. in library science from Columbia University in 1957.

Working as a teacher and librarian in Georgia and South Carolina before and after graduating from Hampton Institute, in 1934 McPheeters joined the

Atlanta Public Library as an assistant librarian at the Auburn Avenue Branch. By 1936 she became head librarian of the Auburn Avenue Branch. While at Auburn Avenue, McPheeters worked to raise low usage numbers and increase the amount of works in the collection focusing on African American history. To do so, she used funds given by the Adult Education Project, sponsored by the American Association of Adult Education, to establish the Negro History Collection.

McPheeters noted that many patrons made use of the Negro History Collection. Responding to the demand on the part of black Atlantans for nonfiction reading material by and for African Americans, McPheeters also made a point to make available African American newspapers and other periodicals. In 1966 McPheeters left the APL and began work as a reference librarian at Georgia State University, where she worked until 1975. From 1977 until 1979 she assisted Pergamon Press with its acquisitions efforts. In 1993 the APL recognized the extraordinary career of McPheeters by renaming one of its branch libraries after her.[47]

THE APL AND COMMUNITY ENGAGEMENT: LIBRARY SERVICE TO ATLANTA AFRICAN AMERICANS EXPANDS

From 1931 to 1934, the CLA participated in a three-year, grant-funded adult education study, which began when the American Association for Adult Education (AAAE) sought ways to provide African American adults with continuing education opportunities. Accordingly, it partnered with the CCNY, which provided the New York Public Library (NYPL) and the CLA with money to fund studies to determine ways communities could best support adult education. According to Barbara Mamie Adkins, the AAAE chose the NYPL and the CLA to gauge the differences between the educational needs of adult African Americans in the North and South. The AAAE might also have chosen the APL as the southern participant in the study because of its leadership in southern public library development and its ability to meet whatever requirements involvement in the program might demand. The CCNY provided $31,000 in funds, while the Julius S. Rosenwald Fund, which also participated in the project, gave $15,000.

A key finding of the study was that Atlanta needed another library to serve the city's African American population. According to Adkins, black Atlantans taking part in the project heard from its organizers the importance and value of the public library, which in turn inspired them to want increased library service.[48] Thus, a citizen group formed to establish a library in Atlanta's University Homes housing project. Now destroyed, University

Homes once stood near the Atlanta University Center and represented one of the first housing projects funded by the federal government. Dr. John Hope, president of the Atlanta University Affiliation (now the Atlanta University Center) originally conceived the idea of the housing project. Hope partnered with Spelman College president Florence Read, W. E. B. DuBois, architect William J. Sayward, and civil engineer O. I. Freeman. This group bought as much land as they could around the Atlanta University Affiliation, an area characterized by poverty and crime, to build public housing for poor African Americans.

Meanwhile, other prominent Atlantans, including Atlanta real estate developer Charles Forrest Palmer, Clark Howell Sr., publisher of the *Atlanta Constitution*, Thorne Flagler, a contractor, architect Flipper Burge, Luther Brittain, president of Georgia Tech, Herbert Choate, president of Atlanta's chamber of commerce, Mayor James L. Key, and George I. Simons, manager of Atlanta city parks, formed and became trustees of Techwood Incorporated. They did so to meet the Public Works Administration's (PWA) requirements for a federal loan to build a white housing project near Georgia Tech called Techwood.

The nature of the relationship between John Hope and Charles Palmer remains unclear, but Hope apparently convinced Palmer to request enough funds from the PWA to also build the University Homes Housing Project as well as the Techwood project.[49] Thus, in 1933 Hope and Palmer went to Washington, D.C. as representatives of Techwood Incorporated to advocate for the establishment of Techwood and University Homes. In October 1933, the PWA sent a letter to Palmer notifying him that it had awarded a $1,062,000 grant to build both housing projects. As part of the process of receiving the grant, Hope and the other members of his group had to give up their ownership of the property around the Atlanta University Affiliation. They transferred their holdings to the Federal Emergency Housing Corporation in 1934. By 1937, construction was finished on the University Homes Housing Project and tenant screenings had begun.[50]

Barbara Mamie Adkins notes that in 1937 a committee made up of librarians, presumably from the APL, and possibly University Homes residents, came together to work toward opening a branch library in the University Homes Housing Project. The APL evidently approved of the effort because in 1937 the University Homes Branch library opened. Annie L. McPheeters recalled that from its beginning, the APL expected the University Homes Branch to serve all of Atlanta's black community, not just University Homes residents.[51] It seems that the APL only provided staff and resources to continue the library's operations, not begin them. The University Homes Housing Project administration provided the space for the branch, as well as its furniture, supplies, and cleaning service. After the library opened, the committee that assembled to obtain the library in the first place continued working to build its collections. For example, in August 1937 the committee sponsored a block party/dance. It asked those attending the event to bring a book to add to the library's collection. The committee collected 188 books. It continued to seek donations through newspaper announcements and word-of-mouth.

Charles Blackmon, an assistant at the Auburn Avenue Branch Library, served as the first University Homes Branch librarian. After Blackmon quit, sometime in the late 1930s, individuals who served on the library committee managed the library for a brief period. Then, librarians hired under the Works Progress Administration (WPA), managed the library until 1941. The University Homes Branch library, in addition to serving as a readily available library to University Homes residents, also acted as an avenue to political participation for those who lived in the housing project. Annie L. McPheeters remembers that for a time the University Homes Branch library, in cooperation with the League of Women Voters and the Negro Women's Voter League, provided voter registration assistance, voter training, and served as a polling place to the residents of the housing project. The University Homes story illustrates that Atlanta African Americans valued library access, as well as political engagement, and would expend significant effort to obtain and protect both.[52]

INTEGRATING LIBRARY PATRONS

After World War II the CLA underwent numerous changes, including becoming known as the Atlanta Public Library (APL) in 1948. Once again, it expanded library service to Atlanta's African Americans. West Hunter, the third branch in Atlanta's library system to serve African Americans, opened in 1949. APL administrators intended the branch to function as the "main" library for black Atlantans.[53] Also in 1949, the APL equalized the pay scale for white and African American workers. Furthermore, the library created a department solely dedicated to administering and developing library service for African Americans. Not only did an African American head the department, but the library paid the department's chief the third highest salary in the library system[54] (figure 4.1).

While these improvements were significant, they were not enough to head off increased efforts to integrate the APL. In 1953 the Atlanta Council on Human Relations (ACHR), which included Whitney Young, sociologist at Atlanta University and civil rights activist, requested that the APL Board of Trustees integrate the library. The board replied by stating that it would study the ACHR's request, but ultimately did nothing.[55] After 1954, activists bombarded the APL with increasingly insistent demands to integrate. On June 8,

"It Is Simply Out of the Question to Eliminate the Colorline" 69

Figure 4.1 Carnegie Library of Atlanta, 1950. *Source:* Atlanta-Fulton Public Library System—Special Collections Department.

1955, John Glustrom, spokesman for Atlanta's American Veterans Committee, and *Atlanta Daily World* managing editor William Gordon, sent a letter to the APL Board of Trustees explaining that no law legalized the library's segregation policy. Furthermore, if the library could not provide a legitimate reason as to why it discriminated against blacks, Gordon would publish a story stating that African Americans could use the downtown library. Glustrom and Gordon closed by remarking that at least thirty other southern cities allowed African Americans to use their public libraries. On July 13, 1955, the APL Board of Trustees responded, pointing out that white and black staff members received equal pay, that APL had a division devoted to library service for African Americans, and that African Americans had access to all library materials through inter-library loan.[56]

Two days after the board's July 13 reply, the *Atlanta Daily World* published an article publicizing the board's decision to keep the APL segregated.[57] Although the meeting minutes and the *Atlanta Daily World* news story make it appear as if the decision to keep the APL segregated represented a relatively straightforward decision, the *Atlanta Journal* revealed that the board had consulted with the city's attorney before responding.[58] Clearly, the APL Board of Trustees understood that it could face a legal challenge. Yet, despite the message sent by the U.S. Supreme Court's landmark decision in the 1954 *Brown v. Board of Education* case, the library board chose to rebuff Glustrom and Gordon's demand.

African American community leaders persisted in their attempts to integrate the APL. On October 9, 1957, the APL Board of Trustees minutes note that a group called the Greater Atlanta Council on Human Relations (GACHR) again requested the APL integrate its facilities and services. Reverend Edwin Cahill, GACHR president and member of the Southern Unitarian Council, and Prof. Whitney Young of Atlanta University were among those presenting the request. Casting about for another delay tactic, the board voted to give its president the power to form a committee to study the possible integration of the APL.[59]

By May 1959 the APL Board of Trustees had no time or tactics left to prevent the library's integration. Minutes of the May 13, 1959, board meeting state that African Americans had increasingly requested service at the main branch of the APL. The minutes also note that the police could do nothing; no segregation law existed which they could enforce. APL administrators had not yet briefed front desk staff on what do when African Americans demanded service, so APL director John Settelmayer suggested that until library administrators could decide how to handle the situation, library staff would "quickly and quietly" serve African Americans asking for service. The board suggested that Settelmayer meet with Mayor William B. Hartsfield, the police chief, and the city attorney, to arrive at a decision about what to do regarding the library's segregated status, which he did.[60]

On May 19, 1959, the APL Board of Trustees, Director Settelmayer, Mayor Hartsfield, the city attorney, and the city police chief met at the elite Atlanta Athletic Club to discuss the attempts to integrate the library. The *Atlanta Journal*, which tried to cover the meeting, could only report, "It was a locked-door luncheon session in a private room at the Atlanta Athletic Club. Negro waiters were excluded after serving the meal. A reporter who knocked was turned away."[61] Board minutes reveal that the mayor, city attorney, and city police chief all acknowledged that no law existed to support the APL's segregation practices. By continuing not to serve African Americans at all city libraries, the city was violating the law.[62]

If legal facts could not convince the library board and city leaders to integrate the library, activists had prepared a discrimination lawsuit. Whitney Young and historian Howard Zinn had already found plaintiffs for the lawsuit: Irene Dobbs Jackson, a Spelman College professor and mother of future Atlanta mayor Maynard Jackson, and Reverend Otis Moss.[63] Jackson agreed to go to the APL's main library and ask for a library card. If the library did not give her one, she would use the denial to prove that the APL practiced segregation, thereby committing an illegal act.[64] In many ways, Jackson was the ideal plaintiff. Not only did she hold a Ph.D. from the University of Toulouse in France, but she and her family had long served as leaders of Atlanta's black community. Her father, John Wesley Dobbs, sometimes called "the mayor of Auburn Avenue," held a government job through his employment at the post office. Atlanta's African Americans sometimes referred to Dobbs as "'the Grand,' after his masonic [sic] title."[65] In short, the Dobbs family possessed considerable influence in Atlanta's black community.[66]

Zinn's published article in the NAACP's magazine, *Crisis*, fully explains how activists integrated the APL. The effort took two forms. The first consisted of nonconfrontational attempts on the part of African American patrons to receive better library service at the APL's main branch. African Americans knew they could receive at least a minimum level of service there, as some black customers had in the past, particularly professionals. Accordingly, black patrons would amiably push for incrementally better service each time they visited the library by adhering to the following formula: they would request a specific book or other item, and white staff would ask if they had searched for the needed item at the system's three African American branches. If the patron said they could not find the item at a black branch, the librarian would offer to locate it and then send it to an African American branch through interlibrary loan.

However, if the African American patron insisted that they needed the item immediately, the librarian might allow them to use it in a basement reading room or some other space within the main library. The other effort involved collecting data supporting their argument that the APL should integrate. The ACHR then sought out individuals who would serve as plaintiffs in a desegregation lawsuit. At this point, Zinn and Young found Jackson and Moss. Somehow, the library's board of trustees found out about the planned lawsuit because on May 18 a library board member called Young and asked him to delay filing the lawsuit. On May 19 at the closed door meeting of the APL Board of Trustees, Mayor Hartsfield, the city attorney, and the city police chief, a decision was reached to desegregate the library.[67]

Press coverage swiftly followed the May 19, 1959, meeting. On Wednesday May 20, the *Atlanta Constitution* quoted Mayor Hartsfield as stating that those attending the meeting made no decision regarding the library's segregated status. Similarly, it quoted APL board member T. Wayne Blanchard as saying the board would study the issue. However, four days later the paper reported that the APL had integrated. Attempting to alleviate white concern, it cast the integration of the library as a minor administrative decision by pointing out that the African American branch libraries had low circulation numbers, thereby implying that few blacks would use the main library.[68] The announcement was so low-key that few people even knew the library had integrated, and the board apparently told library staff to say nothing about its decision. A later newspaper article mentioned that the board supposedly did not decide to integrate until Saturday, May 23.[69]

While the details about this tortuous decision remain sketchy, on May 24, Mayor Hartsfield issued a statement disassociating himself not only from the decision to integrate the library, but from the board as well. His statement, which obscures as much as it illuminates, is worth quoting in full:

> As everyone knows the Atlanta library system is not directly under the Mayor and Board of Aldermen but is operated under a Board of Trustees elected by the Aldermen.
>
> The Board of Trustees, I understand, in a meeting decided to leave this delicate matter of interracial use of the Main Library to the Superintendent Mr. Settelmayer. This probably accounts for the misunderstanding and the unfortunate impression the Board itself had taken some undisclosed action. At this meeting, Mr. Settelmayer, Director, brought out that many cities in the South were already allowing Negro citizens to use facilities of their main and principle libraries. He also brought out the fact that many citizens of Atlanta were sending Negro servants, chauffeurs, and other employees there to procure and return books and other materials. It was also brought out that there were no laws of the State of Georgia or ordinances of the City of Atlanta under which the Board could prevent any citizen from coming to the library. Under these circumstances, the Board very probably left the entire matter to the Superintendent, Mr. John Settelmayer. He is a gentleman of excellent training and great experience, and I am sure he will handle this delicate situation in the same wise and discreet way which we have tried to handle all race problems in Atlanta in the past.
>
> A public library is a symbol of literacy, of education, culture, and progress. If the professional rabble rousers will let that beautiful place alone I am quite sure that this center of culture in Atlanta will be the last place where any unpleasantness will occur, and I am also sure that the good and well-intentioned people of Atlanta will cooperate with us and with the Library Board and the Superintendent to the end of maintaining Atlanta's good reputation in the field of race relations and especially in a place dedicated to progress in the better things in life.[70]

In attempting to decipher William Hartsfield's response to the library's integration, historian Kevin Kruse points out that in the 1950s the nation's press began to view Atlanta as a racially progressive city, especially after Hartsfield provided Atlanta with its famous nickname, "a city too busy to hate." Hartsfield later explained what he meant by the slogan, "We strive to undo the damage the Southern demagogue does to the South. We strive to make an opposite impression from that created by the loud-mouthed clowns. Our aim in life . . . is to make no business, no industry, no educational or social organization ashamed of the dateline 'Atlanta.'"

Accordingly, when efforts to integrate the APL reached their crescendo in 1959, Hartsfield found himself trapped. A moderate stance on race relations had become Hartsfield's modus operandi during his mayoral career. To oppose the library's integration would fly in the face of his long and publicly expressed position on race relations.[71]

Hartsfield also acquiesced to the library's integration to keep intact Atlanta's unique political coalition, a position APL African American librarian Annie L. McPheeters corroborates.[72] In Georgia, African Americans could not vote in primary elections until 1946. Once the court system ruled Georgia's whites-only primary elections law illegal, Atlanta's African American leaders, including John Wesley Dobbs and attorney Austin Walden, formed the All Citizens Registration Committee. The committee helped register black Atlantans to vote. In doing so, it created a large African American voting bloc well-informed about candidates and issues, and able to influence elections. In 1949, Dobbs and Walden also created the Atlanta Negro Voters League (ANVL). For local elections, the group supported Democratic candidates they believed best served black Atlantans' interests. The league also instructed its members to vote for selected candidates. In Atlanta's 1949 mayoral election, the ANVL helped Hartsfield get reelected. From then on, Atlanta's upper- and middle-class whites, and their African American counterparts, worked together and assumed decades-long control over Atlanta politics.

> According to Kruse: Both halves of the new coalition supported progressive politics centered on economic growth, civic pride, and—to the surprise of outside observers—a moderate pace of racial change. Black Atlantans pressed for desegregation for obvious reasons. Affluent whites, meanwhile, acquiesced to limited changes in hopes of presenting a positive public image for themselves, their city, and most important, their business interests.[73]

McPheeters remembered that in addition to its other activities the ANVL also took an interest in the integration of the APL. She recalled that the ANVL partnered with the Atlanta Urban League and "our Friends of the Library" to end library desegregation in Atlanta. McPheeters does not disclose what actions the ANVL and other groups took to integrate the APL. However, she pointed out that she organized the Friends of the Library group. Accordingly, at least in the case of Atlanta, African American librarians sometimes worked to end segregation within their own institutions.[74]

Although most press coverage reported that the library fully and immediately integrated in May 1959, Reverend E. A. Cahill, president of the GACHR, stated otherwise. When he resigned the GACHR presidency in November 1959, he charged the APL had not desegregated its meeting rooms.[75] Although complaints like Cahill's surfaced, the APL seems to have smoothly transitioned to serving African American patrons. However, bringing white and black staff together, as well as hiring additional African American employees, proved challenging.

While the city of Atlanta integrated its public library in the face of a well-coordinated and concerted effort at desegregation, other cities across the South resisted integration of their public libraries in a variety of ways. In Danville, Virginia, for instance, city leaders chose to close the library in May 1960. In September 1960, the Danville Public Library reopened, this time without tables and chairs. Danville, Virginia, would not suffer vertical integration.[76]

Other communities chose more violent and repressive tactics to forestall public library integration. In June, July, and August 1963, African Americans in Anniston, Alabama tried to use the Anniston Public Library and found themselves denied each time. Anniston city leaders, anxious to avoid negative publicity stemming from continued denials of library service to Anniston blacks, decided that on September 15, 1963, African American ministers Quintus Reynolds and William McClain should go to the library and receive service, thereby indicating that the Anniston Public Library had integrated. However, when Reynolds and McClain arrived at the library an angry group of around twenty-five whites met them. The mob beat the ministers with fists, sticks, and even a metal chain. Reynolds and McClain eventually escaped on foot.[77] Because Atlanta leaders had constructed an image of the city as commerce-oriented and "too busy to hate," activists had an opportunity to force the city's hand. Plus, Atlanta regularly found itself at the center of the Civil Rights Movement and accordingly often in the public eye. The national and local media constantly monitored and reported civil rights-related news in the city. However, in smaller southern communities like Anniston and Danville, where activism took place but received less attention than events in cities like Atlanta, city officials and white residents perhaps felt freer to openly resist public library integration.

INTEGRATING LIBRARY STAFF

Although the APL had employed African Americans since the 1920s, outside entities politely pressed for faster integration of the professional staff. In 1965 Atlanta University Library School staff members Dr. Virginia Lacy Jones and Dr. Hallie Brooks wrote to the library asking if it had any open positions. Although Brooks and Jones did not have any students to recommend for jobs, they wanted to make sure that the APL would try to hire more African American staff. The APL's carefully crafted response stated:

Miss Rhea [of the library] reported she had talked by telephone with Dr. Hallie Brooks and Dr. Virginia Lacy Jones of Atlanta University Library School about vacancies in the Main Library, but they did not have qualified applicants to recommend for positions. The Board asked that the conversations be confirmed in writing, stating the Library is anxious to employ capable people in positions in the Main Library. They further suggested that letters be written to the Presidents of the various Negro colleges in the City advising them of professional vacancies and requesting them to encourage anyone interested and qualified to make application.[78]

Hallie Brooks's effort to see African Americans employed at the APL did not constitute her first efforts at working for equality for blacks. Annie L. McPheeters recalls that Brooks also took part in voter registration efforts over the years. McPheeters remembers "Mrs. Brooks was one of the persons that I remember so very well who would come to the library and help teach the people—citizens—how to use those voting machines." McPheeters goes on to say "Mrs. Brooks was one of the women . . . honored for their work in the Negro Women Voters League."[79]

Staff integration, as well as employing more African Americans, slowly proceeded over the next decade. By 1968, African Americans constituted a mere 18 percent of APL employees. During the next several years, the library made significant advances in diversifying its workforce. In 1975, when Atlanta considered classifying the APL's workers as civil service, African Americans made up 44 percent of the library's workforce. Still, as Emma Darnell, Atlanta Commissioner of Administrative Services, pointed out, most of Atlanta's black library workers were in the lowest pay brackets. Only 17 percent of black library employees were in the higher pay ranges.[80]

In terms of extending library service to African Americans, and relations between white and black staff, the APL experienced a rocky desegregation. In December 1970, *Wilson Library Bulletin* selected African American APL librarian John Ferguson as the subject of its monthly column, "Library Front-Liners." Ferguson served as head of the APL's Inner-City Department and coordinated the outreach programs of seven APL branch libraries. Located in high poverty areas, these seven branches provided book mobile service, created storefront libraries, and devised various programs to reach those living in poverty. Although Ferguson's work represented a real effort by the APL to increase its role as a community institution making a meaningful impact in people's lives, the article stated: "he is haunted, frustrated, by the resistance he meets in white and 'integrated' society, some subtle, some of it not so."[81] Although the *Wilson Library Bulletin* celebrated Ferguson and the APL's efforts to serve Atlantans living in poverty, five years earlier, in September 1965, the APL Board of Trustees closed the University Homes Branch even though it had received letters from the University Homes Tenant Association, as well as the Atlanta Housing Authority, pleading with them to keep the branch open.[82]

At some point between 1974 and 1980, the APL's African American employees formed a caucus to address sixty-four acts of perceived discrimination. Some decisions made by the library's administration did seem arbitrary and lacking awareness regarding the tense relations between the library's black and white workers. For instance, Carlton Rochelle, APL director from 1968 to 1976, put an African American employee on probation for six months. When the employee asked why he was on probation, Rochelle explained that although the employee had worked for the library for five years, he had not gone through the probationary period typically imposed when a new worker began employment at the library.[83] In other words, Rochelle retroactively put an employee on probation for no apparent reason.

Despite persistent racial tension at the APL, some African American employees rose to powerful administrative positions. Although Ferguson became a fairly high-level administrator, none rose higher than Ella Gaines Yates. A career librarian, Yates joined the APL in 1972 as Carlton Rochelle's assistant. In November 1976, she became library director after Rochelle resigned.[84] Yates's appointment may have lessened racial tensions among employees, but when Mitchell J. Shields of the *Atlanta Journal and Constitution Magazine* interviewed Yates in 1979, her relationship with the board and city hall was already strained. Although Yates carefully measured her criticism, she spoke at length about the tension between the library board, city hall, and herself. She explained that she often had to go back and forth between the board and city hall. Furthermore, Yates complained that the city would not adequately fund the library. In her words: "Atlanta has never actually funded its library as it should. As far back as you go, reading board minutes or whatever, the hue and cry has been the same. Our budget is too low; we don't have enough staff. . . . That's one of my biggest problems." Shields believed he found other reasons why Yates encountered constant frustrations as APL director: un-named entities considered her unqualified for the directorship due to her sex and race. Shields wrote, "She was a black woman seeking a position previously held only by white males and though power in the city had swung convincingly to a group of black politicians, there was still some uncertainty about whether Yates could do what would be required of her."[85]

The fact that African Americans in Atlanta had begun to increasingly control the city's politics may have caused some of the tension and conflict Yates encountered. In 1974 Atlantans elected the city's first African American mayor, Maynard Jackson, which represented the culminating event in the shifting of political power from whites to blacks. Kevin Kruse remarks that many white business owners fearfully observed the transition of power, noting "Don Sweat, executive director of Central Atlanta Progress (CAP), a powerful organization of downtown businesses, remembered that his colleagues watched Jackson assume the mayoralty with a 'a great sense of apprehension, fear . . . in some cases bordering on panic.'"[86] White business owners found themselves particularly troubled by Jackson's attempts to make commerce more equitable between whites and African Americans. According to Kruse, "A major point of contention came when the new mayor forcefully tried to 'integrate the money' in Atlanta." Jackson withheld $400 million in contracts pertaining to Atlanta's airport until contractors guaranteed African American-owned contracting firms would receive one-fifth of the overall sum. Jackson also informed banks holding city funds that he would withdraw $450 million in deposits if the banks continued to employ discriminatory lending practices.[87]

Yates's appointment as director swiftly followed on the heels of Jackson's first successful bid for mayor. He would gain reelection in 1978. While primary sources remain mostly silent on whether Yates's race had any bearing on her relationship with the board, her annoyance with APL institutional politics also seems a likely source of friction. Shields's article dwells at length on Yates's frustrations regarding the failure of the board to clearly and adequately communicate with her and city hall. The APL Board of Trustees' meeting minutes also contain numerous entries describing the tension between Yates and the board. In any case, two months after the *Atlanta Journal and Constitution Magazine* published Shields's article, the APL Board of Trustees put Yates on probation.

The board minutes regarding her probation illuminate deep divisions among board members regarding Yates and her leadership, but do not state any specific reason as to why the board of trustees put her on probation. Rather, it seems as though Yates became caught in a power struggle among board members. On November 9, 1979, the *Atlanta Constitution* reported that the APL Board of Trustees had put Yates on probation for six months. However, one board member, G. D. Adams, explained that the board had met on October 6 to discuss issues it had with Yates's work performance, but he insisted that "the word 'probation' is certainly a misstatement of the situation." Three days later, the *Constitution* again reported on Yates's probation. This time it quoted Adams as stating: "it was 'unfortunate' that 'we did put in the word 'probation' in the letter to Mrs. Yates, adding that she had already alleviated most of the problems."[88] Seven months after the board placed Yates on probation, and subsequently lifted it, the *Library Journal/School Library Journal* revealed that some of the trustees had put Yates on probation without the other board members knowing it. It also noted that less than the full board of trustees took Yates off probation.[89]

The situation remained strained for more than a year. The March 26, 1980, minutes disclose that some trustees had met unbeknownst to the other members, and had met on October 4, 1979, not October 6, as Adams had reported to the *Atlanta Constitution*. The members present at the October 4 meeting put Yates on probation.[90] In March 1980, less than the full board took Yates off probation. However, even that decision became a minor controversy. The board later chastised Yates because trustees believed that she had leaked to the press their decision to end her probation. She responded by stating that she issued a press release because the board, as a public entity, was required to make all its actions and proceedings open and available to the public. Secondly, many entities had called the library, among them the mayor's office, asking for information about the board's decision to lift Yates's probation.[91]

Although Yates had seemingly come through the probation debacle by early 1980, the APL Board of Trustees continued fighting among themselves, with the city, and with her. On April 15, 1981, Yates finally sent her resignation letter to the board of trustees.[92] After leaving Atlanta, Yates moved to Seattle, Washington, and started her own library consulting company. She also lectured at the University of Washington's library school and took part in many other library-related endeavors. In 1987 she became Virginia's state librarian, and later became interim director of the Robert Woodruff Library at Clark Atlanta University in Atlanta. In 1998 Yates ended her career by returning to the APL, by then known as the Atlanta-Fulton Public Library System (AFPLS), as interim director.[93]

During Yates's 1976–1981 tenure as APL director, racial tensions between staff members cooled. However, in the late 1990s and early 2000s, they rose again to a boiling point when the library was named as the defendant in a costly discrimination lawsuit. In January 2002, a federal judge awarded millions in damages to the plaintiffs after the 11th Circuit Court of Appeals reaffirmed the decision of the lower court, which found that the APL Board of Trustees had demoted several employees due to their race. Three African American trustees and the library system's white director, Mary K. Hooker, were found guilty.[94] Between 2002 and 2004, attorneys for the plaintiffs and defendants, along with the courts, worked out the actual amount of the award. In 2004, the *Atlanta Journal Constitution* reported that Fulton County had agreed to pay $18,000,000 to seven of the eight plaintiffs in the original lawsuit.[95]

The outcome of the lawsuit seems to present a clear case of discrimination. However, *Atlanta Journal Constitution* journalist Cynthia Tucker uncovered a more complicated story. In 1999, when the AFPLS hired Mary K. Hooker as director, she began envisioning a staff reorganization plan to correct what she thought represented a staff imbalance between the main and branch libraries. She felt the main library had too many staff members while the branches had too few. However, AFPLS board members William McClure and Mary Jamerson Ward had a different view. Ward told fellow board member Nancy Puckett that "there were 'too many white faces' in Central Management."[96] McClure pressured Hooker into transferring some white employees from the main library to the branch libraries while shifting African American employees to the main branch. Before going ahead with the staff reorganization plan, Hooker consulted with Fulton County's attorney and personnel director. She did not have complete confidence in the plan to reorganize the AFPLS staff. She felt the plan might transfer senior employees into positions not matching their skills and levels of experience. The county attorney and personnel director each expressed misgivings about the plan for the same reason. Nonetheless, on May 24, 2000, the AFPLS board approved the reorganization plan. This moved twenty-eight people, including fifteen African American and thirteen white employees, from their then-current positions. At this point, seven of the white employees filed a lawsuit. They argued that while their pay had not been cut, they had been stripped of many responsibilities and significant authority. The lawsuit appears to have been the outcome of a long history of miscommunication and conflict between the library board of trustees and more than one director. Tucker reported that former AFPLS director Julie Hunter had resigned in May 1998 due to the board's infighting as well as its overbearing nature toward her. Hunter's temporary replacement, Ella Gaines Yates, also resigned in 1998 for the same reasons.[97]

In keeping with southern progressivism, which often rejected African American participation in public and political life, only whites could regularly use the APL until the 1920s. Black Atlantans had to wage a constant battle to obtain any library service. When it came to integrating the public library, activists faced an even more arduous campaign. However, Mayor William B. Hartsfield unwittingly opened the way. In 1955, he billed Atlanta as the "city too busy to hate." During his long political career he also relied on elite and middle-class white and African American voters to keep him in office. Accordingly, Atlanta's white powerbrokers realized that defending segregation negatively affected business and potentially threatened Atlanta's role as the South's economic leader. Hartsfield built his political career on the platform of creating a city that welcomed business and economic development by downplaying racial strife. Atlanta's businessmen and civic elites, under Hartsfield's leadership, essentially recreated Atlanta's image simply by defining the city as not interested in the racial violence and animosity gripping much of the South during the mid-twentieth century. Black and white activists banked on the power of that new image to stifle any serious attempt to block them from integrating the APL in 1959.

The process of desegregating the APL suggests that variation between its integration and that of other, lesser-sized southern communities existed. In smaller southern cities that received less media attention, like Danville, Virginia, and Anniston, Alabama, whites often seemingly became emboldened to more ferociously resist library integration, even to the point of violence. However, as the vicious and visually jarring 1960 Nashville lunch counter sit-ins indicated, whatever differences that may have existed between the urban New South and rural South did not always translate into a complete divergence in how whites resisted African American efforts to remove segregation from the public sphere.

The years leading up to the integration of the APL, particular before the Supreme Court's decision in the *Brown v. Board of Education* case and after, shows an effort on the part of the library system to adhere to a policy of separate but equal. In 1955, when John Glustrom and William Gordon pushed for the library's integration, the APL pointed to the fact that it opened the West Hunter Branch in 1949—the third branch library in the system to serve African Americans—equalized the pay scales for white and blacks, and created a department focused on developing and managing library service for African Americans. In short, the APL contended that it did not need to integrate because it had worked to follow the spirit and intent of separate but equal.

Ultimately, segregation weighed heavily on the APL and influenced the institution long after its integration in 1959. Past segregation practices created decades of intermittent racial tension among APL staff. Post-integration racial strife between APL employees, including accusations of discrimination and particularly the early 2000s reverse-discrimination lawsuit, illustrate how the consequences of institutional segregation can have damaging effects for decades. The library's attempts to rectify segregation's negative effects at best made slow progress, indicating the residual effects of tenacious, race-based segregation.

NOTES

1. James V. Carmichael, Jr., "Tommie Dora Barker and Southern Librarianship," (PhD diss., Chapel Hill: University of North Carolina, 1987), 6; Mary Edna Anders, "The Development of Public Library Service in the Southeastern States, 1895–1950," (PhD diss., Columbia University, 1958), 49; Betty E. Callaham, "The Carnegie Library School of Atlanta (1905–25)," *Library Quarterly: Information, Community, Policy* 37, no. 2 (April 1967): 153. Librarians from southern cities like Montgomery, Alabama, Charlotte, North Carolina, and Chattanooga, Tennessee, visited Atlanta's public library to receive instruction in library management. Furthermore, Atlanta loaned its workers to southern communities organizing public libraries, including many in Georgia and Alabama. For a time, public libraries in Albany, Newnan, and

Dublin, Georgia, had an Atlanta librarian on staff. Ensley, Selma, and Gadsden, Alabama received similar assistance.

2. Annie L. McPheeters, interviewed by Kathryn L. Nasstrom, June 8, 1992, P1992-09, transcript, Georgia Government Documentation Project, Special Collections and Archives, Georgia State University Library, Atlanta, 4–5.

3. When it opened in 1902 the city named the library the Carnegie Library of Atlanta (CLA). In 1948 the city renamed the library the Atlanta Public Library (APL). In 1983, when Fulton County, Georgia, assumed responsibility for the library, it underwent another name change, this time becoming known as the Atlanta-Fulton Public Library System (AFPLS). This chapter uses APL and CLA to refer to the library, since most of the narrative takes place during these two time frames.

4. "Andrew Carnegie Offers the City of Atlanta $100,000 with Which to Build a Free Library," *Atlanta Constitution*, February 8, 1899.

5. "Andrew Carnegie Offers the City of Atlanta $100,000 with Which to Build a Free Library"; J. R. Nutting, William M. Stanton, and [?] to Andrew Carnegie, letter, December 13, 1899, Carnegie Corporation of New York Records, II, A.1.a, Reel 2 (Atlanta, Georgia), Rare Book and Manuscript Library, Columbia University Libraries, [hereafter cited as CCNY Records]; Anders, "The Development of Public Library Service in the Southeastern States, 1895–1950," 49.

6. "Carnegie Gives $25,000 More to Library Board," *Atlanta Constitution*, November 27, 1899.

7. James V. Carmichael, Jr., "Atlanta's Female Librarians, 1883–1915," *Journal of Library History* 21, no. 2 (Spring 1986): 381; "Marriage of Miss Wallace and Mr. Max F. Howland, *Atlanta Constitution*, February 19, 1908.

8. Carmichael, "Tommie Dora Barker and Southern Librarianship," 8–10, 36.

9. Anders, "The Development of Public Library Service in the Southeastern States, 1895–1950," 49.

10. "Where Shall the New Carnegie Library of Atlanta Be Located?" *Atlanta Constitution*, May 12, 1899; "Carnegie Library Will Be Built Corner of Forsyth and Church," *Atlanta Constitution*, September 24, 1899; "Ground Was Broken Yesterday for the Site of the Handsome Carnegie Library Building," *Atlanta Constitution*, May 16, 1900.

11. Walter M. Kelley to Andrew Carnegie, letter, February 21, 1901, CCNY Records, II.A.1.a, Reel 2 (Atlanta, Georgia).

12. Walter M. Kelley to Andrew Carnegie, letter, October 22, 1898, CCNY Records. II.A.1.a, Reel 2 (Atlanta, Georgia).

13. Bobinski, *Carnegie Libraries*, 13–14; Carmichael, "Tommie Dora Barker and Southern Librarianship," 70.

14. Evan P. Howell served as *Atlanta Constitution* editor and owner from 1876 to 1897 and mayor of Atlanta from 1902 to 1905. "Evan P. Howell," *Georgia Historical Quarterly* 1, no. 1 (March 1917): 56; Chuck Perry, "Atlanta-Journal Constitution," *New Georgia Encyclopedia*, August 8, 2013, accessed October 17, 2015, http://www.georgiaencyclopedia.org/articles/arts-culture/atlanta-journal-constitution; Evan P. Howell to Walter M. Kelley, letter, October or December 28, 1898, CCNY Records, II.A.1.a, Reel 2 (Atlanta, Georgia).

15. William B. Pope, "Big Library Started by 47 Young Men," *Atlanta Journal and Atlanta Constitution*, October 11, 1959; "Carnegie Gives Fund for Library School," *Atlanta Constitution*, April 14, 1905.

16. Callaham, "The Carnegie Library School of Atlanta (1905–25)," 154–55.

17. Carmichael, "Tommie Dora Barker and Southern Librarianship," 78–82.

18. Barbara M. Adkins, "A History of Public Library Service to Negroes in Atlanta, Georgia" (master's thesis, Atlanta University, 1951), 5–6.

19. Carmichael, "Tommie Dora Barker and Southern Librarianship," 72.

20. James Bertram to J. R. Nutting Esq., November 18, 1904, letter, CCNY Records, II.A.1.a, Reel 2 (Atlanta, Georgia).

21. "A Just Claim," *Atlanta Constitution*, February 26, 1917.

22. James Bertram to J. R. Nutting, letter, November 18, 1904; CCNY record of funds awarded to CLA for African American branch library, November 9, 1910, CCNY Records, II.A.1.a, Reel 2 (Atlanta, Georgia). Many applicants who applied for library construction grants handwrote their applications. Carnegie and CCNY staff also often handwrote their comments on the application and responses to the application, sometimes making it difficult to discern the figures on the application form; Carmichael, "Tommie Dora Barker and Southern Librarianship," 41, uses the figure $25,000.

23. Adkins, "A History of Public Library Service to Negroes in Atlanta, Georgia," 6.

24. Delia Foreacre Sneed to James Bertram, letter, October 21, 1914; James Bertram to Delia Foreacre Sneed, letter, October 30, 1914, CCNY Records II.A.1.a, Reel 2 (Atlanta, Georgia); Carmichael Jr., "Tommie Dora Barker and Southern Librarianship," 13.

25. Anonymous, December 1914 [no other date], handwritten transcript of the *Library Journal* announcement that the CCNY awarded the CLA $25,000 with which to build an African American branch library, CCNY Records, II.A.1.a, Reel 2 (Atlanta, Georgia).

26. James Bertram to Delia Foreacre Sneed, letter, December 15, 1914; Delia Foreacre Sneed to James Bertram, letter, December 20 [?], 1914, CCNY Records, II.A.1.a, Reel 2 (Atlanta, Georgia).

27. Tommie Dora Barker to James Bertram, letter, April 29, 1916; James Bertram to Tommie Dora Barker, letter, May 5, 1916; Tommie Dora Barker to James Bertram, letter, May 8, 1916, CCNY Records, II.A.1.a, Reel 2 (Atlanta, Georgia).

28. James Bertram to Tommie Dora Barker, letter, May 18, 1916; Tommie Dora Barker to James Bertram, letter, May 23, 1916; James Bertram to Tommie Dora Baker, letter, May 26, 1916, CCNY Records, II.A.1.a, Reel 2 (Atlanta, Georgia).

29. "Carnegie Library Addition Move Launched as City Celebrates 25th Anniversary," *Atlanta Constitution*, November 16, 1924. After the CLA finished constructing its African American branch library in 1921, it built three more branches for white use: English Avenue (1921), Inman Park (1922), and Stewart Avenue (1924).

30. James Bertram to Tommie Dora Barker, letter, November 9, 1916, CCNY Records, II.A.1.a, Reel 2 (Atlanta, Georgia).

31. Tommie Dora Barker to James Bertram, letter, May 31, 1916, CCNY Records. II.A.1.a, Reel 2 (Atlanta, Georgia).

32. James Bertram to Tommie Dora Barker, letter, November 26, 1918, CCNY Records, II.A.1.a, Reel 2 (Atlanta, Georgia).

33. *Atlanta Georgian*, January 19, 1920; Atlanta City Council Resolution March 1, 1920; James L. Key Proclamation, March 15, 1920; Atlanta city clerk to James Bertram, letter, March 17, 1920, CCNY Records, II.A.1.a, Reel 2 (Atlanta, Georgia).

34. James Bertram to Tommie Dora Barker, letter, June 18, 1920, CCNY Records, II.A.1.a, Reel 2 (Atlanta, Georgia).

35. Tommie Dora Barker to James Bertram, letter, September 28, 1920, CCNY Records, II.A.1.a, Reel 2 (Atlanta, Georgia).

36. Susie Lee Crumley to James Bertram, letter, November 11, 1920, CCNY Records, II.A.1.a, Reel 2 (Atlanta, Georgia); Akilah S. Nosakhere and Sharon E. Robinson, "Library Service for African Americans in Georgia: A Legacy of Learning and Leadership in Atlanta," *Georgia Library Quarterly* 35, no. 2 (Summer 1998): 10; Carmichael, "Tommie Dora Barker and Southern Librarianship," 78.

37. U.S. Department of Commerce and Labor, Bureau of the Census, *Thirteenth Census of the United States: Abstract of the Census . . . With Supplement for Georgia* (1913); *Fourteenth Census of the United States, State Compendium, Georgia* (1924).

38. Bobinski, *Carnegie Libraries*, 13–14; Carmichael, "Tommie Dora Barker and Southern Librarianship," 70.

39. Carmichael, "Tommie Dora Barker and Southern Librarianship," 76; Adkins, "A History of Public Library Service to Negroes in Atlanta, Georgia," 14.

40. Charmichael, "Tommie Dora Barker and Southern Librarianship," 76–77; Cheryl Knott, *Not Free, Not for All: Public Libraries in the Age of Jim Crow* (Amherst: University of Massachusetts Press, 2015), 175.

41. Ibid., Abstract.

42. Annie L. McPheeters, *Library Service in Black and White: Some Personal Recollections, 1921–1980* (Metuchen, NJ: The Scarecrow Press, 1988), 20.

43. Adkins, "A History of Public Library Service to Negroes in Atlanta, Georgia," 18, 20, 22–25.

44. Knott, *Not Free, Not for All*, 224–225.

45. Annie L. McPheeters, interviewed by Kathryn L. Nasstrom, June 8, 1992, 44–46.

46. Ibid., 46–47.

47. Kerrie C. Williams, "Annie L. McPheeters (1908–1994)," *New Georgia Encyclopedia*, July 23, 2018, accessed February 3, 2019, https://www.georgiaencyclopedia.org/articles/education/annie-l-mcpheeters-1908-1994.

48. Adkins, "A History of Public Library Service to Negroes in Atlanta, Georgia," 26–31.

49. Florence Fleming Corley, "Atlanta's Techwood and University Homes Projects: The Nation's Laboratory for Public Housing," *Atlanta History: A Journal of Georgia and the South* 31, no. 4 (Winter 1987–1988): 19–21.

50. Corley, "Atlanta's Techwood and University Homes Projects," 20–29.

51. McPheeters, *Library Service in Black and White*, 51.

52. Annie L. McPheeters, interviewed by Kathryn L. Nasstrom, June 8, 1992, 8–9, 24–27; Adkins, "A History of Public Library Service to Negroes in Atlanta, Georgia," 31–34.

53. "Library Board Denies Use of Main Unit by Negroes," *Atlanta Journal*, July 14, 1955; "How the Public Library Serves People: University Homes Branch Library for the West Side," Special Collections, Atlanta-Fulton Public Library System.

54. Minutes of the Atlanta Public Library Board of Trustees, July 13, 1955, Atlanta Public Library.

55. "The Desegregation of the Atlanta Public Library System," 86–87, Special Collections, Atlanta-Fulton Public Library System.

56. Minutes of the Atlanta Public Library Board of Trustees, June 8, 1955 and July 13, 1955.

57. "Library Denies Use of Facilities to Negroes," *Atlanta Daily World*, July 15, 1955.

58. "City Studying Negroes' Bid to Use Library," *Atlanta Journal*, June 9, 1955.

59. Minutes of the Atlanta Public Library Board of Trustees, October 9, 1957, Atlanta Public Library; "Petition Asks Integration in Library Here," *Atlanta Journal*, October 10, 1957.

60. Minutes of the Atlanta Public Library Board of Trustees, May 13, 1959, Atlanta Public Library.

61. "Library Board Holds Talk on Segregation," *Atlanta Journal*, May 19, 1959.

62. "Library Board Holds Talk on Segregation"; Minutes of the Atlanta Public Library Board of Trustees, May 19, 1959, Atlanta Public Library.

63. "The Desegregation of the Atlanta Public Library System," Special Collections, Atlanta-Fulton Public Library System.

64. "The Desegregation of the Atlanta Public Library System"; M. Pomerantz, "Irene Dobbs Jackson," obituary, *Atlanta Journal and the Atlanta Constitution*, January 20, 1999.

65. Kevin Kruse, *White Flight: Atlanta and the Making of Modern Conservatism* (Princeton: Princeton University Press, 2005), 29.

66. Biography of Irene Dobbs Jackson, Special Collections, Atlanta-Fulton Public Library System.

67. Howard Zinn, "A Case of Quiet Social Change," *Crisis* 66 (1959): 471–76; see also Margaret Shannon, "Atlanta's Biggest Racial Test of 50 Years Near at Hand," *Atlanta Journal and the Atlanta Constitution*, October 11, 1959.

68. "Library Discusses Integration Push," *Atlanta Constitution*, May 20, 1959; "Library Director Sees no Mix Issue," *Atlanta Constitution*, May 24, 1959.

69. "Downtown Library Told to Serve Negroes," *Atlanta Journal*, May 23, 1959.

70. Minutes of the Atlanta Public Library Board of Trustees, May 24, 1959, Atlanta Public Library; Kruse, *White Flight*, 25–26. Despite Hartsfield's politically motivated response to the library's desegregation, he possessed a strong connection to the institution. Too poor to afford law school, he corresponded with law school deans around the country, asking what texts he should read to gain a legal education. With reading list in hand, he headed to the library. According to Kruse, "His alma mater, he later said without shame, was the Atlanta Public Library."

71. As quoted in Kruse, *White Flight*, 40.
72. Annie L. McPheeters, interviewed by Kathryn L. Nasstrom, June 8, 1992, 20.
73. Kruse, *White Flight*, 31–35, quote 35.
74. Annie L. McPheeters, interviewed by Kathryn L. Nasstrom, June 8, 1992, 13, 16, 15–17.
75. "Relations Council Pushes Integration," *Atlanta Constitution*, November 11, 1959.
76. Stephen Cresswell, "The Last Days of Jim Crow in Southern Libraries," *Libraries and Culture* 31, nos. 3–4 (Summer–Fall 1996): 559.
77. Cresswell, "The Last Days of Jim Crow in Southern Libraries," 561–62; Wayne A. Wiegand and Shirely A. Wiegand, *The Desegregation of Public Libraries in the Jim Crow South: Civil Rights and Local Activism* (Baton Rouge: Louisiana State University Press, 2018), 126.
78. "The Desegregation of the Atlanta Public Library System," Special Collections, Atlanta-Fulton Public Library System; Minutes of the Atlanta Public Library Board of Trustees, October 20, 1965, Atlanta Public Library.
79. Annie L. McPheeters, interviewed by Kathryn L. Nasstrom, June 8, 1992, 12–13.
80. John Head, "Bias in Library Jobs Again Argued Here," *Atlanta Journal*, May 8, 1975.
81. "Library Front-Liners: John Ferguson, Outreach Librarian," *Wilson Library Bulletin*, December 1970, 424.
82. Minutes of the Atlanta Public Library Board of Trustees, October 20, 1965, Atlanta Public Library.
83. Minutes of the Atlanta Public Library Board of Trustees, March 26, 1980, Atlanta Public Library.
84. Mitchell J. Shields, "Checking Out the Atlanta Library," *Atlanta Journal and Constitution Magazine*, August 5, 1979, 24; Biography of Ella G. Yates, Special Collections, Atlanta-Fulton Public Library; Alice Murray, "Mrs. Yates New Library Leader," *Atlanta Constitution*, November 24, 1976.
85. Shields, "Checking Out the Atlanta Library," 6, 24, 26, 28.
86. Kruse, *White Flight*, 240.
87. Ibid., 240–41.
88. Raleigh Bryans and Bill Montgomery, "Library Board Tells Director to Shape Up," *Atlanta Constitution*, November 9, 1979; T. I. Wells, "City Library Chief Gets 'Probation,'" *Atlanta Constitution*, November 12, 1979.
89. "Atlanta's New Library to Open Amid Political Chaos," *Library Journal/School Library Journal* 9, no. 23 (June 9, 1980); Minutes of the Atlanta Public Library Board of Trustees, June 1980, Atlanta Public Library.
90. Minutes of the Atlanta Public Library Board of Trustees, March 26, 1980, Atlanta Public Library.
91. Minutes of the Atlanta Public Library Board of Trustees, April 7, 1980, Atlanta Public Library.
92. Minutes of the Atlanta Public Library Board of Trustees, April 1981, Atlanta Public Library.

93. Simeon Booker, "Ticket Tape U.S.A.," *JET* 71, no. 16 (January 12, 1987), 10; Biography of Ella G. Yates, Special Collections, Atlanta-Fulton Public Library; "Library Trustees Name Yates as Interim Library," *Access: A Monthly Guide to Programs and Activities* 8, no. 5 (September 1998).

94. Cynthia Tucker, "Close the Book on Library's Cronyism," *Atlanta Journal Constitution*, January 23, 2002.

95. Paul Clawley, "Chief Librarian Fired, Board Next," *Atlanta Journal Constitution*, May 20, 2004. Clawley states that seven librarians sued the county. Tucker's 2002 article, reports that eight librarians sued the county.

96. *Bogle v. McClure*, 332 F. 3d 1347 (Court of Appeals 11th Circuit, 2003).

97. Tucker, "Close the Book on Library's Cronyism."

Chapter 5

"The Library Cannot Be Opened Indiscriminately to White People and Negroes"

Nashville and the Quest for Integrated Library Service

As in Atlanta, the New South Movement inspired Nashville's quest for a grand public library. From the early 1800s on, different entities in Nashville opened and operated several semi-public and private subscription libraries. Not until the turn of the twentieth century did the quest to construct a public library gain critical mass. The image Nashville created for itself during the New South Era played an instrumental role in the strategy it used to obtain a library construction grant from Andrew Carnegie. Nashville billed itself as a center of higher education in the South. The city did this in part to create a distinction between itself and its dynamic neighbor Atlanta, the New South's leader in many aspects. Accordingly, by the time Andrew Carnegie began awarding library construction grants in the late 1800s, Nashville had its pitch ready.

To the present day, Nashville regards itself as an educational center—among other designations, including a tourism destination and country music production site. Nashville also wanted others to see it as a city practicing segregation in a less-offensive way than other southern communities. David Halberstam, former Nashville journalist and author of *The Children*, which focused on the civil rights movement in Nashville, argues that Nashville's white elites crafted a particular way to practice segregation in order to protect the city's image. Nashville's segregation, in his words, "was largely of a soft kind, administered, it sometimes seemed, not with the passion of angry racist officials, but more as a cultural leftover from the past."[1] Thus, when Nashville's African American community began advocating for desegregation of the Nashville Public Library (NPL) in the mid-twentieth century, the city had to listen. If it did not integrate the library, Nashville would tarnish its self-created image as an education-oriented city that took a moderate stance on race relations.

Similarly, historian Benjamin Houston argues that Nashville practiced segregation in a manner less jarring than in other southern communities. For example, some public facilities, like courtrooms, the post office, and the city's train station, did not have "whites," "colored," or "negro" signs. However, everyone was expected to know that Nashville observed segregation. Accordingly, navigating public space in Nashville prior to integration was tricky. Due to its deep and long-standing association with education, Nashville's power brokers described the city as genteel and elite, professing to reject the raw brand of segregation other southern cities practiced in favor of a more paternalistic version of racial discrimination and restriction.[2] On the one hand, Nashville wanted to preserve its image as a city focused on education, progressivism, and calm race relations. On the other hand, white Nashvillean leaders did not want to alienate other white southerners. Accordingly, Houston claims, many whites in the city self-identified as racial moderates who believed in African Americans' inferiority but still wanted to see them achieve, to the extent it did not threaten white supremacy. In other words, like Atlanta, Nashville's civic leaders realized that publicly defending segregation too strongly could negatively impact the city. Lest his readers believe that segregation in Nashville did not strip away African Americans' dignity, restrict where they could live, limit their economic advancement, and control how they moved in public spaces, Houston points out that blacks living in the city found its segregation practices anything but moderate. They regarded white Nashvillians' supposed racial moderation frustrating at best, humiliating and demeaning at worst.[3]

William H. Chafe's *Civilities and Civil Rights: Greensboro, North Carolina, and the Black Struggle for Freedom* holds particular importance for trying to understand Nashville race relations, so much so that Houston states his study of Nashville race relations builds on and works to extend the conclusions drawn by Chafe. Nashville's race relations, like Greensboro's, emphasized manners and decorum. Politeness and good manners fulfilled a key function in maintaining white privilege. By emphasizing civility in individual interactions with African Americans, Greensboro's whites attempted to avoid directly dealing with the issues posed by segregation and African American attempts to end it. By treating African Americans with courtesy, and blacks returning the deference whites expected, Chafe argues that whites convinced themselves Greensboro had copasetic race relations, when in fact both sides simply played what had become their roles in a long-standing public performance. The public spectacle of manners and deference masked white unease and black frustration.[4] In Greensboro and Nashville, beneath the seemingly calm surface of each city's race relations, African American discontent simmered. It would burst forth in the early 1960s as African Americans in each community attempted to break free from the restraining tokenism of their cities' race relations.

As in Atlanta, white and African American leaders in Nashville formed a political coalition that helped manage race relations in the city. This mixed-race political coalition provided African Americans in Nashville with an opportunity to participate in the city's politics. While Nashville's coalition did not manage politics to the degree that Atlanta's white and African American alliance administered political affairs, Nashville's African Americans wielded influence in some city elections. For instance, while serving in the Tennessee Senate from 1949 to 1951, politician Ben West succeeded in changing the way Nashville elected its city council.

Up to this time, Nashville had chosen its city council by using a city-wide election. After West's legislation passed, each district in Nashville elected its own councilman. This change significantly increased the chance that African American candidates would win election in predominantly African American districts. When West won his 1951 campaign for mayor of Nashville, two African Americans also won election to the city council.[5] This in turn, for a time at least, presumably worked to siphon off some of the frustration African Americans felt regarding their second-class status within the city.

BEGINNINGS

Library service in Nashville developed along the lines mentioned by many scholars of southern libraries. Private libraries following the subscription library model, or devoting themselves to serving a specific user group, came first. In 1813, the Tennessee General Assembly passed legislation incorporating the Nashville Library Company. In 1845 Nashville businessmen formed a library called the Mechanics Institute and Library Association. In 1850 Captain Will Stockell opened a library for firemen on Nashville's College Street. Nashville's Young Men's Christian Association's chapter (YMCA) also took part in Nashville's library boom. In 1855 it opened and began operating a small library. However, the Civil War forced the Nashville YMCA to close its library, which it briefly reopened in 1867. In 1860 a library called the Mercantile Library Association opened. However, it closed in 1863, also because of the Civil War.

The development of numerous private and semi-private libraries in Nashville prior to the Civil War indicated Nashvilleans wanted library service. After the war, new libraries continued to open to meet the unchecked desire for library access. In 1876 the Nashville Library Association established the

Nashville Library. Sources do not clearly indicate if the Nashville Library Association or the YMCA managed the Nashville Library. However, by 1875, only YMCA members could check books out from the Nashville Library, indicating the YMCA exercised a significant degree of control over its operations.[6]

Although several libraries developed in Nashville prior to the Civil War, many did not have the resources to adequately serve more than a small portion of the city's population, or failed to serve many Nashvilleans because they required membership to use them. Accordingly, the need for library service in Nashville remained less than completely fulfilled. In 1887, as Nashville's leaders cast about for a new location to house another library in response to the unquenched demand for more library service, they remembered that deceased businessman Samuel Watkins's will provided space for such a facility in the Watkins Institute in downtown Nashville.

When he died in 1880, Samuel Watkins was one of the richest people in Nashville.[7] Beginning his career as a brick manufacturer and merchant in Nashville in 1827, Watkins swiftly accumulated wealth. He provided brick for the construction of many of Nashville's churches, including First Presbyterian Church, Second Presbyterian Church, and First Baptist. In 1845, Watkins further added to his wealth when he leased a stone quarry to the state as it constructed the new capitol building in Nashville. Although the Civil War caused Watkins to lose over three hundred thousand dollars in personal property, including cattle, crops, slaves, and other assets, he quickly rebounded. During the war he steadily accumulated shares in the Nashville Gas Light Company. By 1868, he had accumulated enough shares to make himself president of the company. During Reconstruction, Watkins expanded his corporate business activities. He served as a director of the Fourth National Bank and the Tennessee Manufacturing Company. In 1871, he took on additional responsibilities when he joined the Church and Spruce Street Railway Company as president. In 1876, Watkins made his will. In it, he set aside $100,000 for the city of Nashville to build a school for the city's poor young people. That school would become the Watkins Institute. In his instructions for setting up the school, Watkins made sure to stipulate that it include a library.[8]

Recognizing the opportunity, Nashville elites installed a library in the Watkins Institute building.[9] Samuel Watkins's will instructed city officials to use the lot he owned at the corner of Sixth Avenue and Church Street, the current site of the NPL, to build a school to educate the city's poor young people. Established at some point between Watkins's death in 1880 and 1887, city officials named the school the Watkins Institute. Watkins's will demanded city officials rent the basement and first floor to provide funds for the school, make the second floor a library, and operate the third floor as a classroom.[10]

In 1887 the library at Watkins Institute opened, and the library's organizers named it Howard Library. They did so because Nashville businessman Hunt

Howard gave the library $15,000 for book purchases. Scholar Mary Ellen McCrary notes that during its earliest days the library functioned as a reference library; patrons could not check books out. Even though the Howard Library initially operated as a reference library, library cards still cost $2.00 per year. In 1898 as the national economy deteriorated, and Howard Library's finances went with it, the Nashville City Council provided the library with $2,500 to keep it open. In April 1901, the Howard Library Board of Directors, also referred to as the Howard Library Executive Committee, made the library totally free to use.[11]

In 1900, the Howard Library Executive Committee began planning how to obtain a library construction grant from Andrew Carnegie. On December 8, they ordered Howard Library librarian Mary Hannah Johnson to attend a library course at the University of Chicago's library school. The Executive Committee also instructed Johnson to visit the Carnegie Library of Atlanta (CLA) and observe how its librarians worked, again speaking to the CLA's influence and leadership in southern public library development. On December 24, Howard Library president and *Nashville Banner* editor Gideon H. Baskette sent a letter to Andrew Carnegie strongly urging him to provide Nashville with a library construction grant. Baskette noted that the Howard Library only had one room in the Watkins Institute building. Furthermore, the library did not possess a permanent claim on that space. In his letter, Baskette made what would soon become a familiar claim in Nashville's attempt to get a library construction grant from Andrew Carnegie: Nashville represented the South's premier educational center. The city needed a proper public library to continue to occupy that position. Baskette stated, "It would be impossible to develop an up-to-date library such as is needed in an educational center like Nashville, without a library building adequate for the purpose."[12]

Other community leaders made the same argument. On July 15, 1901, Vanderbilt University chancellor James H. Kirkland wrote to Andrew J. Carnegie, stating "Nashville is a city of schools and colleges, the very center of educational work in the South. Students gather here in great numbers from every southern state, but there are no adequate library facilities for higher scholarly work."[13] By then, Nashville served as home to many universities and colleges, including Fisk University (1866), Vanderbilt University (1873), Peabody College (1875), the Medical Department of Central Tennessee College (1876, now known as Meharry Medical College), Trevecca College for Christian Workers (1910, now Trevecca Nazarene University), Belmont College for Young Women (1890, now Belmont University), and the Nashville Bible College (1891, now Lipscomb University).

Interestingly, while Nashville elites like Vanderbilt University chancellor James H. Kirkland envisioned a public library in Nashville serving an auxiliary role to the city's many higher educational institutions, Carnegie Library of Nashville (CLN) librarians—after the library's founding in

1904—regarded the library's mission in a perspective clearly influenced by the Progressive Era's emphasis on protecting and improving personal morals, as well as serving as a site of individual uplift. CLN librarian Mary Hannah Johnson expressed her vision for what the library could and should do for the city. She wrote:

> My theory is give the masses good literature and cleanliness and the city will have fewer instances of sorrow, crime, and viciousness on its hands. . . . When people visit the library I believe they should be impressed not only by the literature it contains which should be the best, but they should be impressed with order, cleanliness, neatness, and real culture. If these five things are found, each visitor will receive a stimulus even though he may not be aware of doing so.[14]

In 1901 the Howard Library Executive Committee prepared to directly lobby Carnegie for a library construction grant. A smaller committee would "visit Mr. Carnegie at an early date to secure a donation for the purpose of erecting a library building."[15] As the Howard Library Executive Committee pursued a Carnegie grant, committee chairman Gideon H. Baskette began corresponding with those involved in Atlanta's efforts to obtain Carnegie money. Based on the response he received, it appears Baskette asked how the CLA sought a Carnegie library construction grant, how the process unfolded, how quickly they got their money, and how the city of Atlanta set up its yearly appropriation payments to the CLA.[16] In providing Baskette with this information, the author could not help crowing about the library Atlanta had constructed with Carnegie's money, "We have a beautiful building of white marble, I expect the handsomest building in the South."[17] This braggadocio might have actually sparked a library "arms-race." A few years after Nashville opened its Carnegie-funded library, it asked Carnegie for more funds to expand. The request angered James Bertram, Carnegie's secretary. He chastised Nashville for building, in his eyes, what constituted a grandiose, wastefully designed library.[18]

By late spring 1901, Nashville's leaders were ready to ask Carnegie for a library construction grant. On May 20, a committee representing the Nashville Chamber of Commerce sent Carnegie a letter asking that he fund the city's request for a $50,000 library construction grant. The detailed letter lays out the many reasons the Chamber of Commerce believed Carnegie should provide money. Among its several arguments, the letter claimed that the Howard Library could not adequately serve the city's 100,000 residents and repeated the refrain that an educational center like Nashville needed a library.[19] Almost two months passed before Nashville learned, on July 23, that Carnegie had approved their $50,000 request.[20] When Nashville's leaders finally responded on August 8, they asked for an additional $50,000. Another two months went by before Carnegie responded. On October 4, 1901, Carnegie approved the additional application for funds.[21] For the next three years construction proceeded. Nashville's Carnegie-funded library opened on September 19, 1904.[22]

Immediately after opening, the CLN faced inquiries as to whether it would serve African Americans. On September 19, 1904, J. C. Battle, president of the Nashville-based African American National Baptist Publishing Board, wrote to Mary Hannah Johnson, asking if the library allowed African Americans to use its books, and if so, to what degree. Johnson forwarded the letter to Gideon H. Baskette, who replied that, "for obvious reasons, the library cannot be opened indiscriminately to white people and negroes. The same existing conditions and public sentiment which render necessary the separation of the races in the public schools obtain in this community in regard to libraries."[23]

CLN librarian Mary Hannah Johnson also opposed opening the library to African Americans. More than just an administrator solely dedicated to the CLN's day-to-day operations, Johnson thought broadly about southern public libraries and their development. Around 1905 she wrote an essay titled "Southern Libraries." In it, she argued that southern public library development had proceeded slowly for a few key reasons, including slavery. Slavery had concentrated the South's monetary and cultural wealth in the slaveholders' hands, and she contended that because they possessed so much wealth, slaveholders had developed private libraries for their exclusive use. Before the Civil War, they saw no need to create public libraries. After the war, when the South had recovered enough to spend money on public projects, southern whites chose to establish public schools first for whites and later for African American students.[24]

While defending, or at least explaining, the South's slow and late public library development, Johnson stated that she understood the hypocrisy in building a public library and then excluding African Americans from it. However, she argued, very few towns and cities in the South would accept integrated public libraries, the same argument Evan P. Howell and Walter M. Kelley made regarding the CLA's potential integration during its construction. In her essay Johnson expressed an opinion clearly shaped in part by the South's then dominant perspective on segregation and African American personality traits:

> There are those that may regard this disposition of southern whites to be served with negroes as a manifestation of race prejudice that is inconsistent with a right conception of educational progress. But this view does not comprehend the true situation. Race prejudice exists undoubtedly but it is not prejudice alone that makes the mingling of the races obnoxious and unwise in a library service. The

social line is drawn in the South between the whites and blacks unalterably. This line has been made and kept distinct in the public schools and the wisdom of such separation has been clearly demonstrated. The consensus of opinion in the south is that this separateness should be maintained in libraries as well as schools. The masses of negroes are ignorant and unmannered. Many who have acquired a smattering of learning are conceited and affected and eager to assert themselves in a manner that is objectionable.[25]

Johnson conceded that not all African Americans who acquired an education acted boastful. She contended that if blacks acted in a more restrained manner, southern public libraries could devise schemes to provide them with service. However, Johnson remained steadfast in her belief that white southerners would not stand for integrated libraries. Integrated libraries invited disaster, she argued; whites would stop coming, cities would stop financially supporting them, and libraries would wither and die.[26]

Johnson's thoughts on the question of the CLN serving African Americans represents a position largely at odds with the supposedly moderate, refined racism and segregation that Benjamin Houston and David Halberstam argued Nashville practiced, or tried to appear as if it did. Perhaps Johnson truly believed what she wrote, or maybe she recognized that the CLN, in its infant state, needed as much white support as it could gather to survive. Regardless of what motivated her to write those words, and whether or not she believed them, Johnson's raw, direct, and unabashed opinion indicated that the development of library service for blacks in Nashville would at best slowly occur.

However, the CLN, and later the NPL, would sometimes serve African Americans, a fact activists reminded the library board of in the late 1940s as they worked to integrate the library.[27] Furthermore, black Nashvilleans did not stand by waiting for whites to extend library access to them. For example, Nashville African American politician James C. Napier worked hard to provide Nashville blacks with library service. Born in Nashville in 1845 to free African American parents, James C. Napier became a dynamic force in Nashville's African American community after the Civil War. In the early 1870s he attended law school at Howard University in Washington, D.C. After his legal education, he returned to Nashville. From 1878 to 1886, he served as a Nashville city councilman, during which time he strongly advocated for black education and the establishment of a black fire department. From 1911 to 1913, Napier served as Register of the United States Treasury.[28]

In 1906, Napier delivered a speech at the festivities commemorating the twenty-fifth anniversary of Tuskegee Institute. Andrew Carnegie also attended the event. According to Napier, Carnegie in passing mentioned the CLN's construction. Napier saw the opportunity to advocate on behalf of Nashville African Americans who wanted library service. He apparently asked Carnegie to provide funds to build a branch library for blacks in Nashville. Carnegie told Napier once Nashville guaranteed it would support an African American branch library; he would provide the funds to construct it.[29] Nothing immediately came of Napier's effort, but by presenting Carnegie with his initial request, Napier laid the groundwork for future communication with Carnegie about the possibility of him building an African American branch library in Nashville.

SYSTEM GROWTH AND THE DEVELOPMENT OF AFRICAN AMERICAN LIBRARY SERVICE IN NASHVILLE

By 1907, the CLN's Board of Directors had decided to expand the library building. On February 28, Tennessee Secretary of State J. W. Morton wrote Andrew Carnegie and asked if he would provide the CLN with another $100,000. In reply, James Bertram, Carnegie's secretary, wrote: "Mr. Carnegie considers that $100,000 was ample to cover the cost of a Central working Library Building for the city of Nashville and that anything larger than that must be wanted not primarily as a working Library but as an architectural feature of the city." Bertram went on to state that if Nashville civic leaders wanted the money to build branch libraries, Carnegie would consider the request.[30] Whether Morton asked for more money to cosmetically enhance the CLN's main branch, or for another reason, Bertram had already experienced a similar request. In 1901, before building construction was finished, the Carnegie Library of Atlanta had requested more funds because they used expensive building materials. Accordingly, Bertram became defensive about communities asking for more money to expand their Carnegie-funded libraries.

Although the CLN asked for more money for the stated goal of expanding its building, it may have had other objectives in mind. Nashville built a beautiful, but flawed, library building. By January 1905, about three and a half months after it opened, the building started to physically deteriorate. Water seeped, presumably through the roof, down interior ceilings and into walls. Johnson reported to library building committee chairman William L. Dudley that water leaks threatened the plaster on the walls and ceiling. It seemed the CLN had opted for beauty over sound craftsmanship (see figure 5.1).[31]

After their 1907 request for more Carnegie money, the CLN did not pursue the issue for three years. However, in March 1910, the CLN Board of Directors again asked Bertram for additional Carnegie money. As in 1907, the board wanted the funds to expand the library. Bertram, in reply, asked the board to provide the architectural plans used to build Nashville's library.

Figure 5.1 **Carnegie Library of Nashville Building.** *Source*: Courtesy of Metro Nashville Archives.

After receiving the plans, Bertram sent a second letter severely criticizing the board for selecting what he deemed a space-wasting plan. Ruthless in his criticism, he pointed to tall ceilings and wide hallways as the chief culprits in the CLN's space issues, not heavy use by Nashvillians.[32]

Although Bertram strongly chastised the CLN's Board of Directors for selecting what he believed represented a poor architectural design, the directors sent a strongly worded letter back in response, indicating that they would not give up the quest for additional Carnegie money.[33] On May 19, 1910, CLN librarian Mary Hannah Johnson wrote a separate letter to Bertram asking for additional funds. Johnson began by telling Bertram how the CLN represented an invaluable institution fostering culture and education in Nashville. Turning to the feud between Bertram and the CLN Board of Directors, she argued that Bertram had too harshly treated them. They only wished to do what they believed represented the best for the CLN. Once again, she referenced Nashville's reputation as a center of higher education:

> There have been already a number of requests for branch libraries which should be granted sooner or later but it is of those who have studied the question that

it is a more practical idea just now to build a great central library which is well equipped for all branches of study and fitted to be the court of last resort for the number of colleges and universities around Nashville. . . . Nashville is growing rapidly and she wants this great central library and at the same time branch libraries also, but of course if we cannot get the addition to the central Library then we shall have to be content with branch libraries alone. We sincerely believe that one of the best things possible to be done for the upbuilding of Nashville educationally, is to have this great central Library which will not only be an influence in Nashville but will stimulate more educational endeavors throughout the state.[34]

On June 9, Bertram replied to Johnson. Using a milder tone that his previous letters, he nonetheless maintained his position that Nashville did not need to expand its central library: "Central Library Buildings are inevitably intended by the City to be architectural features even more than accommodation for books and for their being read."[35]

For a year, the CLN stopped asking Bertram for more money. However, on April 28, 1911, Johnson sent another letter. This time, she asked for funds to build three branch libraries, two white and one African American. However, she really wrote to yet again advocate for the CLN's main library's expansion. She bemoaned Bertram's past refusals: "Why can't you with the facts laid before you intercede with Mr. Carnegie to enlarge this building. . . ." She also proposed various schemes to expand the library, some more logical than others. For instance, Johnson noted that the library could buy a lot adjacent to the CLN's main branch and expand sideways, or it could add two stories to the existing structure.[36] In the battle to see who possessed a more stubborn temperament, Bertram again won out. On May 3, Bertram reiterated that Andrew Carnegie did not want to fund main library expansion projects.

For another year the CLN's Board of Directors and director sulked. Meanwhile, James C. Napier continued to press Carnegie to provide the money to build a black branch library in Nashville. On February 6, 1912, Napier wrote Andrew Carnegie, reminding him about his 1906 promise to give Nashville the funds to construct an African American library, if the city would guarantee to support the new branch. A day later James Bertram replied to Napier's letter, stating that until Nashville's mayor and city council made a formal application for funds, the CCNY could do nothing regarding building an African American library in Nashville.[37] With this information in hand, Napier apparently convinced Mayor Hillary Howse to support building an African American library. On February 14, 1912, Howse sent a letter to James Bertram officially requesting $25,000 to build an African American branch library, and $25,000 to construct a white branch library.[38] According to Robbie D. Jones, Napier and Howse supported each other politically.[39] For a few months Nashville waited for a response to Howse's letter. Finally, on April 8, Bertram replied, stating the CCNY would fully fund both of the mayor's requests.[40]

Even before Bertram informed the CLN that the CCNY would provide money to build branch libraries, the Nashville media knew the library would pursue additional Carnegie funding. In February, the African American *Nashville Globe* published a lengthy column about the CLN's effort to build branch libraries, including one for African Americans. The story reported Mary Hannah Johnson saying, "To make the free public library of Nashville all it should be, and reach all of the people, both grown as well as children, and the Negroes also, there must be branches in the four sections of the city, and a special library for the Negroes."[41] It seems the CLN did not have a clearly thought out plan for expansion. Since the CCNY remained insistent that it would only provide funds for branch libraries in Nashville, Johnson evidently felt compelled to publicly support building branch libraries, when expanding the CLN's main and, at the time, only building, represented her real objective.

After receiving notification in spring 1912 that the CCNY would provide funds to construct an African American branch, CLN president Gideon H. Baskette did not send architectural plans for the library to the CCNY until May 20, 1914. Perhaps the search for property on which to build the library, or the drawing up of architectural plans, delayed Baskette. This would make sense, given that CLN seemed to lack an organized, coherent plan for the library system's expansion. The CLN's Board of Directors asked Nashville's Negro Board of Trade, the black counterpart to the city's white Board of Trade, to select the library's site. Some Nashville African Americans wanted to locate the library near Fisk University or black Pearl High School. Eventually, the Negro Board of Trade selected a property at the corner of Twelfth Avenue North and Hynes Street, a location near much of Nashville's African American population.

The CLN Board of Directors demanded that Nashville's African American community contribute $1,000 toward the lot's $6,000 purchase price. The city paid the remaining $5,000. Once the CLN selected a site for the library, the CCNY authorized payments for construction. In September 1914 builders laid the library's cornerstone. Nashville's African American branch library, named by the CLN as the Negro Branch Library, opened in February 1916. In 1910, two years before Nashville received the money to build an African American branch library, 36,523 African Americans lived in the city, constituting 33.1 percent of its overall population. In 1920, four years after the Negro Branch Library opened, Nashville's black population slightly declined to 35,633.[42] However, despite the modest decline, Nashville's single black branch still served, in theory, an incredible number of people.

The CLN hired twenty-nine-year-old Nashvillean Marian M. Hadley as librarian, and Hattie L. Watkins as her assistant. Before she assumed her duties, Hadley paid her own way to Louisville to receive additional library training, affirming Thomas Blue's importance in early library education for African Americans living in the South. Recall that Blue also trained Alice Carey, the librarian at Atlanta's African American branch, Auburn Avenue.[43]

Hadley's appointment as librarian at the CLN's Negro Branch Library launched a lengthy career in public service. In 1919 she resigned her position at the library to become the first executive secretary of the Nashville's Young Women's Christian Association (YWCA). While working for the YWCA, Hadley helped establish Nashville's Blue Triangle chapter, which served as Nashville's YWCA's African American branch. After working at the YWCA, Hadley moved to Chicago in the 1930s. For nearly twenty years Hadley worked as a librarian in Chicago until her retirement in 1959.[44]

Although the CLA may have led public library development in the South during the early twentieth century, the CLN's Negro Branch Library opened five years before Atlanta's Auburn Avenue Branch. Black Atlantans took notice. John Wesley Dobbs, father of Irene Dobbs Jackson—who volunteered to serve as plaintiff in the case to integrate the Atlanta Public Library—worked as a mail clerk in Atlanta. Sometimes he worked the mail train running between Atlanta and Nashville. When working on the mail train, Dobbs would check out books from Nashville's Negro Branch Library, as well as Fisk University's library, for his family, returning them when he came back to Nashville on another mail run.[45]

INTEGRATION AND OTHER CHANGES

During the 1920s and 1930s, the CLN expanded library service to the city's African Americans. The library set up subbranches for blacks in the Andrew Jackson Courts and J. C. Napier Courts housing projects, the African American schools Clifton and Meigs, and the South Street Community Center.[46] Much like the CLA's African American branch library, Auburn Avenue, the CLN's Negro Branch Library assumed a community-center-like role in black Nashville. The Girl Scouts, Parent-Teacher Association, and other community organizations held meetings there. In 1949, the Negro Branch Library expanded its services to include lending books to African Americans in the hospital and sanatorium.[47]

However, despite these efforts, Nashville's African Americans wanted full access to NPL's main branch. In the late 1940s, they would commence working to integrate the library. How they would do so reflected a keen understanding of the city's racial climate and segregation practices. Benjamin Houston claims Nashville's racial practices influenced the ways whites resisted African American efforts to achieve equality and how Nashville blacks attacked segregation and white paternalism in the city. African American leaders used letters, meetings with NPL's administration, compromise, and private negotiating out of the public's eye to achieve the library's integration. In time then, Nashville's supposedly refined segregation practices became the weapon Nashville blacks used to integrate the NPL.[48]

On December 9, 1947, prominent Nashville African Americans met with the NPL Board of Directors to point out that the Negro Branch Library's book collection was small in size and in poor condition. The group included Negro Branch Librarian Ophelia Lockhart, Fisk University Comptroller W. D. Hawkings, Girl Scout executive Josephine Holloway, Fisk University Dean of Men Reverend W. J. Faulkner, Fisk University Librarian Arna Bontemps, Tennessee State University Librarian Lois Daniel, Ford Green City School Principal W. H. Ford, and several other community leaders.[49] Due to the library's meager and substandard resources, the group suggested that the board allow African Americans to use the main branch in downtown Nashville. The board demurred. To forestall integrating the main library, the board of directors considered purchasing a bookmobile to provide more library service to African Americans. It also decided that too many African Americans had moved away from the Negro Branch Library for it to remain useful to Nashville's black population and agreed to start thinking about selling the property.[50]

NPL's director during this time, Robert S. Alvarez, recorded a lengthy account of the meeting in his diary, providing an insider's view of the confrontation contemporary with the event. However, using Alvarez's diary as a source requires caution as he was still alive when it was published and the possibility exists he edited the diary prior to publication. Alvarez had a vested interest, particularly in relation to the integration of the NPL, to cast himself in as positive a light as possible.[51] According to Alvarez, the group first met with him in October 1947 and politely criticized the library for poorly stocking the shelves of the Negro Branch Library. They complained that they could never find the books they wanted. They argued that if NPL administrators considered the Negro Branch Library to be the main library for blacks, since it was the only public library available to African Americans in the city, they would have accordingly stocked it like a main library. If the NPL did sell the Negro Branch Library, they wanted the new library for Nashville blacks located downtown, away from Fisk University and Tennessee State University (TSU), so it would be easier for all Nashville African Americans to visit. Also, the leaders told Alvarez that Nashville blacks did not use the existing Negro Branch Library because the NPL excluded them from the system's main library.[52]

Nashville's African American leaders wanted to know why they could not use the system's main library. After all, they pointed out, they could use the Tennessee State Library and Archives, why not the Nashville Public Library?

To advance their cause, Alvarez wrote, "they pointed out, only the educated Negroes would use the building, not the masses that people see sitting in front of dilapidated frame houses and all those they picture when hearing the word 'negro.'"[53] Interestingly, this argument is essentially the same one made by an anonymous white southern public librarian when asked why she did not oppose southern public libraries integrating.[54]

Alvarez reported that he asked the group how many African American readers the city had. They estimated there were 4,000 black college students, 400 university and college faculty and staff, at least 150 clergy, and 7,500 school-age children. They also pointed out that four African American publishers maintained offices in Nashville. In the end, the group asked Alvarez to arrange a meeting between them and the NPL Board of Directors, which he agreed to do. After they met with him, Alvarez reflected on the African American leaders' requests. He thought Nashville's black community would struggle to integrate NPL's main library because its board of directors would oppose it. However, Alvarez believed that if NPL desegregated its main library, it would save the library system significant monetary sums, and positively contribute to Nashville's race relations.[55]

According to Mary Ellen McCrary's 1959 master's thesis, Nashville's African American leaders met with the NPL Board of Directors at some point in 1947.[56] Alvarez states that he presented a letter written by the group to the directors at their meeting of December 9, 1947. However, when black Nashville's complaints regarding the library reached the NPL Board of Directors, they caused an animated discussion. Two board members did the most speaking, Alvarez remarked, strongly arguing against integrating the library. Alvarez did not name the board members but characterized their attitudes, in his words, as believing that if the board granted African Americans access to the library, they would "overrun the main library once they got their foot in the door."[57] Alvarez felt other directors might have held more moderate positions regarding integration, but were mostly cowed by their colleagues' strong stance against it. Still, a minister who served on the board asked what would Christ do. Alvarez remarked "Certainly no one could doubt what Christ's way—The Way—would be, but if the group thought of this matter they did not let such realization affect their argument."[58] It appears from Alvarez's diary that no one responded to the minister's question; however, he reflected on a female board member, who noted that African Americans could use the post office, try on clothes just touched by white women, freely move within downtown Nashville's stores, but could not use the public library.

Alvarez's diary makes clear that since they mostly remained opposed to integration, the NPL Board of Directors knew they would have to make some concessions to Nashville's African American leaders or risk spurring black Nashville to publicly work to integrate the library, and accordingly embarrass the library's administration. Thus, the board of directors agreed to provide Nashville's African American community with better, but not integrated, library service. For instance, the board promised to upgrade the Negro Branch Library's book collection. It also agreed to meet with Nashville's African American leaders at the January 1948 board meeting.[59] The question of whether Alvarez voiced his thoughts and opinions on the matter at the December 9, 1947, meeting remains unanswered, at least by his diary. His diary suggests his presence at the meeting was mostly as an observer. However, he did present the letter written by Nashville's African American leaders. This surely, to a degree, drew him into the ensuing conversation and debate.

The next meeting between NPL's board and representatives from Nashville's black community did not take place until February 4, 1948. Alvarez wrote that four African Americans attended the meeting, where they politely asked the library board to permit blacks to access the NPL's main branch downtown. According to Alvarez, one of the four African Americans, whom he does not identify, stated: "Our people are allowed to go into liquor stores all day long to get that which destroys one's soul, but they are not permitted to enter the library to get the books that would feed their minds and souls." After the four African Americans pled their case, they left, and the board debated their request. Regarding the four African Americans and their petition, Alvarez wrote, "They spoke with such sincerity and put their request in such a nice way that I was very sorry that they were not going to get what they came for." However, Alvarez remarked that the board seriously discussed the request, finally concluding that they could not give in to it because they believed the time was not right to integrate the library, as well as the fact they believed President Harry Truman's civil rights agenda had caused social unrest.[60]

In late November 1948, NPL administrators and library director Alvarez met with representatives from four African American organizations, including the Solid Block, Woman's Club, a group referred to only as ASACP, and the Ministers Alliance. Charles Dinkins represented the ASACP, which may have referred to the NAACP, because in 1949 he served as president of Nashville's NAACP chapter.[61] A special NPL report covering the meeting indicated that the representatives wanted the NPL to build two facilities for African American use, one near 18th Avenue and Jefferson Street in north Nashville, and the other in the southwest Nashville neighborhood of Edgehill. However, the report also noted that the African American community representatives believed NPL administrators should take no action toward selecting a site for the new African American library for three to six months.[62]

Meanwhile, between the February and November 1948 meetings, the NPL sold the Negro Branch Library building and lot to the Buchi Plumbing

Company for $42,000. The Nashville Electric Service later acquired the property, demolished it, and built its headquarters on the site.[63] The plan to sell the Negro Branch Library had its origins in 1946. In October that year the then newly hired Alvarez visited the branch. He found a small, worn-out collection badly in need of weeding. He also discovered the branch had low circulation numbers. When the African American North Nashville Community Council requested a library outpost in the neighborhood's Ford Green School, two days a week from 3:00 p.m. to 9:00 p.m., Alvarez proposed to Negro Branch Librarian Ophelia Lockhart that she close the Negro Branch during those two days. Lockhart opposed the plan.

On October 18, 1946, Alvarez met with the NPL Board of Directors. Not only did he present the same proposition he made to Lockhart, but he also suggested closing the Negro Branch at 6:00 p.m. instead of 9:00 p.m. Furthermore, Alvarez asked the board to reconvene a committee they had previously formed to sell the Negro Branch Library. Privately, he acknowledged that while black Nashvilleans may not have checked out many books from the Negro Branch Library, African American organizations in Nashville held their meetings there, yet another example of how African Americans used libraries as community centers.[64] Still, Alvarez decided to move forward with his attempt to sell the Negro Branch Library. He wanted to use the proceeds to build African American branch libraries in north, east, and south Nashville. When he made his plan known to the NPL Board of Directors, they wholeheartedly supported the idea.[65]

After the library sold the Negro Branch Library, it began providing Nashville's African Americans with bookmobile service. The *Tennessean* article covering the library's sale and bookmobile service's beginning noted that the black bookmobile could hold 850 books at a time.[66] However, even providing bookmobile service to African Americans did not occur without controversy. In April 1947, over a year before the NPL would sell its Negro Branch Library, the NPL Board of Directors met and discussed providing bookmobile service to whites and African Americans. In his diary Alvarez stated he believed both white and black Nashvilleans should receive bookmobile service. However, some NPL board members believed white Nashvilleans would object to using books "going into colored people's homes. To settle the issue, the board decided to purchase a vehicle exclusively providing bookmobile service to Nashville African Americans" (see figure 5.2). In its first year, African Americans checked out 19,579 books from NPL's black bookmobile, doubling the Negro Branch Library's circulation numbers.[67]

After selling the Negro Branch Library's building and site, the NPL Board of Directors relied on realtor V. H. Dixon, a member of the group that in 1947 asked the library to integrate, to locate a temporary location for the Negro Branch Library. By October 1948, Dixon had found a provisional site. On October 13

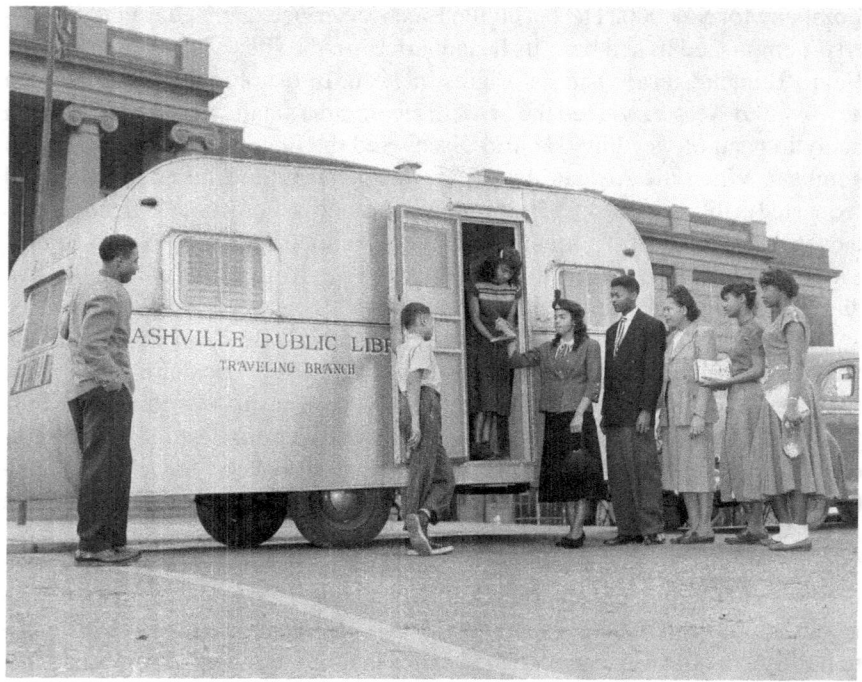

Figure 5.2 Nashville Public Library Bookmobile, date unknown. *Source*: Courtesy of Metro Nashville Archives.

Alvarez wrote to E. W. D. Isaac, secretary of the National Baptist Training Union (NBTU), and informed him that the library wanted to rent three rooms on the ground floor of his organization's building.[68] At the same time, NPL administrators were seriously considering a permanent location in west Nashville's Hadley Park neighborhood, located near Tennessee State University.

While construction of a new branch library was under discussion, Charles L. Dinkins wrote a letter, in June 1949, to NPL Board Chairman Judge Albert G. Ewing calling for the NPL's desegregation. Dinkins argued that Nashville's NAACP chapter knew NPL's main branch in downtown Nashville had on occasion served African Americans. On August 31, the library responded to Dinkins, stating that Nashville's city council had recently appointed a committee to provide the library's board of directors with advice. The letter also stated that NPL administrators would discuss his integration request with the city council-appointed advisory committee.[69]

On August 2, 1950, the NPL entered into a ninety-nine year lease with Nashville's Board of Park Commissioners to build and operate a library in

Hadley Park, located adjacent to TSU.[70] Meanwhile, according to McCrary, the NPL Board of Directors decided to integrate the system's main library in January 1950.[71] However, neither the *Tennessean* nor the *Nashville Banner* published the decision to integrate. As Alvarez later explained in a 1958 letter to Memphis State University's Dr. Rowland M. Hill, the library board never actually voted to desegregate the library. According to Alvarez, "the Library Board had discussed opening the Library to Negro readers a number of times before but two of our elder members were against it and no other action was taken. However, when one of these two men died and the other resigned in the late 1940s the matter then could be discussed again." Alvarez told Hill he asked the board of directors at one of their meetings if anyone objected to him instructing NPL's librarians to provide African Americans with books. No board members objected, and the library integrated.[72]

On Easter Sunday 1952, NPL opened the Hadley Park branch. Nashville mayor Ben West, as well as the presidents of Fisk University and TSU, attended the opening ceremony. Hadley Park represented the first branch library in Nashville built in thirty-five years.[73] According to Mary Ellen McCrary, the library selected Hadley Park as a replacement for the Negro Branch Library because it was near housing projects as well as Jefferson Street, the heart of Nashville's African American business district until the city built Interstate 40 through it, located adjacent to TSU, and within walking distance of Fisk University and Meharry Medical College.[74]

David Halberstam's and Benjamin Houston's arguments regarding the way Nashville practiced segregation helps explain why the NPL integrated, how it integrated, and why as well as where it built the branch library to replace the Negro Branch Library. According to Halberstam, Nashville's more moderate type of segregation was almost like "a cultural leftover from the past," meaning that whites in Nashville paternalistically practiced a southern-style noblesse oblige.[75] Houston contends that Nashville used its "moderate" segregation practices to control where African Americans could live in the city and how they moved about it.[76] Thus, the NPL remained committed to Nashville's brand of segregation until the city's African American leadership began pushing hard for the integration of the library. In short, the library integrated to protect the city's image. The meetings, letters, negotiations, and compromise—all out of the eyes of the press—reflect the library's commitment to practicing a more moderate type of segregation. However, it remains important to remember that what constitutes "moderate" is in the eye of the beholder, and although often described that way, Nashville's segregation practices still existed to keep whites more powerful than the city's African Americans. The location of the branch library that replaced the old Negro Branch Library proves this point. The NPL located the new branch library in a black neighborhood near a historically black college and university. While the selection of this location for the new branch library came about after negotiations between the library and Nashville's African American leaders, its location meant it would serve a largely, if not entirely, black clientele. This was not entirely a bad thing since that neighborhood otherwise would not have had a public library. However, it also demonstrates that Nashville's "moderate" segregation still controlled where African Americans could live in the city.

When the NPL did desegregate in 1950, the civil rights movement had yet to erupt the way it would from the mid-1950s to the late 1960s. Nineteen-fifty Nashville race relations remained relatively calm. NPL's director and board of directors felt that the library could desegregate because it would make few waves. On the surface at least, integration occurred with hardly any notice from Nashvilleans, but this was perhaps because the NPL did not publicize its decision to integrate. Nashville's two daily newspapers, the *Tennessean* and the *Nashville Banner*, appear to have not published a single story about the library's integration.

Although many factors contributed to the NPL's relatively smooth desegregation process, some stand out more than others. First, the organized civil rights movement had not yet erupted across the South. The Supreme Court's ruling in *Brown v. Board of Education* would not take place for another four years, and the Montgomery Bus Boycott remained five years in the future. Secondly, Nashville, to differentiate itself from other cities, particularly Atlanta with its large industrial, manufacturing, and railroad transportation base, created for itself an identity as an educational center. Nashvillians also might have wanted to distinguish their city from its neighbor to the south, Birmingham, whose rise was based on the heavy industries of iron and steel production as well as coal extraction.

Thirdly, defending segregation in an ugly manner, which occurred later during the Nashville sit-ins, as evidenced by the documentary *Eyes on the Prize*, would call into question Nashville's image as a genteel, refined, and education-focused city. The Nashville sit-ins, as well as related civil rights activities that took place in Nashville in the 1960s, demonstrated that, for some blacks, partial or gradual desegregation was not enough. Put under pressure, Nashville's "moderate" segregation practices did not exist as a cultural leftover but as a way to preserve the power of whites. However, African Americans did score early victories working within the boundaries of Nashville's moderate segregation.

Fourthly, as evidenced in the late 1940s negotiations to desegregate the NPL, a unique white and African American civic power coalition existed in Nashville, as was true in Atlanta. Both sides of the coalition did not want to disrupt the delicate equilibrium they had achieved. Furthermore, Nashville's emphasis on developing and fostering higher educational institutions within its boundaries, as well as its commitment to characterizing the city as genteel and cultured, also influenced the NPL to desegregate in 1950. As Benjamin Houston argues, Nashville practiced a peculiar brand of race relations. The Nashville Way ultimately led to the NPL's integration as the city's African American leaders used compromise, private negotiations, and constant communication to desegregate the library.

In 1960, the Nashville and Davidson County City-County Planning Commission published a report titled "Books for Metropolitan Nashville." The report argued that Nashville needed a new downtown public library as well as more branch libraries in the city's suburbs. Consequently, in 1963, Nashville tore down its Carnegie library to build a new facility in its place.[77] The new building eventually became known as the Ben West Library.

In 1998, the city engaged in talks with the owners of Watkins Institute, NPL's first home, about erecting a new library where their building then stood.[78] Construction began later that year, and on June 9, 2001, the facility opened. Fronting on Church Street, the massive structure takes up the entire block between Sixth and Seventh avenues. The Metropolitan Government of Nashville and Davidson County provided $50,000,000 to build the 300,000 square foot facility. Another $65,000,000 was authorized to construct five new suburban branches as well as remodel three other libraries in the system.[79]

NOTES

1. David Halberstam, *The Children* (New York: Random House, 1998), 110.

2. Benajamin Houston, *The Nashville Way: Racial Etiquette and the Struggle for Social Justice in a Southern City* (Athens: The University of Georgia Press, 2012), 3, 4.

3. Houston, *The Nashville Way*, 4.

4. William A. Chafe, *Civility and Civil Rights: Greensboro, North Carolina, and the Black Struggle for Freedom* (New York: Oxford University Press, 1980), 5, 8–10.

5. Don Doyle, "Ben West," *Tennessee Encyclopedia of History and Culture*, January 1, 2010, accessed November 8, 2015, https://tennesseeencyclopedia.net/entry.php?rec=1492.

6. "History of Nashville Public Library, 1813–1965," Nashville Public Library Records, Nashville Metro Archives.

7. Cornelia Walker, "Watkins Institute," *Tennessee Encyclopedia of History and Culture*, January 1, 1010, accessed November 1, 2015, https://tennesseeencyclopedia.net/entry.php?rec=1476.

8. George C. Grise, "Samuel Watkins," *Tennessee Historical Quarterly* 6, no. 3 (September 1947): 252–53, 255, 257, 259.

9. Margaret Kerchevel, Untitled History of Carnegie Library of Nashville, Speeches and Addresses, Carnegie Library Records, Nashville Metro Archives.

10. Walker, "Watkins Institute"; Grise, "Samuel Watkins," 258–59.

11. Mary Ellen McCrary, "A History of Public Library Service to Negroes in Nashville, Tennessee, 1916–1958" (master's thesis: Atlanta University, 1959), 13–15; [?] to Theo W. Koch, letter, August 31, 1903, Carnegie Library Records, Nashville Metro Archives.

12. G. H. Baskette to Andrew Carnegie, December 24, 1901, letter, Carnegie Library Records, Nashville Metro Archives; David E. Sumner, "Nashville Banner," *Tennessee Encyclopedia of History and Culture*, February 23, 2011, accessed November 1, 2015, https://tennesseeencyclopedia.net/entry.php?rec=965.

13. James H. Kirkland to Andrew Carnegie, letter, July 15, 1901, Carnegie Corporation of New York Records. II.A.1.a, Reel 21 (Nashville, Tennessee), Rare Book and Manuscript Library, Columbia University Libraries [hereafter cited as CCNY Records].

14. Mary Johnson to Major Lewis, letter, December 13, 1905, Carnegie Library Records, Nashville Metro Archives.

15. "Records of the Executive Committee of the Howard Library Association, January 8, 1900–November 30, 1901," Carnegie Library Records, Nashville Metro Archives.

16. ? to G. H. Baskette, letter, October 23, 1901, Carnegie Library Records, Nashville Metro Archives. This letter to Baskette contains the sender's name. However, deciphering the sender's handwriting to determine their identity proved impossible.

17. Ibid.

18. James P. Bertram to G. H. Baskette, letter, April 2, 1910, CCNY Records, II.A.1.a, Reel 21, (Nashville, Tennessee).

19. Nashville Chamber of Commerce to Andrew Carnegie, letter, May 20, 1901, Carnegie Library Records, Nashville Metro Archives.

20. Nashville Library Board of Directors to Andrew Carnegie, letter, August 8, 1901, CCNY Records, II.A.1.a, Reel 21 (Nashville, Tennessee).

21. Carnegie Corporation of New York, notes on Nashville, CCNY Records, II.A.1.a, Reel 21 (Nashville, Tennessee).

22. Carnegie Library of Nashville to Carnegie Library of Nashville Board of Directors, letter, May 2, 1905, CCNY Records, II.A.1.a, Reel 21 (Nashville, Tennessee).

23. J. C. Battle to Carnegie Library of Nashville, September 19, 1904; Carnegie Library of Nashville president to J. C. Battle, September 22, 1904, both Carnegie Library Records, Nashville Metro Archives. The National Baptist Publishing Board became one of, if not the, largest African American owned publishing company by 1910, employing over 100 workers. It published religious literature, including full-length sermons, short homilies, song sheets, hymnals, etc.; see Paul Harvey, "National Baptist Publishing Board," *Tennessee Encyclopedia of History and Culture*, January 1, 2010, accessed November 2, 2015, https://tennesseeencyclopedia.net/entry.php?rec=980.

24. Mary Hannah Johnson, "Southern Libraries," Carnegie Library Records, Nashville Metro Archives.

25. Johnson, "Southern Libraries."

26. Ibid.

27. Charles L. Dinkins to Judge Albert G. Ewing, letter, June 15, 1949, Nashville Public Library Records, Nashville Metro Archives.

28. Herbert Clark, "James C. Napier," *Tennessee Encyclopedia of History and Culture*, February 23, 2011, accessed October 31, 2015, https://tennesseeencyclopedia.net/entry.php?rec=961. Napier died in 1940.

29. James C. Napier to Andrew Carnegie, letter, February 6, 1912, CCNY Records, II.A.1.a, Reel 21 (Nashville, Tennessee).

30. James Bertram to John W. Morton, March 4, 1907, letter, CCNY Records, II.A.1.a, Reel 21 (Nashville, Tennessee).

31. Mary Johnson to William L. Dudley, letter, January 13, 1905, Carnegie Library Records, Nashville Metro Archives. for more information on Vanderbilt University chemistry professor, as well as the university's chemical laboratories director and medical school dean William L. Dudley, see "William Lofland Dudley," *Vanderbilt University Quarterly: A Record of University Life and Work* 14, no. 4 (October–December 1914): 259–84 ; "Carnegie Library," *Nashville Banner*, April 27, 1903.

32. G. H. Baskette to James Bertram, letter, March 19, 1910; James Bertram to G. H. Baskette, letter, March 28, 1910; James Bertram to G. H. Baskette, letter, April 2, 1910, all CCNY Records, II.A.1.a, Reel 21 (Nashville, Tennessee).

33. G. H. Baskette to James Bertram, letter, April 9, 1910, CCNY Records, II.A.1.a, Reel 21 (Nashville, Tennessee).

34. Mary Johnson to James Bertram, letter, May 19, 1910, CCNY Records, II.A.1.a, Reel 21 (Nashville, Tennessee).

35. James Bertram to Mary Johnson, letter, June 9, 1910, CCNY Records, II.A.1.a, Reel 21 (Nashville, Tennessee).

36. Mary Johnson to James Bertram, letter, April 28, 1911, CCNY Records, II.A.1.a, Reel 21 (Nashville, Tennessee).

37. James Bertram to J. C. Napier, letter, February 7, 1912, CCNY Records, II.A.1.a, Reel 21 (Nashville, Tennessee).

38. Hillary Howse to James Bertram, letter, February 14, 1912, CCNY Records, II.A.1.a, Reel 21 (Nashville, Tennessee); Robbie D. Jones, "'What's in a Name?': Tennessee's Carnegie Libraries & Civic Reform in the New South, 1889–1919" (master's thesis, Middle Tennessee State University, 2002),123.

39. Jones, 129.

40. James Bertram to Gideon H. Baskette, letter, April 8, 1912, CCNY Records, II.A.1.a, Reel 21 (Nashville, Tennessee).

41. "Library for Negroes," *Nashville Globe*, February 2, 1912.

42. United States Bureau of the Census, *Fourteenth Census of the United States[:] State Compendium[,] Tennessee* (1925).

43. Carnegie Library of Nashville Annual Report, January 1, 1916, Carnegie Library Records, Nashville Metro Archives; James V. Carmichael Jr., "Tommie Dora Barker and Southern Librarianship" (PhD diss., Chapel Hill: University of North Carolina, 1987), 6; Mary Edna Anders, "The Development of Public Library Service in the Southeastern States, 1895–1950," (PhD diss., Columbia University, 1958), 76.

44. Carol F. Kaplan, "Nashville's Negro Carnegie Library, 1916–1949" (paper presented at the Nashville Public Library's Nashville Room, February 12, 1997), Hadley, Marian-Librarian, Vertical Files, Special Collections Division, Nashville Public Library; *Nashville Banner*, September 13, 1931; Nina Mjagki, ed., *Organizing Black America* (New York: Garland Publishing, 2001), 306. In writing about the Blue Triangle, Bobby Lovett implies that it acted as Nashville's African American YWCA; see Bobby L. Lovett, *The African-American History of Nashville, Tennessee, 1780–1930: Elites and Dilemmas* (Fayetteville: University of Arkansas Press, 1999), 123.

45. Robert Churchill, "Dobbs Story Tells of Local Libraries," *Nashville Banner*, January 28, 1970.

46. Meigs High School represented the first high school for African Americans built in Nashville. Meigs High School first opened in 1886 and closed in 1897. In 1958 the school reopened and closed in 1969. In 1970 Meigs became a junior high school and in 1983 a magnet school. In the early 2000s the original Meigs school building was demolished for a new school. Schools: M., Subject Files, Special Collections Division, Nashville Public Library.

47. "Librarian's Report [1949]," Nashville Public Library Records, Nashville Metro Archives.

48. Houston, *The Nashville Way*, 4, 6.

49. McCrary, "A History of Public Library Service to Negroes in Nashville, Tennessee, 1916–1958," 21–22.

50. Ibid., 22.

51. Alvarez received his library education at the University of Chicago Library School. He became director of the NPL in 1946. In 1959, Alvarez quit so he could become director of the Berkeley Public Library in California; see "Nashville Public Libraries," Nashville Public Library Records, Nashville Metro Archives.

52. Robert S. Alvarez, *Library Log: The Diary of a Public Library Director* (Foster City, CA: Administrator's Digest Press, 1991), 281.

53. Alvarez, *Library Log*, 282.

54. Danton, "South Does Less Restricting," 990; Birmingham Public Library, "Birmingham Public Library: 50th Anniversary," Department of Archives and Manuscripts, Birmingham Public Library.

55. Alvarez, *Library Log*, 282.

56. McCrary, "A History of Public Library Service to Negroes in Nashville, Tennessee, 1916–1958," 21–22.

57. Alvarez, *Library Log*, 305.

58. Ibid., 305–306.

59. Ibid., 306.

60. Ibid., 325.

61. Dinkins, Charles L., Vertical Files, Special Collections Division, Nashville Public Library; Perre Magnus, "LeMoyne Owen College," *Tennessee Encyclopedia of History and Culture*, February 21, 2011. During the time he lived in Nashville, and later Memphis, Dinkins played an important role in those cities' black communities. In Nashville, Dinkins served as East Nashville Baptist Church's pastor, and president of the National Association for the Advancement of Colored People's

(NAACP) Nashville chapter. Although Nashville produced numerous famous Civil Rights Movement leaders, including Diane Nash, Bernard Lafayette, John Lewis, Marian Barry, and Z. Alexander Looby, the lesser-known Dinkins deserves credit as an advocate who worked quietly behind the scenes to obtain rights for Nashville's African American community. Born in Selma, Alabama, in 1920, he attended college at Selma University. He then attended divinity school at Oberlin College's Graduate School of Theology in Oberlin, Ohio. In 1943 Dinkins moved to Nashville and assumed employment at the National Sunday School Publishing Board of the National Baptist Convention, USA. He served as interim pastor at the East Nashville Baptist Church from 1949 to 1951, and as pastor from 1951 to 1957. In 1959, he left Nashville to become president of Memphis's Owen College. When Owen College and Lemoyne College merged in 1968, Dinkins became the college's director of development. From 1968 to 1994 he served as pastor of Memphis's First Baptist Church, Lauderdale. Dinkins died on November 1, 1996.

62. "A Special Meeting of the Joint Committee on the Improvement of Library Service to Negroes," Nashville Public Library Records, Nashville Metro Archives.

63. Negro Branch Report + Cornerstone, Carnegie Library of Nashville Records, Nashville Metro Archives.

64. Ibid., 139.

65. Alvarez, *Library Log*, 90, 98.

66. "Negro Branch of Library Sold to Plumbing Firm," *Tennessean*, August 12, 1948.

67. Alvarez, *Library Log*, 223; "Librarian's Report [1949]," Nashville Public Library Records, Nashville Metro Archives.

68. "Negro Branch of Library Sold to Plumbing Firm," *Tennessean*, August 12, 1948; "Plans Discussed For Negro Library," *Tennessean*, October 3, 1948; Robert S. Alvarez to E. W. D. Isaac, letter, October 13, 1948, Nashville Public Library Records, Nashville Metro Archives; R. H. Boyd Publishing Corporation, "Our History," accessed November 20, 2015, http://www.rhboydpublishing.com/content/our-history.asp; "National Baptist Congress," accessed November 20, 2015, http://www.nationalbaptistcongress.org/; McCrary, "A History of Public Library Service to Negroes in Nashville, Tennessee, 1916–1958," 22.

69. Charles L. Dinkins to Judge Albert G. Ewing, letter, June 15, 1949; Nashville Public Library Board of Directors to Charles L. Dinkins, letter, August 31, 1949, both Nashville Public Library Records, Nashville Metro Archives. Albert G. Ewing also served on the Watkins Institute's Board of Commissioners starting in 1941, the institution first housing what became the NPL. In 1947 he became the Watson Institute's Board of Commissioners' chairman; see Ewing, Albert, Vertical Files, Special Collections Division, Nashville Public Library.

70. Ordinances Enacted by City Council, Bill No. 50-400, August 2, 1950, City of Nashville.

71. McCrary, "A History of Public Library Service to Negroes in Nashville, Tennessee, 1916–1958," 15.

72. Robert S. Alvarez to Rowland M. Hill, letter, June 10, 1958, Nashville Public Library Records, Nashville Metro Archives. Rowland Hill wanted to know how the

NPL integrated because he became involved in the effort to integrate the Memphis Public Library (MPL). A professor at Southwestern at Memphis (now known as Rhodes College), Hill worked to integrate the MPL by gathering signatures for petitions asking the library integrate. Apparently he wrote Alvarez to gain information for his effort. Wayne Dowdy, *Crusades for Freedom: Memphis and the Political Transformation of the American South* (Jackson: University of Mississippi Press, 2010), 61–63.

73. 1952 Report of Progress, Nashville Public Library Records, Nashville Metro Archives.

74. McCrary, "A History of Public Library Service to Negroes in Nashville, Tennessee, 1916–1958," 23.

75. Halberstam, *The Children*, 110.

76. Houston, *The Nashville Way*, 2.

77. "Nashville Public Libraries," Nashville Public Library Records, Nashville Metro Archives; "Library's Demolition Scheduled for Summer," *Nashville Banner*, February 26, 1963.

78. Rob Moritz and Bill Carey, "New Downtown Library May Displace Watkins," *Tennessean*, March 20, 1998.

79. Amber Austin, "New Nashville Library Follows National Trend," *The Associated Press*, June 3, 2001.

Chapter 6

"This We Believe"
Local Black Activism, the National Civil Rights Movement, and the Integration of the Birmingham Public Library

Birmingham, like Atlanta and Nashville, serves as an excellent example of a New South city. In just a few years it grew from a community of 1,000 in Alabama's Jones Valley to an urban center of steel, iron, and coal production. However, Birmingham's relationship with its public library differed from that of Atlanta and Nashville. While city leaders often spoke about a public library's positive contributions, they did not take action to obtain one as Atlanta and Nashville's elites did. Birmingham's boomtown quality during its early years probably contributed to the lack of widespread desire to establish a public library. Still, the Birmingham Public Library (BPL) eventually grew into a large, multi-branch library system and confronted the same issues of providing a public service in a rigidly segregated society that the APL and NPL dealt with.

Like Atlanta's and Nashville's public libraries, the BPL did provide Birmingham's African Americans with segregated library service prior to its integration. Also similar to Atlanta and Nashville, Birmingham provided library service to blacks by developing a separate African American library system. However, the BPL more aggressively worked to stave off desegregation. Unlike Nashville, and to a lesser degree Atlanta, the BPL integrated in response to direct, very public lobbying by African Americans and the national attention Birmingham received as a result of the infamous 1963 civil rights campaign in the city.

National and local quests for civil rights often intersected during the civil rights movement. While groups like the Southern Christian Leadership Conference (SCLC) and the National Association for the Advancement of Colored People (NAACP) worked on a national level to obtain civil rights legislation, local groups and individuals worked to achieve their own objectives. Birmingham fit this mold. Rev. Fred Shuttlesworth, an SCLC founder, and co-founder of the Alabama Christian Movement for Human Rights (ACMHR), provided uncompromising leadership. Others who played key roles in Birmingham's civil rights campaign included James Bevel, director of SCLC's direct action and nonviolent education programs, and students at Miles College, a historically black college. In 1962, Miles College students organized a boycott of Birmingham businesses practicing segregation. Students from the college also participated in sit-ins to demand the BPL's integration.[1]

In the spring of 1963, from April 3 to May 8, Martin Luther King Jr., Fred Shuttlesworth, Wyatt T. Walker, James Bevel, Andrew Young, and others, took part in SCLC'S campaign to attack segregation in Birmingham. During the campaign, Birmingham police arrested thousands of protestors, including King. While imprisoned, King wrote the well-known "Letter from a Birmingham Jail." The Birmingham campaign also saw the Birmingham police turning firehoses and police dogs on student protestors in an effort to break up demonstrations. These tactics led to some of the most iconic images of the civil rights movement.[2] SCLC's campaign focused the nation's attention on Birmingham. As Miles College students sat-in at the library, BPL's administrators knew that the media would likely cover the event and cast the library in a negative light, especially if the police arrested the students and the library resisted integration. Accordingly, in spring 1963, national and local events came together in Birmingham in such a way as to enable young black activists to integrate the BPL.

BEGINNINGS

In the 1850s, Alabama's state geologist studied the land in central Alabama and found massive coal, iron, and limestone deposits. Meanwhile the Alabama and Chattanooga Railroad and the Louisville and Nashville Railroad snaked toward each other, eventually intersecting at Birmingham's present-day site. In December 1870, ten men formed the Elyton Land Company in Montgomery, Alabama. The group named their company after the small community with the same name in Alabama's Jones Valley, where Birmingham would soon exist. One group member, John T. Milner, worked for the South and North Alabama Railroad (later controlled by the Louisville and Nashville Railroad). He ensured that the Alabama and Chattanooga (later named the Southern Railway System) and Louisville and Nashville railroads would intersect where the Elyton Land Company owners wanted them to, not at Elyton, but slightly to the east of town. While forming the company, the group also mapped out Birmingham's city plan.[3]

In 1871 Birmingham incorporated as a city with a population of around 1,000. For its first seven years Birmingham slowly grew. However, in 1878, when the Pratt Mines (coal), the Alice Furnaces, and shortly thereafter the Sloss Furnaces opened, the city boomed. Soon, other furnaces opened. Many manufactured pig iron, a combination of iron ore, coke (a fuel made from coal), and limestone. In 1899, Birmingham mills commenced manufacturing steel. By 1920, Birmingham's population had grown to 178,806. In 1900, African Americans made up forty percent of the city's population. A city founded to extract and exploit the coal, iron, and limestone in the surrounding area, Birmingham became an industrial city focused on steel and pig iron production.[4]

In 1884 the Birmingham Library Association formed. The association gathered books and other reading materials, planning to run a library. However, the group soon became overwhelmed with the task. By 1886, they had turned their materials over to Birmingham Superintendent of Schools Dr. John Herbert Phillips to see what he could do with them. Phillips made the association's reading matter available to Birmingham High School students in a single room located outside his office in the school's first location at Third Avenue and Nineteenth Street. In 1890 the library founded by the Birmingham Board of Public Education became among the first in the state to receive funding from tax dollars.[5]

In 1891 the Birmingham Board of Education, high school, and superintendent's office moved to a refurbished hotel at Sixth Avenue and Twenty-first Street. That year the library became known as the BPL.[6] Students could freely use the library at its new location. Nonstudents paid two dollars a year to check books out, although Phillips did not strictly enforce the two-dollar fee. Even so, like the NPL and APL, early on in its history the BPL relied on the subscription library model. By 1909, the BPL became totally subscription free.[7]

Unlike Atlanta and Nashville, Birmingham never received a library construction grant from Andrew Carnegie or the Carnegie Corporation of New York (CCNY). In their history of the BPL, Virginia Pounds Brown and Mabel Thuston Turner noted that in 1901 Birmingham's Commercial Club attempted to obtain a library construction grant. James Bertram, Carnegie's secretary, responded by sending the group an information form to complete. Six months later the Commercial Club's W. N. Malone returned the form, explaining that the city would not guarantee funds to support the library. Since Birmingham could not meet Carnegie's requirement for ongoing city support, the Commercial Club failed to obtain a Carnegie library construction grant.[8] However, surrounding suburbs, which Birmingham eventually annexed, including Avondale, Bessmer, Ensley, and West End, did receive Carnegie library construction grants. Ensley, in northwest Birmingham, applied for a Carnegie grant in late 1904 and received it in 1905. Avondale, in southeast Birmingham, applied for and received its grant in 1907. West End, a western suburb of Birmingham, applied for and received its grant in 1909. Avondale, Ensley, and West End eventually became BPL branch libraries.[9]

Until Birmingham's city hall burned in April 1925, the city at best gave only passing notice to the BPL. Nonetheless, the library had a constant advocate in pediatrician Thomas D. Parke, who had moved from Selma to Birmingham in 1887 and became actively involved with the library shortly thereafter. Eventually, the city began to give the library slightly more notice, although it would not guarantee funds in 1901 when the Commercial Club tried to pursue a Carnegie construction grant on the city's behalf. However, in 1903 Birmingham built a new city hall, and in 1904 the library moved to this structure. Even so, the city jail was below the library, and across the street at the city market, "the killing of chickens disturbed the children in quiet study."[10]

Lila May Chapman, formerly a student at the Carnegie Library School of Atlanta (CSLA), was hired to catalog the BPL's books. She became the BPL's assistant director in 1913, and by 1926 became the system's overall director, a post she held until her retirement in 1947. In 1907, along with other community leaders, Dr. Parke formed the Birmingham Public Library Association.[11] Soon after, in 1911, the Birmingham Public Library Association incorporated Ensley's Carnegie-funded library into the BPL system. In 1912, West End's library also became part of the system.

Perhaps because it took notice of the BPL's expansion, or due to efforts by Thomas Parke, in 1913 the City of Birmingham assumed control of the library. After taking over the library, the city created a board to govern it. Parke served on the BPL's first board after the city takeover. Meanwhile, the library continued to expand, bringing Avondale's library into the system in 1913.[12] The fact that the city only assumed responsibility for the library after it expanded multiple times, and not during its earliest years when it most needed help, illustrates that it did not want the responsibility of financing and managing the BPL's earliest development. During the BPL's embryonic years, the city's priorities clearly lay elsewhere.

Perhaps attempting to emulate Atlanta, in August 1920 the BPL announced it would open its own library school. The newspaper article reporting the story stated that the library wanted to start the school to meet its demand for librarians, as well as requests for trained librarians from public libraries across Alabama. Library director Lloyd W. Josselyn and chief cataloger Caroline Engstfeld were to serve as the primary faculty. The story reported that Josselyn and Engstfeld "will give a large number of the lectures and plan the practice work of the different students." The curriculum would consist of cataloging, classifying, library science, economics, and bibliography.[13]

However, it seems that the BPL's ambitious plan to start a library school did not last long. The brief mention in the newspaper is as far as the plan ever went.

On April 25, 1925, Birmingham's city hall caught fire, causing $800,000 in damage. The catastrophe gave force to a standing call for a new library building. By late May 1925, the Birmingham City Commission had approved plans for a new $650,000 library.[14] Prior to the 1925 fire, the BPL library board worked to generate support for a bond issue to build a stand-alone library. Board members, including Thomas D. Parke, advanced two arguments. First, fire insurance on Birmingham's city hall cost seven and a half times more than the neighboring building, indicating its high fire risk. Second, the library's location on the city hall's fourth floor would make it difficult for people to get out if the building caught fire.[15]

For two years the city housed the library in temporary quarters at Birmingham's old post office building located at Second Avenue and Eighteenth Street. In 1927 the library's new building opened, located on Woodrow Wilson Park, now known as Linn Park.[16] This structure, now known as the Linn-Henley Research Library, currently houses the BPL's Archives and Manuscripts department, as well as other special collections departments.

AFRICAN AMERICANS AND THE BIRMINGHAM PUBLIC LIBRARY

While the BPL developed, Birmingham's African Americans advocated for and worked toward establishing their own library. For years, African American teachers held various fundraising events to generate money to open a library for black use. Finally, by 1898, the teachers acquired enough money. Sources vary on the amount raised, from $350 to $4,144.17. Whatever the sum, the money enabled Superintendent Dr. John Herbert Phillips to buy books and refurbish a room in the African American Slater School to serve as the library.[17] In the beginning, the Slater School library was open for only six hours a week, compared to the fifty-five hours a week at the BPL.

Later, African American residents tried other approaches to gain increased library service. In 1913 African American doctor Ulysses G. Mason wrote to the Carnegie Corporation of New York (CCNY) and complained that it had provided Avondale, Ensley, and West End with funds to construct their public libraries, but gave no money to construct an African American library in Birmingham. In 1917 Mason again made the same complaint to the CCNY.[18]

Mason's efforts to obtain a branch library for Birmingham's African Americans provides yet another example of the centrality of black professionals to the efforts to provide and expand library service to blacks in the urban

South. Overall, the pre-1954/1955 work of activists to expand library service to southern blacks, as well as to integrate southern public libraries, does not comfortably fit within the civil rights movement's traditional time frame. The earliest efforts to expand library service to southern blacks, often beginning immediately after communities opened their public libraries, is evidence that African American attempts to break down segregation in southern public libraries span multiple phases of the black freedom movement.

At its January 9, 1918 meeting, the BPL Board for the first time considered opening a branch library to serve African Americans. However, the board tabled a decision on the matter for two months due to the upcoming military draft to provide soldiers for U.S. involvement in World War I. In March 1918 the board again discussed opening an African American branch library, this time referencing "the young colored woman from Birmingham, who is now in training at Louisville for library work with her people, [who] will by June 1st have completed her course, and wishes to return to Birmingham as soon as the colored branch can be launched."[19] As was the case with the NPL Board minutes discussing Marian Hadley, the BPL Board minutes do not disclose whether the African American librarian-in-training was directly studying under Thomas Blue at the Louisville Public Library. However, she obviously studied at the library education program he established. Again, Thomas Blue's influence in early library education for southern African Americans made its presence felt.

Mattie Herd, the young woman the BPL Board selected to manage the BPL's branch, did not suddenly appear on the scene. Birmingham African American school principals met in 1913, along with Booker T. Washington and BPL director Carl Milam, to pick an African American high school student who would finish her regular schooling, work at the BPL after school hours, attend the Louisville Public Library's training program after graduation, and then return to Birmingham to lead the BPL's black branch. At the meeting, participants selected Mattie Herd, daughter of an African American railroad switchman.[20]

On July 10, 1918, the BPL Board decided to open an African American branch library and find a location for it. Accordingly, it decided to interview Mattie Herd to ascertain her ability to serve as the black branch's librarian.[21] It remains unclear what happened with Mattie Herd in the five-year interval between her selection as the branch's eventual librarian and her interview in 1918. Still in school in 1913, perhaps Herd focused on her studies until called forth by the library in 1918.

On July 29, 1918, librarian Emily Miller Danton reported to the board that the library had found a twenty-five-by-one-hundred-foot building at 1715 Third Avenue for $55 a month, indicating the library's preference to rent as opposed to buying. On August 2, 1918, the BPL Board voted to name the library the Lincoln Branch, a name suggested by Superintendent of Education Dr. John Herbert Phillips.[22] However, on August 14, the board decided to change the name to the Booker T. Washington Branch.[23] Also at the August 2 meeting, the board discussed what to do about loaning books from the system's main branch to the African American branch. The board decided to try and refrain from doing so, unless absolutely necessary. If the system did loan a book from the main branch to the black branch, the board instructed the main branch to purchase a new copy of the loaned item.[24] This policy indicates that Birmingham had already begun travelling down the path of becoming one of the South's most intensely segregated cities, and that no institution, including the public library, remained untouched by segregation. It also illustrates the irrationality of segregation.

Other southern cities and their public libraries, including those that claimed adherence to a moderate brand of segregation, also had similar policies. In April 1947 the Nashville Public Library's (NPL) board met to explore the possibility of providing bookmobile service to whites *and* African Americans. However, some board members disagreed with serving whites and blacks from the same bookmobile, because white Nashvilleans might oppose books "going into colored people's homes." The NPL accordingly purchased another bookmobile to exclusively serve African Americans.[25]

What to call Mattie Herd also posed an issue as revealed by the August 14, 1918 BPL Board meeting minutes. Dr. Thomas D. Parke brought up the issue, and BPL director Carl Milam suggested assigning Herd the title of Acting Librarian because of her youth. He believed that the library might have to replace her with someone older. Although the board discussed the matter, it made no decision until November when it decided that the Washington Branch needed a male librarian.[26] The BPL intended to have a grand opening for the Booker T. Washington Branch on October 8, 1918, but could not due to the city's ban on public gatherings because of a flu epidemic. Instead, the library quietly opened at 2 p.m. the next day. When it opened, the branch served as the only library for African American use in Alabama, including the 70,230 blacks living in Birmingham. In 1923, when the BPL lost the lease on this property, the Booker T. Washington Branch moved from its Third Avenue location to the Colored Masonic Temple on 1630 Fourth Avenue North (figure 6.1).[27]

INTEGRATION COMING

Other than the April 25, 1925, fire that destroyed the BPL's main branch and city hall, and the subsequent construction of the new main branch building, little seems to have occurred between the fire and the early 1940s. However,

Figure 6.1 Interior of Booker T. Washington Branch. *Source*: Hill Ferguson Papers, Birmingham Public Library Archives.

with the coming of the 1940s, library service to African Americans in Birmingham and Jefferson County slowly expanded. In 1940 or 1941 (sources conflict) the library opened another African American library at the Slossfield Center in North Birmingham in the vicinity of the American Cast Iron Pipe Company, locally known as Acipco. The company played a direct role in the library's creation, and the BPL later became involved. Jacob Eagan, president of Acipco, strongly believed in corporate welfare. As such, Eagan and Acipco provided its white workers with various services intended to create a better quality of life, including library service. Acipco's white workers received library service in the form of an Acipco-backed YMCA library located, it seems, on or near the company's property in North Birmingham. However, Eagan also desired to provide Acipco's black workers with library access. Initially, it seems as if the black branch was located in the same building as the Acipco-sponsored white branch. According to Patterson Toby Graham, "Services for whites were provided on the first floor with a door in front. Acipco provided black services on the second floor with a door from the rear of the building."[28] Shortly thereafter, Eagan took advantage of available space in the National Youth Administration (NYA) facility in Slossfield to establish a library for the company's African American workers.[29]

According to Graham, the NYA chapter in Slossfield began as a boys club in the 1930s through a private donation of a house in the neighborhood.

In 1939, the Slossfield NYA acquired further space. That same year Eagan wrote to the BPL suggesting it open a black branch library in Slossfield. Under his plan, the Acipco Negro Auxiliary, considered the premier African American community group in Slossfield, would fundraise and advocate for the branch library; Acipco and the Negro Auxiliary would provide books and equipment for the new library; and the NYA would provide the space. Acipco even paid the salaries of the branch's librarian, Daisy Jones, as well as her eventual replacement, Ludie Brown. The BPL simply had to administer the new library. However, as a result of this arrangement, the BPL provided almost no funds for the branch until 1944.[30]

On October 12, 1944, BPL director Lila May Chapman reported to the press that the library planned to construct six African American branch libraries in the Jefferson County Library System, which the BPL administered.[31] The Jefferson County Commission provided the funds to build the facilities, although the commission intended its appropriation to serve as a general contribution to the BPL and nothing more. However, the BPL "found it possible to use the additional appropriation for this purpose [constructing the black branches]." Further, Chapman announced, "$50 a month will be spent for books for the Negro libraries, and this will be supplemented by donations from the third district of the Federation of Women's Clubs." The article also reported that the new African American branches would separately exist from the white branches and books between the two would not mix.[32]

The white Federation of Women's Clubs in Alabama had a history of developing public library service. For instance, in 1899 the organization, formed in 1895, created travelling libraries that it sent to communities across Alabama. Later, the group sent the libraries to schools that did not have a library. In 1905, the Alabama Library Association took over the administration of the travelling libraries.[33] Meanwhile, the National Association of Colored Women's Clubs (NACWC), formed in 1896, launched numerous social welfare efforts across the nation. The NACWC especially worked to respond to the needs of those newly moved to cities and other large urban areas, creating daycare centers as well as kindergartens and playgrounds for children, establishing health clinics, and working to reduce overcrowding in African American schools.[34] Although it remains unclear which women's clubs, African American, white, or both, pledged to contribute books to the planned new libraries, women in Birmingham cared about increased library service to African Americans.

Born in Dadeville, Alabama, in 1872, Lila May Chapman received her higher education at Wesleyan College in Macon, Georgia. After graduation, she became a teacher until the CLSA opened in 1905, at which point she enrolled in the school. Chapman and nine others made up the CLSA's first class. Even before graduating, Chapman found work in Alabama libraries. While enrolled at the CSLA, she went to Ensley, Alabama, and helped organize the collection at the town's Carnegie-funded library. After graduation, Chapman worked as a cataloger at the Gadsden Public Library, in Gadsden, Alabama, then as a librarian at the public library in Corsicana, Texas, before becoming a librarian at the BPL in 1909. While at the BPL, she steadily moved up the administrative hierarchy. In 1913, she became the library's assistant director. In 1914, she became vice director. From 1926 until her retirement in 1947, she served as the BPL's director.[35]

After Chapman retired, Emily Miller Danton became the BPL's director. In 1948, she published an article titled "South Does Less Restricting" in *Library Journal*. In her piece Danton analyzed data she collected through a survey of southern librarians to determine their attitudes toward serving African Americans and working with black library staff members. Her research revealed that many white librarians had no problem providing some level of service to black patrons, or working with African American coworkers. Furthermore, Danton's survey revealed that southern librarians viewed segregation in libraries as antiquated and at odds with a library's mission.[36] Although Danton only surveyed twenty-two libraries across the South, and her results are best viewed as qualitative data, they do provide interesting insights into the attitude among white librarians on race and segregation in southern public libraries. However, an editorial comment attached to Danton's article represents perhaps its most intriguing aspect for what it says and the questions it raises:

> Mrs. DANTON is entirely Southern, in ancestry, birth, and upbringing, but her long residence in Middle-Western and Eastern cities, while it has in no way dimmed her affection and loyalty to the South, has perhaps made her more objective in viewpoint than are many southerners. She is concerned with the inequalities in library service to the two races in the South, and hopes to increase library facilities for Negroes in Birmingham.

Even though *Library Journal*, a professional publication, published Danton's article, thereby implicitly stating its soundness, whoever wrote the editorial comment felt it necessary to state that Danton had the authority to study and comment upon segregation in southern public libraries. The legitimacy, at least according to the author of the comment, came in the form of Danton's birth and upbringing in the South. The comment reveals much, including an implication that only "southerners" could analyze southern race relations because they lived every day immersed in them. This theme hearkens at least back to the New South Era, during which southerners wanted to fully economically rejoin the rest of the nation but retain some element of distinctiveness while doing so. Of course, that distinctiveness could no longer come in the form of a defense of slavery; the Civil War, Reconstruction, and the New South Movement saw to that. The distinctiveness came partly from the ability to proclaim and defend one's "southerness." At the same time, Danton's article and the editorial comment attached to it, also suggest that while living outside the South her views on race had expanded, although Danton may have always held opinions on race that differed from many southerners.

Legitimate southerner or not, Danton and her article, as well as Chapman's 1944 effort to increase support of black libraries and library service in Birmingham and Jefferson County, suggests less than total adherence to Birmingham's fanatical public support of segregation. Chapman's attempt to better serve African Americans came at the end of her career. Perhaps she saw an opportunity to expand library service to African Americans and took it. Danton, in writing her article, may have had the same objective. In any case, both Chapman and Danton used their status as directors of the BPL to improve public library service to African Americans.

Although the push to expand library service to Birmingham's African Americans began in 1939 and slowly increased in the 1940s, a 1950 anonymous editorial in the *Birmingham News* calling for expanded library service to Birmingham blacks ushered in the last, albeit long, phase in the BPL's history before it integrated. Questions relating to this editorial abound. Who wrote it? Was the author white or black? What did such an editorial in one of the South's most segregated cities mean? These questions remain difficult to answer because the newspaper only identified the author as "Vulcan": the city's huge statue of the Roman god of fire, metalworking and the forge, which stands atop Birmingham's Red Mountain.[37] The *Birmingham News* then and now represented the dominant newspaper in Birmingham. Accordingly, the Vulcan editorial, very likely widely read by the city's residents, suggests that some in Birmingham believed African Americans in the city deserved better access to certain city services. The editorial stated its support for Emily Miller Danton's efforts to have a new African American branch library built. The anonymous author wrote, "I am proud of our library system here. But I would like to see the library services to Negroes expanded. Negro youth could be much better served through a better and larger library."[38]

In the years following "Vulcan's" editorial, the BPL made a prolonged, concerted effort to increase the library service it provided to African Americans living in Birmingham. In March 1952 an African American named John H. Anderson, representing several African American organizations, asked the library to consider building an African American main branch in downtown Birmingham, situated in Ingram Park.[39] Although the BPL would eventually build three more African American branch libraries, it did not build the downtown library requested by Anderson. However, a month after Anderson made his request, the BPL Board initiated a plan to place books in white and African American county schools that did not have any. This program came about after the Booker T. Washington Branch provided the black Forty-Second Street School with one hundred books.[40]

At its September 1953 meeting the BPL Board listed the improvements it wanted to make to the system, including asking the city for $300,000 to build a central African American branch downtown.[41] However, it seems the board never forwarded the request to the city. The BPL also assembled a "Negro advisory committee." This decision came about in July 1953 after the board learned that the Booker T. Washington Branch's circulation figures had significantly declined.[42] Carol H. Hayes, director of Birmingham's African American schools, E. Paul Jones, director of Jefferson County's Division of Negro Education, and Mrs. M. L. Gaston, head of the Booker T. Washington Business College, made up the committee. Advising the board on how to expand library service to African Americans in Birmingham and throughout Jefferson County served as the committee's purpose.

The Negro Advisory Committee developed multiple strategies to increase African American use of the city's black library branches. Regular speaking engagements to increase awareness of the libraries represented one approach. The advisory committee's Publicity and Speakers Subcommittee planned to send speakers to black churches, schools, social clubs, and other African American organizations to talk about the libraries. In return, the advisory committee made it clear that it expected the BPL to provide African Americans with better library service if library usage increased.[43]

Whether created in concert with the Negro Advisory Committee or not, the BPL Board in 1953 put forth an ambitious program to provide Birmingham blacks with better library service. For example, the board proposed to install five book deposit stations in African American housing projects. Furthermore, the Birmingham City Commission also supported the idea to build a new, downtown African American branch library as the Booker T. Washington Branch remained in a rented facility.[44] In December 1953, after receiving a donation from a Mrs. Horace Hammond, the BPL purchased a bookmobile to serve African Americans. Although the newspaper does not expressly say so, it appears the bookmobile represented the first to serve Birmingham blacks. Hammond had given to the library in the past. In 1952 she provided funds that helped the library purchase a bookmobile for white use, as well as expand its dance and ballet collection. In 1953, along with the money she gave to help the library buy a bookmobile for African Americans, she also gave $1,000 so the library could again expand its dance collection. The *Birmingham News* reported that between 1952 and 1953, Hammond, along with her daughter, gave the library almost $19,000.[45]

The BPL's efforts to increase the quantity and quality of library service it provided to African Americans, beginning in the late 1930s but especially by the early 1950s, indicates it knew segregation in public institutions would increasingly come under attack. As the Supreme Court's 1954 ruling in *Brown v. Board of Education* loomed, the BPL expanded its efforts to create a separate-but-equal library system for African Americans. However, the BPL knew the attempt might prove futile and thus exercised limits on how far it would go in trying to develop that system. In January 1954, with the decision of the Supreme Court pending, the library chose to put on hold its plans to build the $300,000 African American branch library downtown until the Supreme Court issued its decision. The library knew that if the Supreme Court ruled in favor of the plaintiff, building a $300,000 branch for African Americans would constitute a waste of money. Anticipating the court's decision, one board member, a Mrs. Evans, even suggested integrating the BPL's main building. However, the board as a whole wanted to determine the effects the Supreme Court's decision would have on libraries before it made any big decision regarding the construction of African American branch libraries. The BPL Board minutes note: "no definite commitments should be made until such time as a ruling is handed down by the Supreme Court on the matter of segregation."[46]

On May 17, 1954, the Supreme Court ruled that segregated schools violated the equal protection clause of the Fourteenth Amendment. However, the Supreme Court's decision came and went with little if any discernible impact on the BPL. The library did not revisit the idea to build the $300,000 African American branch, yet by 1955, the BPL was planning to build a black branch on Birmingham's Southside at Sixth Avenue South and Center Street. The proposed new branch would cost $80,000, to be funded through a $500,000 bond issue taking place that year. Construction on the new facility did not begin until 1957. In the two years between announcement and construction, the BPL built three other branch libraries: two white, Park Memorial and Ensley, and one African American, Smithfield. When Smithfield opened in 1956, the BPL intended it to replace the Booker T. Washington branch[47] (figure 6.2).

Meanwhile, African Americans began pressing for desegregation. In May 1956, the library received a petition with over one hundred signatures asking it to desegregate its main branch by June 30, 1956. The board seriously considered the request, knowing it now had no legal foundation supporting its segregated status. Proceeding cautiously, the board asked the city attorney if integrating the library would violate any city laws. While the board waited for an opinion from the city attorney, it considered building another African American branch library on the city's south side, which it began constructing in 1957.[48]

Figure 6.2 Storytime at the Booker T. Washington Branch. Ca. 1950. *Source:* Birmingham, Ala. Public Library Archives.

After the 1956 petition for integrated service, African Americans' quest for better library service temporarily quieted. However, in 1959, Elias Hendricks, speaking for Birmingham's Northside Civic League, Elsberry League, and Finley Avenue Civic League, appeared before the library board and asked it to consider building a new branch library in the Acipco plant area in North Birmingham. Hendricks believed the African American branch library located in the Slossfield Community Center could no longer provide suitable service due to its location. The minutes do not explain what Hendricks meant by his statement. Perhaps he intended to say that a significant amount of the black population once living near the branch had moved, a situation similar to Nashville's Negro Branch Library. In any case, the board replied to Hendrick's request by noting that the BPL wanted to build a new library near the Acipco plant and had made the city aware of its desire. However, it cautioned Hendricks that the city might not provide money for the branch. The board then essentially stated that if the city did not allocate funds to build a new black branch library in North Birmingham, it would have to make some difficult decisions. While the library waited on the city's reply, the board suggested to Hendricks that the organizations he represented take steps to improve the Slossfield branch by planting new foliage and beautifying its grounds. Hendricks apparently relayed the suggestion. The November 12, 1959, board minutes note that the Northside Civic League bought a drinking fountain for the Slossfield branch.[49]

From the minutes it remains difficult to discern board members' individual feelings regarding segregation. However, the minutes do reveal an awareness regarding the broader mood in Birmingham toward segregation and issues of race. The board's decision to continue building black and white branch libraries reflects that mood, and constituted a direct challenge to federal law. However, the board also aptly perceived that events in the larger context would impact the library, even if they could not immediately figure out how or when. The board's careful watching of the Supreme Court in early 1954, as well as its deliberate, considered actions during and in response to events during the 1963 civil rights campaign in the city would prove that.

By 1961, the BPL's days as a segregated institution were drawing to a close. On November 8, 1961, a federal judge ruled illegal a Birmingham city ordinance segregating theaters, auditoriums, playgrounds, athletic facilities, and all other forms of public entertainment. However, the ruling exempted some institutions for sixty days. During the exemption period, entities like the BPL had to make a case as to why they should remain segregated. Amazingly, the BPL continued to survive as a segregated institution past the sixty-day exemption period, even building another African American branch library in 1961, the Georgia Road branch.[50]

INTEGRATION ARRIVES

In 1963, civil rights movement leader Martin Luther King Jr., along with other SCLC activists, including James Bevel and Andrew Young, came to Birmingham at the behest of local movement leader Fred Shuttlesworth to arrange and put into motion a plan to attack segregation in the city. The campaign began in April and lasted until May. Initially, City Commissioner of Public Safety Eugene "Bull" Conner stifled the campaign's efforts. In response, James Bevel, a King lieutenant, suggested organizing Birmingham's children and youth for a march. From May 2 to 5, hundreds of young people marched. Bull Conner used fire hoses, police dogs, and mass incarceration to combat the marches, leading to some of the civil rights movement's most iconic images.

As the Birmingham campaign began, the BPL soon found itself affected by it. On April 9 and 10, 1963, African American students sat-in at the BPL's main branch. The April 11 board minutes note that twelve black students came to the library on April 10, sat at various tables, stayed for forty-five minutes, and then left. U. W. Clemon, a former U.S. District Judge for Northern Alabama, participated in the library sit-in. He later recalled that he and his friends went to Birmingham's Sixteenth Street Baptist Church to receive instructions from Andrew Young on how to conduct the sit-in. Clemon also recalled that the Birmingham police had the group under surveillance while in the library, although he remained unaware of this until 1996 when someone showed him pictures of the sit-in. Nonetheless, Clemon believed the police did not arrest them because they thought their adult chaperon was white. When asked what book he read while sitting-in at the library, Clemon said he did not remember but stated, "that was some fake reading."[51]

Clemon and his fellow protestors attended Miles College. Likewise, the adult accompanying them, Addine "Deenie" Drew, worked at the college. Miles and its students had already played a key role in attacking segregation in Birmingham before the 1963 campaign. In 1962 students from the college protested segregation by economically boycotting many white-owned stores in Birmingham. Drew also played an important role in the BPL's integration.

Before the Miles College students sat-in at the library, they needed information about it; none of them had ever entered the building. Accordingly, SCLC organizer Wyatt Walker asked Drew to visit the library. Walker selected Drew because of her fair skin; she could pass as white. Drew did more than scout the library; she accompanied the Miles students to the April 9 sit-in. Clemon, Sandra Edwards, and Catherine Jones made up the Miles students sitting-in on April 9. On April 10, Walker sent twelve students to sit-in at the library. Police monitored the April 10 sit-in, but did not arrest the protestors.[52]

By not turning them away, library director Fant Thornley believed he served the students. At the April 11 board meeting, Thornley asked the trustees if they approved of his decision to serve the protesting students. The board crafted a resolution stating they disapproved of people using the library as a protest site, but that they supported the director's actions. Furthermore, the board decided to integrate the library, even though Birmingham mayor Art Hanes pledged he would integrate the city's libraries only at gunpoint. The library board's minutes note: "The Board (1) approves the action of its Director in serving said demonstrators on April 10 and (2) directs that no persons be excluded from the use of the public library facilities except in the cases and under the circumstances set forth in the rules and regulations of the Library adopted and published January 18, 1962."[53]

After the BPL integrated, it had to adjust to the changes brought about by its decision to do so. For example, a month after the library integrated, library director Thornley had to inform the branch libraries that any person with a library card could use them. Two months after the library integrated, the library board minutes indicate that no reported incidents had occurred. Soon after the BPL integrated, distinctive African American library use patterns emerged. The BPL's Ensley branch, in West Birmingham, received many African American library card applications. In fact, the Ensley branch's user numbers so increased that Director Thornley recommended building another branch in the area. The BPL Board accordingly authorized the library to purchase a lot in the Ensley area for an amount not exceeding $7,500.[54]

In December 1963, Thornley received a federal subpoena to appear in court and testify in the case of *Hendricks vs. City of Birmingham*, a case filed in 1962 prior to the library's integration. The plaintiffs, Reverend Herbert Oliver and Lola Hendricks, claimed the library refused to issue them a library card. However, the case actually encompassed more institutions than just the library, and more plaintiffs than Oliver and Hendricks. Six plaintiffs, including N. H. Smith Jr., J. S. Phifer, both clergymen, W. E. Shortridge, Charles Ewbank Tucker, Hendricks, and Oliver, sued Birmingham to desegregate its airport motel and all public buildings, including libraries. Hendricks argued that when she tried to check out a book at the BPL's main branch, a librarian refused her service and told her she could check out the book at one of the system's African American branches. However, by the time the case came to trial, the plaintiff's case had become moot. Thornley, in his report regarding the case to the library board, reported that Oliver had admitted he had received a library card since filing the case and had used it many times.[55]

POST-INTEGRATION

Following the BPL's integration, the system experienced numerous changes. The library initiated many developments to better serve African American patrons, from programming to bringing African Americans onto the BPL Board. Additionally, the city mandated that a certain amount of contracts go to minority-owned contracting firms. Birmingham worked to shed its former whites-only status. For example, in 1965 the Birmingham City Commission appointed Miles College instructor Imogene Murchison to a five-year term on the BPL Board.[56] The library also developed an affirmative action plan intended to raise the percentage of minorities on its workforce to the percentage of minorities in the general population. Between 1977 and 1987, the percentage of African Americans who worked at the BPL rose from 30 percent to 55 percent. In the late 2000s, the library reported African Americans made up 55 percent of its staff.[57]

However, the transition to becoming a more inclusive institution did not always smoothly occur. In the early 1980s Birmingham's first African American mayor, Richard Arrington, and the BPL Board engaged in a public tussle regarding the level of minority participation in the contract to construct a new building for the central library. On May 7, 1982, when the story first broke, Arrington wanted minority-owned contracting firms to receive a greater percentage of the contract to build the new library building. Arrington also wanted to delay construction so that Champion, the firm awarded the $8.6 million contract, could increase the amount of money it had set aside, only $110,000, for minority firm participation.[58]

On May 9, Arrington got his stay in the awarding of the contract. However, it caused tense relations between him and the BPL Board. Board member Don Long described Arrington's effort to increase minority participation in the contract as a "total failure." The library argued that it had tried to increase minority participation in the contract. However, as the *Birmingham News* reported, when the BPL held a meeting to announce its desire to construct a new building and release bidding information, only three minority-owned firms attended. The mayor countered by inquiring why then did the library not hire a firm specializing in bundling subcontracts in such a way to ensure minority participation. A representative of Parametric, a company that did just that, reported having spoken with acting library director Dan Wilson in 1981, but nothing happened.[59]

At its April 1982 meeting, the BPL Board recognized Champion's bid to build the new library as the lowest. However, the library also acknowledged Champion's offer did not meet the city's minimum requirement for minority participation in city-awarded contracts. The board actually voted to not pick Champion's bid as the winning bid until it could acquire more information about the city's requirement that a minimum amount of a city-awarded contract to go to minority firms.[60]

For around a month the media reported nothing more about the spat between Arrington and the BPL Board. However, in early June, the *Birmingham News* reported that Arrington had presented the library board with six different plans intended to increase the amount of money going to minority-owned subcontracting firms. The *Birmingham News* also questioned some of Arrington's suggestions, noting that if the library implemented four of the six strategies the mayor suggested, it would add nearly $100,000 to the new library building's construction costs.[61]

Nonetheless, Arrington's strategy worked. By June 8, Champion had raised the amount of money it planned to award to minority subcontractors from $110,000 to $250,000. Apparently satisfied with the additional amount, the library accepted the bid. However, some Birmingham city council members regarded the $250,000 set aside for minority firms as a pittance. At the June 8 Birmingham City Council meeting, councilman Jeff Germany literally tossed cracker crumbs at three African American leaders to illustrate how little he believed $250,000 to represent. Germany stated, "To grant $250,000 in an $8.7 million construction contract to black subcontractors 'is a direct insult to the black leaders who campaigned for the bond issue and black citizens who overwhelmingly supported the bond issue [to raise money to build the new library].'"[62]

In July 1982, another story about the black contractor experience appeared in the *Birmingham News*. The paper asked several African American contractors working in Birmingham what represented their biggest hurdles to winning contracts. The contractors replied that many black-owned contracting firms struggled to get financing and bonding, insurance guaranteeing a firm will complete a job. The contractors also mentioned they often could not win contracts because they simply did not have the resources necessary to accomplish a large job.

The lack of minority participation in Birmingham-awarded contracts came to a head in 1976 when black contractors won only $476 of $20,000,000 in contracts awarded by the city. From that point on, then Mayor David Vann required ten percent of each city-awarded contract to go to minority firms. However, in 1982, apparently shortly after Arrington demanded the BPL Board increase the amount of funds awarded to minority subcontracting firms, the Associated General Contractors of Alabama sued Birmingham, intending to end its policy of awarding a minimum level of city-awarded contracts to minority firms.[63]

While the BPL's constant expansion of library service to African Americans from the 1940s on provided the city's blacks with more and better library service, the system had other goals in mind as it went on an African American branch library building spree in the 1950s. Building an excessive number of African American branch libraries supported segregation. The BPL clearly attempted to fulfill the concept of "separate but equal." Furthermore, many city leaders believed in and worked to preserve segregation, including Art Hanes, Birmingham mayor from 1961 to 1963. Hanes's comment about integrating the libraries only at gunpoint may have had something to do with the BPL not integrating sooner; the library did not want to bite the hand feeding it. Thus, in 1981, the BPL caused a public outcry when it announced it would close several branches due to redundancy. In explaining the library's decision, library director George Stewart stated, "Historically, many of these branch libraries were built during the late 1950's [sic] and early 1960's [sic] to prevent racial integration.... Consequently, there are several examples of needless and expensive duplication."[64]

Historically, library segregation in Birmingham represented an extremely complicated situation. Some entities earnestly believed in segregation and worked to defend it. Others adhered to segregation because they felt they had to. Thus, African Americans initially demanded their own libraries, and BPL administrators built branch libraries partly in response to this demand. However, not everyone believed in segregating the library, as evidenced by the Vulcan editorial, as well as Emily Miller Danton's 1948 article and Lila May Chapman's efforts in the 1940s to expand library service to African Americans. Furthermore, as this chapter has shown, still others determinedly worked to integrate the BPL.

The BPL's desegregation also illustrates that, individual efforts aside, events in the larger context played just as large, or larger, role in affecting the situation. The 1963 civil rights campaign in Birmingham provided the needed event to break the stalemate between those wishing to keep the BPL segregated and those wishing to integrate it. SCLC's 1963 campaign in the city proved the largest single factor influencing how Miles College students chose to try and integrate the library. It brought the right amount and combination of tension and media attention—enough to cause the BPL administration to want to avoid unpleasant scenes. The Miles College students successfully used sit-ins to integrate the BPL. Indeed, the BPL's integration demonstrates the civil rights movement's local and national levels could come together in such a way to make achieving seemingly difficult or impossible goals possible.

The dispute between Mayor Richard Arrington and the BPL's Don Long over the total amount, in monetary terms, set aside for minority contractors illustrates not ingrained racism on the library's part, but the long-term impact that segregation had on minority businesses. Simply put, few African American-owned contracting firms existed, and the ones that did generally were prohibited from bidding because they were too small to handle large jobs. Arrington's efforts to increase the amount of funds minority-owned contracting firms received from the contract to build the BPL's new main library building represented an attempt to heal some of the effects of segregation in Birmingham. Although it caused tension between him and the BPL Board, particularly board member Don Long, Arrington clearly believed, as did his predecessor Mayor David Vann, he had to take active steps to begin to address segregation's effects in the city. As the Atlanta case study also shows, determining how to deal with an institution or community having long-practiced segregation represents a complex undertaking, with outcomes not immediately clear.

The outcomes of efforts to combat segregation's effects, like Arrington and Vann's, depend on many variables. Among them include who holds power, in terms of making the decision to address the legacy of an institution's segregated past, and deciding what steps to take. Increasing the number of African Americans on the BPL's staff represents one way to deal with the library's past segregation practices. Although not without its own complications—see the case study on the APL—achieving a more accurate representation of the general population's demographics serves as one way to begin to address a past history of segregation. As for working to overcome the long history of economic segregation in Birmingham, that represents an even more complex and difficult issue to deal with. Like dealing with library segregation, it depends on who holds the power and how willing they are to work to resolve continuing economic inequalities or address the legacy of past ones.

NOTES

1. Andrew Manis, "Fred Lee Shuttlesworth," August 27, 2014, accessed December 15, 2015, http://www.encyclopediaofalabama.org/article/h-1093.

2. Adam Fairclough, *Better Day Coming: Blacks and Equality, 1890–2000* (New York: Penguin Books, 2001), 273–76.

3. Marjorie Longenecker White, Richard Sprague, and G. Gray Plosser, Jr., eds., *Downtown Birmingham: Architectural and Historical Walking Tour Guide* (Birmingham: Birmingham Historical Society, 1977), 4.

4. William T. Miller, "Library Service for Negroes in the New South: Birmingham, Alabama, 1871–1918," *Alabama Librarian* 27, no. 1 (November/December 1975): 5, 6.

5. Virginia Pounds Brown and Mabel Thuston Turner, "History of the Birmingham Public Library," Chapter 1, pp. 4–6 (Manuscript), Newspaper Clipping Files, Department of Southern History and Literature, Birmingham Public Library; Kenneth R. Johnson, "The Early Library Movement in Alabama," *Journal of Library History* 6, no. 2 (April 1971): 123.The Alabama Supreme Court Law Library, founded in 1828, represents the first library in Alabama to receive funds from tax dollars.

6. Miller, "Library Service for Negroes in the New South," 7.

7. Brown and Turner, "History of the Birmingham Public Library," Chapter 1, pp. 4–6, Chapter 2, pp. 2 (Manuscript); Miller, "Library Service for Negroes in the New South," 7.

8. Brown and Turner, "History of the Birmingham Public Library," Chapter 3, pp. 1–2 (Manuscript).

9. Ensley, Alabama, Application and Approval for CCNY construction grant, September 1, 1904 and March 15, 1905, Carnegie Corporation of New York Records, Columbia University Libraries [hereafter cited as CCNY Records] II A.1.a, Reel 10 (Ensley, Alabama); Avondale, Alabama, Application and Approval for CCNY Construction grant, October 10, 1907 and December 13, 1907, CCNY Records, II, A.1.a, Reel 2 (Avondale, Alabama); West End, Alabama Application for CCNY construction grant, January 23, 1909, CCNY Records, II, A.1.a, Reel 34 (West End, Alabama); James Bertram to S. Norwood, letter, February 1, 1909, CCNY Records, II, A.1.a, Reel 34 (West End, Alabama); "A Great Free Library for Birmingham; Actually a University for the People," *Birmingham News*, May 7, 1922. The majority of newspaper articles cited from Birmingham, Alabama newspapers in this monograph came from the Birmingham Public Library Scrapbooks.

10. Brown and Turner, "History of the Birmingham Public Library," Chapter 3, pp. 3.

11. James L. Baggett, "Birmingham Public Library," May 12, 2011, accessed December 12, 2015, http://www.encyclopediaofalabama.org/article/h-1406.

12. W. L. Murdoch, "Vision of Pioneers Realized as New Public Library Makes Dreams Come True," *Birmingham News*, April 10, 1927; Brown and Turner, "History of the Birmingham Public Library," Chapter 3, pp. 3; Birmingham Public Library Board Minutes, November 12, 1959, and Birmingham Public Library, "50th Anniversary," both Department of Archives and Manuscripts, Birmingham Public Library; "History of Birmingham Public Library," December 29, 2014, accessed December 10, 2015, http://www.bplonline.org/about/history/; Baggett, "Birmingham Public Library."

13. "To Inaugurate Library School," *Birmingham Age-Herald*, August 16, 1920.

14. "Work on Library to Begin July 15" and "Revenue Board Gives Final Approval to Building Plan," *Birmingham News*, May 23, 1925; W. J. Boles, "Public to Occupy 'Palace of Books,'" *Birmingham News*, April 10, 1927.

15. "A Central Library for Birmingham," n.d., n.p., Newspaper Clipping Files, Department of Southern History and Literature, Birmingham Public Library; "50,000 Now Using Library and Yet City Has No Central Building," *Birmingham Age-Herald*, May 21, 1922.

16. "City Hall Is Almost in Ruins after Sweep of Noonday Fire," *Birmingham News*, April 24, 1925; "Library to Use Old Post Office," *Birmingham News*, April 25, 1925; "New City Hall to Face Woodrow Wilson Park," *Birmingham News*, April 24, 1925.

17. Robert C. Kaufmann, "Library Service to Negroes in Birmingham, Alabama," n.d., n.p., Newspaper Clipping Files, Department of Southern History and Literature, Birmingham Public Library.

18. Miller, "Library Service for Negroes in the New South," 7.

19. Birmingham Public Library Board Minutes, January 9, 1918, and March 13, 1918, Department of Archives and Manuscripts, Birmingham Public Library.

20. Miller, "Library Service for Negroes in the New South," 7–8.

21. Birmingham Public Library Board Minutes, July 29, 1918, Department of Archives and Manuscripts, Birmingham Public Library.

22. Birmingham Public Library Board Minutes, August 2, 1918.

23. Ibid., August 14, 1918.

24. Ibid., August 2, 1918.

25. Robert S. Alvarez, *Library Log: The Diary of a Public Library Director* (Foster City, CA: Administrator's Digest Press, 1991), 223; "Librarian's Report [1949]," Nashville Public Library Records, Nashville Metro Archives.

26. Birmingham Public Library Board Minutes, August 14, 1918, Department of Archives and Manuscripts, Birmingham Public Library; Patterson Toby Graham, *A Right to Read: Segregation and Civil Rights in Alabama's Public Libraries* (Tuscaloosa: University of Alabama Press, 2002), 14.

27. United States Bureau of the Census, *Fourteenth Census of the United States[:] State Compendium[,] Alabama* (1924); "Colored Library Is Not to Open Soon," *Birmingham News*, October 8, 1918; "Formal Opening Plans Abandoned," *Birmingham Ledger*, October 8, 1918; Oscar W. Adams, "What Negroes Are Doing," *Birmingham News*, October 9, 1943; Marcella White, "Concerning Negroes," *Birmingham Post-Herald*, October 23, 1947; Historic American Buildings Survey, "Masonic Temple (Colored), 1630 Fourth Avenue North, Birmingham, Jefferson County, AL," Library of Congress, accessed December 13, 2015, http://www.loc.gov/pictures/item/al0969/.

28. Graham, *A Right to Read*, 44.

29. Marcella White, "Concerning Negroes," *Birmingham Post-Herald*, October 23, 1947; "Plan of Action Proposed by Advisory Board on Library Service to Negroes, From August 1, 1953 to August 1, 1954," 2, n.d., n.p., Newspaper Clipping File, Department of Southern History and Literature, Birmingham Public Library.

30. Graham, *A Right to Read*, 45–47; "Plan of Action Proposed by Advisory Board on Library Service to Negroes, From August 1, 1953 to August 1, 1954," 2.

31. The Jefferson County Library System continues to exist in the form of the Jefferson County Library Cooperative (JCLC). Community libraries in Jefferson County, including the BPL, make up the JCLC membership. The JCLC has its main office in the BPL's central branch in Birmingham. The JCLC derives its funds primarily from grants, state monies, and membership fees. Until 2011, the JCLC also received funds from the Jefferson County Commission; see Jefferson County Library Cooperative, "History and Purpose," July 2013, accessed February 29, 2016, http://www.jclc.org/aboutjclc/history.aspx.

32. "Six Negro Libraries to Be Established," *Birmingham News*, October 12, 1944.

33. Johnson, "The Early Library Movement in Alabama," 121, 126.

34. Gerda Lerner, "Early Community Work of Black Club Women," *Journal of Negro History* 59, no. 2 (April 1974): 162–63.

35. Brown and Turner, "History of the Birmingham Public Library," Chapter 4, pp. 4.

36. Danton, "South Does Less Restricting," 990–92.

37. Mike Dixon-Kennedy, *Encyclopedia of Greco-Roman Mythology* (Santa Barbara, CA: ABC-CLIO Inc, 1998), 319–20.

38. Vulcan, "From Where I Stand," *Birmingham News*, November 27, 1950.

39. Birmingham Public Library Board Minutes, March 12, 1952, Department of Archives and Manuscripts, Birmingham Public Library.

40. Birmingham Public Library Board Minutes, April 9, 1952.

41. Ibid., September 10, 1953.

42. Ibid., July 9, 1953.

43. "Plan of Action Proposed by Advisory Board on Library Service to Negroes," 4.

44. "Library Board Here Names Negro Advisory Committee," *Birmingham News*, July 25, 1953.

45. "Birmingham Negroes Will Soon Have Bookmobile of Their Own," *Birmingham News*, December 22, 1953.

46. Birmingham Public Library Board Minutes, January 5, 1954, Department of Archives and Manuscripts, Birmingham Public Library.

47. "Branch Library for Negroes to Cost $80,000," *Birmingham News*, November 26, 1955; "Branch Library for Negroes OK'd," *Birmingham News*, January 11, 1957; "Library Facilities for Negroes Expand," *Birmingham News*, May 24, 1957; Kaufmann, "Library Service to Negroes in Birmingham, Alabama," 4.

48. Birmingham Public Library Board Minutes, May 10, 1956, Department of Archives and Manuscripts, Birmingham Public Library.

49. Birmingham Public Library Board Minutes, July 9, 1959, and November 12, 1959.

50. "Second City Law on Mixing Voided," *Birmingham News*, November 9, 1961; Baggett, "Birmingham Public Library."

51. U. W. Clemon, interview by Jim Baggett, Birmingham, Alabama, Birmingham Public Library, January 26, 2009, accessed December 12, 2015, https://www.youtube.com/watch?v=Y23IhDBAXZ4&index=6&list=PLD5BCE279B8392D57.

52. Graham, *A Right to Read*, 87–89.

53. Birmingham Public Library Board Minutes, April 11, 1963, Department of Archives and Manuscripts, Birmingham Public Library; Baggett, "Birmingham Public Library."

54. Birmingham Public Library Board Minutes, May 16, 1963; June 13, 1963; July 18, 1963.

55. Birmingham Public Library Board Minutes, December 12, 1963; "Negroes File Mixing Suit," *Birmingham Post-Herald*, July 11, 1962.

56. "Council Fills Board Vacancies," *Birmingham Post-Herald*, November 24, 1965.

57. Birmingham Public Library, "History of Birmingham Public Library," December 29, 2014, accessed June 15, 2016, http://www.bplonline.org/about/history/.

58. Jay Hamburg, "Library Contract Delayed By Lack of Minority Firms," *Birmingham Post-Herald*, May 7, 1982.

59. Kitty Frieden, "Mayor, Board Collide on Black Subcontractors," *Birmingham News*, May 9, 1982.

60. Birmingham Public Library Board Minutes, April 23, 1982, Department of Archives and Manuscripts, Birmingham Public Library.

61. "Arrington Asks Added Black Role in Library," *Birmingham News*, June 2, 1982.

62. Jay Hamburg, "Minority Plan Leads to Library Board Bid OK," *Birmingham News*, June 8, 1982; "Germany Says Blacks Getting a Crumby Deal," *Birmingham News*, June 8, 1982.

63. Andrew Kilpatrick, "'Just . . . Overlooked' Is Big Minority Problem," *Birmingham News*, July 6, 1982; "Minority Contracts Put 'Out of the Ball Game,'" *Birmingham News*, July 13, 1982.

64. Birmingham Public Library, "Library Board Proposes Sweeping Re-organization," June 22, 1981, Newspaper Clipping Files, Department of Southern History and Literature, Birmingham Public Library.

Conclusion

The establishment of public libraries across the nation represented a reform effort born of the Progressive Era. However, many southern communities also founded their public libraries to prove that the New South economic development agenda worked and could sustain civic culture in many forms. Nonetheless, the development of southern public libraries fit within the broader narrative of national public library development, which philanthropy, especially Andrew Carnegie's, greatly influenced. Carnegie eventually provided enough funds to construct 1,679 public libraries across the country.[1]

Despite Carnegie's contributions to southern public library development, women and women's organizations drove the growth of southern public libraries. While the support of government and philanthropic agencies constitute an important component of southern public library development, these entities in many ways built upon the foundations laid by women and women's groups. Women's involvement in libraries and librarianship, especially, stems from their participation in women's clubs. There, in clubs, women crafted strategies that enabled them to use Progressive Era societal stereotypes of them—as nurturers and protector of morals—to enter public life. By couching the mission of public libraries in Progressive Era language and goals, women could use participation in the development and management of public libraries as a way to participate in public life and pursue their own goals.

While Andrew Carnegie made a substantial investment in southern public libraries, other philanthropic entities, including the General Education Board, the Rosenwald Fund, and the Board of Education for Librarianship, among others, played central roles in developing southern public libraries, as well as supporting library access and education for African Americans. Besides philanthropic organizations, government entities like the Tennessee Valley

Authority and the Works Progress Administration significantly contributed to the development of southern public libraries. In sum then, women and women's organizations, as well as federal government and philanthropic support, represent a defining characteristic of the first fifty to sixty years of southern public library development.

Carnegie, other philanthropists and philanthropic groups, women and women's organizations, and later the federal government believed libraries provided substantial educational benefits to those who would take advantage of them. Carnegie stated, "I choose free libraries as the best agencies for improving the masses of the people, because they give nothing for nothing-they help those who help themselves. . . ."[2] At Carnegie's insistence, and later the Carnegie Corporation of New York's (CCNY), communities receiving construction grants had to "help themselves" by annually appropriating library maintenance and operation funds. By insisting communities continue to support their public libraries, Carnegie and the CCNY ensured public libraries would become fixtures of the civic landscape and an accepted feature of American public life.

In Atlanta and Nashville, accepting Carnegie library construction grants helped these cities realize their particular reform, educational, and economic development objectives.[3] However, it also enabled them to institutionalize segregation and racism. While Carnegie did give money for the construction of African American branch libraries in Atlanta and Nashville, as well as other cities across the South, the size of those grants paled in comparison to the magnitude of funds given to construct whites-only public libraries. The willingness of Carnegie and the CCNY to provide communities with significant sums of money to construct public libraries without challenging Jim Crow practices gave southern whites a tool to extend the subjugation of African Americans. While discrimination against African Americans contradicted the idea of libraries as sites of personal improvement and uplift, it did not contravene southern progressivism. As Dewey W. Grantham argues, many southern progressives believed diminishing the involvement of African Americans in southern political and public life as much as possible constituted a progressive action.[4]

David Carr in *The Promise of Cultural Institutions* argues that cultural institutions represent humanity.[5] They closely resemble the society in which they exist. Thus, for example, southern public libraries generally practiced racial segregation when most of southern society did so as well. By the same token, African American efforts to integrate the APL, BPL, and NPL occurred because blacks in Atlanta, Birmingham, and Nashville believed that they had the right to use their cities' public libraries. The close relationship between cultural institutions and society constitutes one reason why public libraries became focal points for desegregation.

African American efforts to integrate southern public libraries represented a key factor in their integration, institutional growth, and increase in societal value. African Americans, as well as white supporters like Reverend Edwin Cahill and Howard Zinn in Atlanta, constantly pressured the APL, BPL, and NPL to provide blacks with better library service. By the 1950s, and even the late 1940s in Nashville, activists no longer demanded better service; they wanted fully integrated public libraries. African American's relentless struggle for better, and eventually integrated, library service, resulted in the full integration of all three libraries.

The larger context came into play when activists worked to determine what tactics they would use to integrate the APL, BPL, and NPL. However, local contexts especially determined the approaches activists used in their work to integrate public libraries in their communities. With respect to the APL and NPL, Atlanta and Nashville elites' commitment to creating and maintaining a specific image of their respective cities played a significant role in determining how activists worked to integrate the libraries in these locales. In Nashville's case, the city's elites focused on crafting and maintaining an image of the city as an educational center, and to a lesser degree, a financial one. Barring people from using a public library in a city billing itself as an educational center undermined Nashville's attempts to create and uphold the vision of the city its elites had in mind. Historian Benjamin Houston argues that because Nashville elites endeavored to create an image of the city as educated, genteel, and refined, its elites committed to practicing a supposedly "moderate" form of race relations.[6] From the late 1940s when attempts to integrate the NPL earnestly got underway, until 1950 when the library integrated, activists used Nashville elites' desire for others to view the city as an educational center characterized by moderate race relations against the library. Activists employed letters, private meetings, and compromise, all while avoiding the press, to integrate the NPL.

When the APL integrated in 1959, Atlanta mayor William B. Hartsfield had already declared the city "too busy to hate."[7] Knowing Hartsfield and other Atlanta elites' commitment to a vision of the city as a commercial hub, activists pressed their advantage. However, those attempting to integrate the APL did more than use the city's image as leverage. Activists exhibited a willingness to risk direct confrontation. In 1959, activist and professor Whitney Young, president of the Greater Atlanta Council on Human Relations, threatened a lawsuit to integrate the library. At the city's behest, Young agreed to delay filing the lawsuit to give the library an opportunity to integrate on its own. However, to see if the city and library administration would honor its promise to integrate, Young and Howard Zinn asked Spelman College professor Irene Dobbs Jackson to go downtown and attempt to get a library card, which she did, without incident.

Conclusion

The tactics African American activists used to integrate the BPL in 1963 differed in comparison to those used by activists to integrate the APL and NPL in at least two ways: a willingness to use the media to their advantage to the fullest extent possible and to take direct confrontation to its limit. During the late 1940s and 1950s, activists in Birmingham attempted to use compromise and negotiations to secure expanded library service and work toward the integration of the BPL. However, events in the larger context dramatically changed activists' tactics. In April 1963, the infamous Birmingham campaign began. For two months, April and May 1963, civil rights movement leaders and activists, including Martin Luther King Jr., Fred Shuttlesworth, Wyatt Walker, James Bevel, and Andrew Young, among many others, campaigned to attack segregation in Birmingham. The campaign led to some of the most iconic images of the civil rights movement as Birmingham's Commissioner of Public Safety "Bull" Conner turned fire hoses and police dogs on protesters. The campaign also provided activists working to integrate the BPL with the perfect amount of leverage. Instead of using compromise and negotiations, Miles College student activists staged two sit-ins at the BPL. At the second sit-in, reporters sat at a table in the library observing. Wishing to avoid the type of confrontation and publicity following the events that had already occurred in the Birmingham campaign, and the incidents that would soon follow, BPL administrators integrated the library.

Integration at the APL, NPL, and BPL occurred in specific local contexts and at different moments in the overall struggle for African American equality. However, in all three instances, highly educated people participated in the efforts. In Nashville, the city's African American elite, which included educators, businesspeople, and even politicians like James C. Napier, worked to improve and then provide integrated library access for the city's African Americans. In Atlanta, the effort to integrate the library again came from African American elites. However, the struggle to integrate the APL also included a few white participants, including professor Howard Zinn and Reverend Edwin Cahill. The participants in the final push to desegregate the BPL were all college students, with the exception of one adult chaperone.

That most cultural institutions share a common set of values partly originating in the wider society remains an essential point to consider in the desegregation of the APL, NPL, and BPL. Not all southern public library workers, from librarians in the branches up to library board members, believed segregation morally correct. This study's three case studies provide examples of librarians, library directors, and board members in Atlanta, Nashville, and Birmingham who believed segregation wrong, unethical, a waste of time and resources, a hindrance, and ultimately unworkable. However, the degree to which the professional staff and governing boards of the APL, NPL, and BPL contributed to de-institutionalizing segregation in their respective cities is hard to discern. Although, at least in the qualitative example of Annie L. McPheeters, it is clear that some librarians, including African American librarians, actively worked to end segregation in their library systems.

While the APL's and NPL's integrations represented victories activists could point to as they worked to integrate other places in Nashville and Atlanta, their ability to use the desire of civic leaders to maintain certain images for their respective cities had a greater impact. In Birmingham's case, the 1963 civil rights campaign directly led to the BPL's integration, in large part because Miles College students had already honed their activism skills in the 1962 economic boycott of Birmingham merchants.

In addition to their place in the history of the South, the Black Freedom Movement, and southern public libraries, the APL, NPL, and BPL integration stories fit within the context of the recent historiographical debate concerning the civil rights movement. According to Sundiata Keita Cha-Jua and Clarence Lang, the first wave of scholars claimed the civil rights movement spontaneously occurred and had few, if any connections, to African Americans' prior quests to obtain civil rights. Among other things, second wave historians contended that grassroots activists and leaders represented the movement's heart and soul. Third wave scholars argue the movement had certain key characteristics, particularly African Americans' use of personal agency, as well as the ability to capitalize on the opportunity the Cold War provided them to obtain their objectives. According to Cha-Jua and Lang, the common belief that the civil rights movement took place from 1954–1955 to 1965 unifies the first three waves. They also take issue with Jacquelyn Dowd Hall and other fourth wave scholars, who argue that the movement began in the 1930s and continued into the 1980s. Lang and Cha-Jua believe extending the civil rights movement's timeframe erases important demarcations in space and time. They claim that expanding the timeframe of the civil rights movement sucks the meaning out of what scholars once considered a discreet period in the long history of the black struggle for equality.[8]

The early and unceasing efforts of activists to gain any sort of African American library service at the APL, NPL, and BPL, as well as their near-constant attempts to integrate these institutions long before the civil rights movement's traditional timeframe, indicate that the 1954–1955 to 1965 framework does not have enough elasticity to accommodate pre-1954 efforts to integrate public libraries in major southern cities. It also validates Cha-Jua and Lang's thesis. In studying activists' efforts to integrate the APL, NPL, and BPL, as well as when these institutions actually desegregated, it becomes apparent each did so at distinctly different points in the overall effort to achieve black equality.

Nashville's integration occurred on the eve of the beginning of the traditional timeframe of the civil rights movement. Activists' efforts to use diplomacy revealed a commitment to the ideology of respectability that the movement's youth would challenge as it made its way through the 1960s. Rebecca de Schweinitz, in *If We Could Change the World: Young People and America's Long Struggle for Racial Equality*, argues that middle- and upper-class African Americans defined respectability as adhering to middle-class values, particularly emphasizing the importance of the family, home, culture, and education—in short, Progressive Era infused notions of refinement. De Schweinitz points out middle- and upper-class African Americans adhered to and advocated on behalf of these values as a way to dispel stereotypes about African Americans.[9] Access to public libraries helped achieve, as well as demonstrate, black commitment to these ideals. Such efforts had a discernible impact on white librarians, including one who remarked:

> You have to realize that the class of Negroes who want to use the library is a pretty high class. Just like the whites who use the library are high class. What made it easy was that the class who would oppose Negroes does not use the library. . . . There are two classes of people. Library users are seekers of knowledge. The rough class of either race doesn't go to the library.[10]

The integration of the APL reveals a commitment to respectability and an increasing turn toward direct confrontation and skillful use of the media. Activists' approach to integrating the APL indicates that their efforts had gained momentum since what scholars once considered the start of the civil rights movement (1954), and that they sought ways to extend the gains they had already made. It also demonstrates that the movement had begun to transition to a different phase in which direct confrontation became the tactic of choice as activists worked to tear down segregation in the South. The integration of the BPL shows a complete acceptance of the use of direct confrontation and media to achieve library desegregation.

The integration of southern public libraries played a key role in the civil rights movement and the overall Black Freedom Movement. At the same time, integrating public libraries represented just one of the civil rights movement's objectives. Middle- and upper-class African Americans, as well as students, especially cared about ending segregation in these institutions. Achieving the integration of public libraries mattered to these groups because they clearly saw the ability to access them as a necessity in a democratic society.

In 2001, award-winning children's author Patricia C. McKissack published *Goin' Someplace Special*. McKissack's book explains how much the library meant to her, how badly segregation in Nashville made her feel, and the joy she felt going to the library. To McKissack, the integrated Nashville Public Library represented a refuge from the segregation outside its walls, a place to escape segregation's dignity-stripping reality. For television host, producer, business person, and more, Oprah Winfrey, reading, and by extension, books, also held a deeply personal meaning. In a speech to the Association of American Publishers in 2003, Winfrey reflected on what books meant to her as a young person living in Mississippi and in her present life, "Books allowed me to see that there was a world beyond my grandmother's front porch. That everybody didn't have an outhouse, that everybody wasn't surrounded by poverty, that there was a hopeful world out there and that it could belong to me. [Books were] an open door to dwell in possibility . . . ." Winfrey went on to describe books and engrossing herself in them as "my comfort, it is my solace[.]"[11]

NOTES

1. David Nasaw, *Andrew Carnegie* (New York: The Penguin Press, 2006), 585–86, 607.
2. As quoted in Thomas Augst and Wayne Wiegand, *Libraries as Agencies of Culture* (Madison: University of Wisconsin Press, 2003), 11.
3. The City of Birmingham never directly received a Carnegie library construction grant. However, Avondale, Ensley, and West End, Alabama, which Birmingham early in its history annexed, did receive Carnegie grants.
4. Dewey W. Grantham, *Southern Progressivism: The Reconciliation of Progress and Tradition* (Knoxville: The University of Tennessee Press, 1983), xv.
5. David Carr, *The Promise of Cultural Institutions* (Walnut Creek, CA: AltaMira Press, 2003), XVI.
6. Benjamin Houston, *The Nashville Way: Racial Etiquette and the Struggle for Social Justice in a Southern City* (Athens: The University of Georgia Press, 2012), 3, 4.
7. Kevin M. Kruse, *White Flight: Atlanta and the Making of the Modern Conservatism* (Princeton: Princeton University Press, 2005), 40.
8. Sundiata Keita Cha-Jua and Clarence Lang, "The 'Long Movement' as Vampire: Temporal and Spatial Fallacies in Recent Black Freedom Studies," *Journal of African American History* 92, no. 2 (Spring 2007): 266–67.
9. Rebecca de Schweinitz, *If We Could Change the World: Young People and America's Long Struggle for Racial Equality* (Chapel Hill: University of North Carolina Press, 2009), 15–17.
10. International Research Associates, *Access to Public Libraries: A Research Project*, Prepared for the Library Administration Division, American Library Association, International Research Associates, Inc. (Chicago: American Library Association, 1963).
11. Oprah Winfrey, "Oprah on 'The Fire for Reading,'" *Publishers Weekly*, March 10, 2003, accessed February 6, 2019, https://www.publishersweekly.com/pw/print/20030310/26705-oprah-on-the-fire-for-reading.html.

Bibliography

ARCHIVES AND MANUSCRIPT SOURCES

Atlanta-Fulton Public Library System Special Collections.
Birmingham Public Library, Archives and Manuscripts Division.
Birmingham Public Library Board Minutes, 1913–1989, AR 511
Birmingham Public Library Scrapbooks, 1913–1985, AR1325
Subject Files, 1960–1969.
Birmingham Public Library, Department of Southern History and Literature. Clippings Files.
Carnegie Corporation of New York Records. Rare Book and Manuscript Library. Columbia University Libraries.
   *Note: Many, if not all, of the Nashville Public Library (NPL)-produced records used in this study remain unprocessed. Accordingly, below are listed the current box title and box number the records cited pertaining to the NPL came from. Some boxes had no title. When this happened, the bibliographic citation also included the name of the document. It is possible the box numbers and titles will change as archivists process the records.
Nashville Metro Archives.
Speeches and Addresses, Series II, Sub-Series II, 1912–1920, Box 3.
Accessions, Circulation Volumes, Scrapbooks, 1901–1928, Box 7.
Bound Records of Howard + Carnegie Library, 1901–1941, Box 8.
Director's Correspondence 1948–1960, Box 10.
History of NPL, Nashville Public Library Clippings/Directors, Box 15.
1900–1960 Carnegie Library Reports, Correspondence, Box 19.
Director Correspondence 1948–1960, Box 23.
Director Correspondence 1948–1960, Box 24.
Library Documents-1937–1977, Box 31.
Library Correspondence 1905, Carnegie Library, Box 32.
1913–1916 Branches: North, South, Negro, Box 33.

Reports + Correspondence Robert Alvarez 1953–1957, Box 40.
Public Library (Unprocessed), Box 42.
Annual Reports-1949–1950, Public Library (Unprocessed), Box 42 Reports, Box 45.
Nashville Public Library, Special Collections Division.
Vertical Files.
Subject Files.

NEWSPAPERS

Associated Press
Atlanta Constitution
Atlanta Daily World
Atlanta Georgian
Atlanta Journal
Atlanta Journal-Constitution
Birmingham News
Birmingham Post-Herald
Nashville Globe

MISCELLANEOUS

Bogle v. McClure. 332 F. 3d 1347 (Court of Appeals 11th Circuit, 2003).
Brown et al. v. Board of Education of Topeka et al. 349 U.S. 294 (1955).
Clemon, U. W. Interview by Jim Baggett. Birmingham, Alabama. Birmingham Public Library. January 26, 2009. Accessed December 12, 2015. https://www.youtube.com/watch?v=Y23IhDBAXZ4&index=6&list=PLD5BCE279B839 2D57.
McPheeters, Annie L., Interviewed by Kathryn Nasstrom, 8 June 1992, P1992–09, Series J. Black and White Women in Atlanta Public Life, Georgia Government Documentation Project, Special Collections and Archives, Georgia State University Library, Atlanta.
Nashville, City of. Ordinances Enacted by City Council, Bill No. 50-400, August 2, 1950.
U.S. Bureau of the Census.
    Thirteenth Census of the United States (1910).
    Fourteenth Census of the United States (1920).

BOOKS AND PUBLISHED REPORTS

Alvarez, Robert S. *Library Log: The Diary of a Public Library Director.* Foster City, CA: Administrator's Digest Press, 1991.
American Library Association. *Books for the South.* Chicago: American Library Association, 1933. Accessed July 22, 2015. HathiTrust.

Bibliography

Anderson, Eric, and Alfred A. Moss, Jr. *Dangerous Donations: Northern Philanthropy and Southern Black Education, 1902–1930.* Columbia: University of Missouri Press, 1999.

Anderson, James D. *The Education of Blacks in the South, 1860–1935.* Chapel Hill: University of North Carolina Press, 1988.

Anderson, Karen. *Little Rock: Race and Resistance at Central High School.* Princeton: Princeton University Press, 2010.

Augst, Thomas, and Wayne Wiegand. *Libraries as Agencies of Culture.* Madison: University of Wisconsin Press, 2003.

Battles, David M. *The History of Public Library Access for African Americans in the South: Or, Leaving behind the Plow.* Lanham, MD: The Scarecrow Press, Inc., 2009.

Blackmon, Douglas. *Slavery by Another Name: The Re-enslavement of Black People in America from the Civil War to WWII.* New York: Doubleday, 2008.

Blair, Karen J. *The Clubwoman as Feminist: True Womanhood Redefined, 1868–1914.* New York: Holmes & Meier Publishers, Inc., 1980.

Bobinski, George S. *Carnegie Libraries: Their History and Impact of American Public Library Development.* Chicago: American Library Association, 1969.

Bryan, Ferald J. *Henry Grady or Tom Watson?: The Rhetorical Struggle for the New South, 1880–1890.* Macon, GA: Mercer University Press, 1994.

Carr, David. *The Promise of Cultural Institutions.* Walnut Creek, CA: AltaMira Press, 2003.

Chafe, William H. *Civilities and Civil Rights: Greensboro, North Carolina, and the Black Struggle for Freedom.* New York: Oxford University Press, 1980.

Cronon, William. *Nature's Metropolis: Chicago and the Great West.* New York: W. W. Norton & Company, 1991.

Davis, Donald G. and Cheryl Knott Malone. "Reading for Liberation: The Role of Libraries in the 1964 Mississippi Freedom Summer Project." In *Untold Stories: Civil Rights, Libraries, and Black Librarianship*, edited by John Mark Tucker, 110–125. Champaign, IL: University of Illinois Graduate School of Library and Information Science, 1998.

Davis, Donald G. and Ronald C. Stone Jr. "Poverty of Mind and Lack of Municipal Spirit: Rejection of Carnegie Public Library Building Grants by Seven Southern Communities." In *Carnegie Denied: Communities Rejecting Carnegie Library Construction Grants, 1898–1925*, edited by Robert Sidney Martin, 137–173. Westport, CT: Greenwood Press, 1993.

Davis, Harold E. *Henry Grady's New South: Atlanta, A Brave and Beautiful City.* Tuscaloosa: University of Alabama Press, 1990.

Davis, Kenneth S. *FDR: The New Deal Years, 1933–1937.* New York: Random House, 1986.

De Schweinitz, Rebecca. *If We Could Change the World: Young People and America's Long Struggle for Racial Equality.* Chapel Hill: University of North Carolina Press, 2009.

Dixon-Kennedy, Mike. *Encyclopedia of Greco-Roman Mythology.* Santa Barbara, CA: ABC-CLIO Inc., 1998.

Dowdy, G. Wayne. *Crusades for Freedom: Memphis and the Political Transformation of the American South.* Jackson: University of Mississippi Press, 2010.

Doyle, Don H. *Nashville in the New South, 1880–1930.* Knoxville: University of Tennessee Press, 1985.

———. *New Men, New Cities, New South: Atlanta, Nashville, Charleston, Mobile, 1860–1910.* Chapel Hill: University of North Carolina Press, 1990.

Durham, Walter T. *Reluctant Partners: Nashville and the Union, July 1, 1863 to June 30, 1865.* Nashville: Tennessee Historical Society, 1987.

Fairclough, Adam. *Better Day Coming: Blacks and Equality, 1890–2000.* New York: Penguin Books, 2001.

Frankel, Noralee, and Nancy S. Dye, eds. *Gender, Class, Race, and Reform in the Progressive Era.* Lexington: The University Press of Kentucky, 1991.

Gleason, Eliza Atkins. *The Southern Negro and the Public Library: A Study of the Government and Administration of Public Library Service to Negroes in the South.* Chicago: The University of Chicago Press, 1941.

Gould, Lewis W. *America in the Progressive Era, 1890–1914.* New York: Longman, 2001.

Graham, Patterson Toby. *A Right to Read: Segregation and Civil Rights in Alabama's Public Libraries, 1900–1965.* Tuscaloosa: University of Alabama Press, 2002.

Grantham, Dewey W. *Southern Progressivism: The Reconciliation of Progress and Tradition.* Knoxville: The University of Tennessee Press, 1983.

Greene, Christina. *Our Separate Ways: Women and the Black Freedom Movement in Durham, North Carolina.* Chapel Hill: University of North Carolina Press, 2005.

Halberstam, David. *The Children.* New York: Random House, 1998.

Harvey, Bruce G. *World's Fairs in a Southern Accent: Atlanta, Nashville, and Charleston, 1895–1902.* Knoxville: University of Tennessee Press, 2014.

Hogan, Wesley C. *Many Minds, One Heart: SNCC's Dream for a New America.* Chapel Hill: University of North Carolina Press, 2007.

Houston, Benjamin. *The Nashville Way: Racial Etiquette and the Struggle for Social Justice in a Southern City.* Athens, GA.: University of Georgia Press, 2012.

International Research Associates. *Access to Public Libraries: A Research Project, Prepared for the Library Administration Division, American Library Association, International Research Associates, Inc.* Chicago: American Library Association, 1963. Accessed July 31, 2015. HathiTrust.

Johnson, Joan Marie. *Southern Ladies, New Women: Race, Region, and Clubwomen in South Carolina, 1890–1930.* Gainesville, FL: The University Press of Florida, 2004.

Jones, Theodore. *Carnegie Libraries Across America: A Public Legacy.* New York: Preservation Press, 1997.

Knott, Cheryl. "The Publication and Reception of *The Southern Negro and the Public Library.*" In *Race, Ethnicity and Publishing in America*, edited by Cécile Cottenet, 51–76. New York: Palgrave Macmillian, 2014.

Kruse, Kevin. *White Flight: Atlanta and the Making of Modern Conservatism.* Princeton: Princeton University Press, 2005.

Link, William A. *The Paradox of Southern Progressivism, 1880–1930.* Chapel Hill: University of North Carolina Press, 1992.

Longenecker, Marjorie, Richard Sprague, and G. Gray Plosser, Jr., eds. *Downtown Birmingham: Architectural and Historical Walking Tour Guide.* Birmingham: Birmingham Historical Society, 1977.

Lovett, Bobby L. *The African-American History of Nashville, Tennessee, 1780–1930: Elites and Dilemmas.* Fayetteville: University of Arkansas Press, 1999.

Martin, Robert Sidney. "Introduction." In *Carnegie Denied: Communities Rejecting Carnegie Library Construction Grants, 1898–1925,* edited by Robert Sidney Martin. Westport, CT: Greenwood Press, 1993.

McPheeters, Annie L. *Library Service in Black and White: Some Personal Recollections, 1921–1980.* Metuchen, NJ: The Scarecrow Press, 1988.

Morgan, Francesca. *Women and Patriotism in Jim Crow America.* Chapel Hill: The University of North Carolina Press, 2005.

Nasaw, David. *Andrew Carnegie.* New York: The Penguin Press, 2006.

Russell, James Michael. *Atlanta, 1847–1890: City Building in the Old South and the New.* Baton Rouge: Louisiana State University Press, 1988.

Shaw, Stephanie J. *What a Woman Ought to Be and to Do: Black Professional Women Workers during the Jim Crow Era.* Chicago: University of Chicago Press, 1996.

Stanford, Edward Barrett. *Library Extension Under the WPA: An Appraisal of an Experiment in Federal Aid.* Chicago: University of Chicago Press, 1944.

Sullivan, Peggy. *Carl H. Milam and the American Library Association.* New York: H. W. Wilson, 1976.

Taylor, Nick. *American-Made: The Enduring Legacy of the WPA: When FDR Put the Nation to Work.* New York: Bantam Books, 2008.

Van Slyck, Abigail. *Free to All: Carnegie Libraries & American Culture, 1890–1920.* Chicago: University of Chicago Press, 1995.

Wiegand, Wayne A. *Part of Our Lives: A People's History of the American Public Library.* New York: Oxford University Press, 2015.

Wiegand, Wayne A. and Shirley A. Wiegand. *The Desegregation of Public Libraries in the Jim Crow South: Civil Rights and Local Activism.* Baton Rouge: Louisiana State University Press, 2018.

Wilson, Louis Round and Mary Milzewski. *Libraries of the Southeast: A Report of the Southeastern States Cooperative Library Survey, 1946–1947.* Chapel Hill: University of North Carolina Press, 1949.

Wilson, William H. *The City Beautiful Movement.* Baltimore: The Johns Hopkins University Press, 1989.

Woods, Jeff. *Black Struggle, Red Scare: Segregation and Anti-Communism in the South, 1948–1968.* Baton Rouge: Louisiana State University Press, 2004.

DISSERTATIONS AND THESES

Adkins, Barbara M. "A History of Public Library Service to Negroes in Atlanta, Georgia." Master's thesis, Atlanta University, 1951.

Anders, Mary Edna. "The Development of Public Library Service in the Southeastern States, 1895–1950." PhD diss., Columbia University, 1958.

Carmichael Jr., James V. "Tommie Dora Barker and Southern Librarianship." PhD diss., Chapel Hill: University of North Carolina, 1987.

Jones, Robbie D. "'What's in a Name?': Tennessee's Carnegie Libraries & Civic Reform in the New South, 1889–1919." Master's thesis, Middle Tennessee State University, 2003.
McCrary, Mary Ellen. "A History of Public Library Service to Negroes in Nashville, Tennessee, 1916–1958." Master's thesis, Atlanta University, 1958.
Mitchell-Powell, Brenda. "A Seat at the Reading Table: The 1939 Alexandria, Virginia, Public Library Sit-in Demonstration—A Study in Library History, 1937–1941." PhD diss., Simmons College, 2015.
Pethel, Mary Ellen. "Athens of the New South: College Life in Nashville, a New South City, 1987–1917." PhD diss., Georgia State University, 2008.

ARTICLES

Anonymous. "Evan P. Howell." *Georgia Historical Quarterly* 1, no. 1 (March 1917): 52–57.
Anonymous. "William Lofland Dudley." *Vanderbilt University Quarterly: A Record of University Life and Work* 14, no. 4 (October–December 1914): 259–287.
Callaham, Betty E. "The Carnegie Library School of Atlanta (1905–25)." *Library Quarterly: Information, Community, Policy* 37, no. 2 (April 1967): 149–179.
Carmichael Jr., James V. "Atlanta's Female Librarians, 1883–1915." *Journal of Library History* 21, no. 2 (Spring 1986): 376–399.
Cha-Jua, Sundiata Keita and Clarence Lang. "The 'Long Movement' as Vampire: Temporal and Spatial Fallacies in Recent Black Freedom Studies." *Journal of African American History* 92, no. 2 (Spring 2007): 265–288.
Corley, Florence Fleming. "Atlanta's Techwood and University Homes Projects: The Nation's Laboratory for Public Housing." *Atlanta History: A Journal of Georgia and the South* 31, no. 4 (Winter 1987–1988): 17–36. Accessed February 14, 2016. http://album.atlantahistorycenter.com:2011/cdm/compoundobject/collection/AH Bull/id/19686/rec/2.
Cresswell, Stephen. "The Last Days of Jim Crow in Southern Libraries." *Libraries and Culture* 31, nos. 3–4 (Summer–Fall 1996): 557–573.
Danton, Emily Miller. "South Does Less Restricting." *Library Journal* 73, no. 13 (July 1948): 990–992.
Dumont, Rosemary Ruhig. "Race in American Librarianship: Attitudes of the Library Profession." *Journal of Library History* 21, no. 3 (Summer 1986): 488–509.
Fultz, Michael. "Black Public Libraries in the South in the Era of De Jure Segregation." *Libraries and the Cultural Record* 41, no. 3 (Summer 2006): 337–359.
Grise, George C. "Samuel Watkins." *Tennessee Historical Quarterly* 6, no. 3 (September 1947): 251–264.
Hall, Jacquelyn Dowd. "The Long Civil Rights Movement and the Political Uses of the Past." *Journal of American History* 91, no. 4 (March 2005): 1233–1263.
Holden, Ann. "The Color Line in Southern Libraries: A Progress Report." *New South* 9, no. 1 (January 1954): 1–4.
Johnson, Kenneth R. "The Early Library Movement in Alabama." *Journal of Library History* 6, no. 2 (April 1971): 120–132.

Lerner, Gerda. "Early Community Work of Black Club Women." *Journal of Negro History* 59, no. 2 (April 1974): 158–167.

Lewis, W. David. "The Emergence of Birmingham as a Case Study of Continuity between the Antebellum Planter Class and the Industrialization in the 'New South.'" *Agricultural History* 68, no 2 (Spring 1994): 62–79.

Malone, Cheryl Knott. "Autonomy and Accommodation: Houston's Colored Carnegie Library, 1907–1922." *Libraries & Culture* 34, no. 2 (Spring 1999): 95–112.

———. "Books for Black Children: Public Library Collections in Louisville and Nashville, 1915–1925." *Library Quarterly: Information, Community, Policy* 70, no. 2 (April 2000):179–200.

———. "Quiet Pioneers: Black Women Public Librarians in the Segregated South." *Vitae Scholasticae* 19, no. 1 (2000): 59–76.

———. "Unannounced and Unexpected: The Desegregation of the Houston Public Library in the Early 1950s." *Library Trends* 55, no. 3 (Winter 2007): 665–674.

Martin, Robert Sidney, and Orvin Lee Shiflett. "Hampton, Fisk, and Atlanta: The Foundations, the American Library Association, and Library Education for Blacks, 1925–1941." *Libraries & Culture* 31, no. 2 (Spring 1996): 299–325.

Mickelson, Peter. "American Society and the Public Library in the Thought of Andrew Carnegie." *Journal of Library History* 10, no. 2 (April 1975): 117–138.

Miller, William T. "Library Service for Negroes in the New South: Birmingham, Alabama, 1871–1918." *Alabama Librarian* 27, no. 1 (November/December 1975): 6–8.

Nosakhere, Akilah S., and Sharon E. Robinson. "Library Service for African Americans in Georgia: A Legacy of Learning and Leadership in Atlanta." *Georgia Library Quarterly* 35, no. 2 (Summer 1998): 9–12.

Passet, Joanne E. "Men in a Feminized Profession: The Male Librarian, 1887–1921." *Libraries & Culture* 28, no. 4 (Fall 1993): 385–402.

Pickens, William. "The American Congo-The Burning of Henry Lowry." *Nation* (March 23, 1921).

Rubinstein, Stanley and Judith Farley. "Enoch Pratt Free Library and Black Patrons: Equality in Library Services, 1882–1915." *Journal of Library History* 15, no. 4 (Fall 1980): 445–453.

Van Slyck, Abigail, A. "The Lady and the Library Loafer: Gender and Public Space in Victorian America." *Winterthur Portfolio* 31, no. 4 (Winter 1996): 221–242.

Watson, Paula D. "Carnegie Ladies, Lady Carnegies: Women and the Building of Libraries." *Libraries & Culture* 31, no. 1 (Winter 1996): 159–196.

REFERENCE WORKS

Baggett, James L. "Birmingham Public Library." *Encyclopedia of Alabama*. May 12, 2011. Accessed December 12, 2015. http://www.encyclopediaofalabama.org/article/h-1406.

Clark, Herbert. "James C. Napier." *Tennessee Encyclopedia of History and Culture*, February 23, 2011. Accessed October 31, 2015. https://tennesseeencyclopedia.net/entry.php?rec=961.

Doyle, Don. "Ben West." *Tennessee Encyclopedia of History and Culture*, January 1, 2010. Accessed November 8, 2015. https://tennesseeencyclopedia.net/entry.php?rec=1492.

Harvey, Paul. "National Baptist Publishing Board." *Tennessee Encyclopedia of History and Culture,* January 1, 2010. Accessed November 2, 2015. https://tennesseeencyclopedia.net/entry.php?rec=980.

Magnus, Perre. "LeMoyne Owen College." *Tennessee Encyclopedia of History and Culture*, February 21, 2011. Accessed March 20, 2016. https://tennesseeencyclopedia.net/entry.php?rec=778.

Manis, Andrew. "Fred Lee Shuttlesworth." *Encyclopedia of Alabama.* August 27, 2014. Accessed December 15, 2015. http://www.encyclopediaofalabama.org/article/h-1093.

Perry, Chuck. "Atlanta-Journal Constitution." *New Georgia Encyclopedia*. August 8, 2013. Accessed October 17, 2015. http://www.georgiaencyclopedia.org/articles/arts-culture/atlanta-journal-constitution.

Sumner, David E. "Nashville Banner." *Tennessee Encyclopedia of History and Culture,* February 23, 2011. Accessed November 1, 2015. https://tennesseeencyclopedia.net/entry.php?rec=965.

Walker, Cornelia. "Watkins Institute." *Tennessee Encyclopedia of History and Culture*, January 1, 2010. Accessed November 1, 2015. https://tennesseeencyclopedia.net/entry.php?rec=1476.

Williams, Kerrie C. "Annie L. McPheeters (1908–1994)." *New Georgia Encyclopedia*. July 23, 2018. Accessed February 3, 2019. https://www.georgiaencyclopedia.org/articles/education/annie-l-mcpheeters-1908–1994.

WEBSITES

American Library Association. "Past Executive Directors & Secretaries." Accessed July 25, 2015. http://www.ala.org/aboutala/history/past-executive-directors.

Atlanta-Fulton Public Library System. "History." Accessed October 20, 2015. http://www.afpls.org/history.

Birmingham Public Library. "History of Birmingham Public Library." Last modified December 29. Accessed December 10, 2015. http://www.bplonline.org/about/history/.

Historic American Buildings Survey. "Masonic Temple (Colored), 1630 Fourth Avenue North, Birmingham, Jefferson County, AL." Library of Congress. Accessed December 13, 2015. http://www.loc.gov/pictures/item/al0969/.

Jefferson County Library Cooperative. "History and Purpose." Last Modified July 2013. Accessed February 29, 2016. http://www.jclc.org/aboutjclc/history.aspx.

Old Chapel Hill Cemetery. "Louis Round Wilson." Accessed July 26, 2015. http://www.ibiblio.org/cemetery/university/wilson.html.

R. H. Boyd Publishing Corporation. "National Baptist Congress." Accessed November 20, 2015. http://www.nationalbaptistcongress.org/.
———. "Our History." Accessed November 20, 2015. http://www.rhboydpublishing.com/content/our-history.asp.
Tennessee Valley Authority. "From the New Deal to a New Century." Accessed August 1, 2015. https://www.tva.com/About-TVA/Our-History.
Winfrey, Oprah. "Oprah on 'The Fire for Reading,'" *Publishers Weekly*, March 10, 2003. Accessed February 6, 2019. https://www.publishersweekly.com/pw/print/20030310/26705-oprah-on-the-fire-for-reading.html.

Index

AAAE. *See* American Association of Adult Education
Access to Public Libraries report, 49
ACHR. *See* Atlanta Council on Human Relations
Acipco. *See* American Cast Iron Pipe Company
ACMHR. *See* Alabama Christian Movement for Human Rights
Adams, G. D., 77–78
Adkins, Barbara M., 61, 66–67
AFPLS. *See* Atlanta-Fulton Public Library System
African American branch libraries, 95, 99, 118–19; circulation within, 71–72; funding for, 97; locations of, 105–6
African American history, 66
African American library access, xi, 26, 37, 46–47, 55–56, 100, 121
African American library development, 37–40, 42–45
African American library education, 45, 51, 63, 99
African American National Baptist Publishing Board, 93
African Americans, ix; BPL and, 117–19; depictions of, xiv; disfranchisement of, 3; educational needs of, 66; employment for, 74; as inferior, 8; in leadership, 99; politeness towards, 88; segregation fought by, 51; voting rights for, 73
airports, 77
ALA. *See* American Library Association
Alabama Christian Movement for Human Rights (ACMHR), 114
Alabama Library Association, 121
Alexandria Public Library (Virginia), xi
Alice Furnaces, 115
All Citizens Registration Committee, 73
Alvarez, Robert S., 100–103, 110n51
American Association of Adult Education (AAAE), 66
American Cast Iron Pipe Company (Acipco), 120
American Library Association (ALA), xviii, 26, 45, 48
Anders, Mary Edna, x, 2; on economic development, 8; on funding, 40–41; on southern public library development, 20, 25–28
Anderson, John H., 123–24
Andrew Jackson Courts housing projects, 99
Anniston Public Library, 74
ANVL. *See* Atlanta Negro Voters League

APL. *See* Atlanta Public Library
Arrington, Richard, 129, 132
Association of American Publishers, 143
Atlanta Commissioner of Administrative Services, 75
Atlanta Compromise, 59
Atlanta Council on Human Relations (ACHR), 68–69
Atlanta Daily World, 65, 69
Atlanta-Fulton Public Library System (AFPLS), 78–79
Atlanta Housing. Authority, 76
Atlanta Journal and Constitution Magazine, 59, 67, 69–70, 76–79
Atlanta Manufacturers Association, 4
Atlanta Negro Voters League (ANVL), 56, 73
Atlanta Public Library (APL), xi, xv, xviii; board of trustees, 61; branches of, 56; Carnegie library construction grant for, 55; changes within, 68; community engagement and, 66–68; desegregation efforts for, 79–80; employment by, 55; founding of, 57; history of, 56; integration of, 48, 139–41; Knott on board of trustees for, 64; leadership role of, 51; library segregation within, 59, 79–80
Atlanta's American Veterans Committee, 69
Atlanta University, 44
Atlanta University Affiliation, 67
Atlanta University Library School, 74–75
Atlanta Urban League, 73
Auburn Avenue Branch Library (Atlanta), 56, 63–66, 99
Augst, Thomas, 21

Baldwin, William H., Jr., 41
Barker, Tommie Dora, xv, 45, 56; advisory committee and, 64; appreciation for, 63; funding sought by, 60–62

Barry, Marian, 110n61
Baskette, Gideon H., 91–93, 108n16
BEL. *See* Board of Education for Librarianship
Belmont University, 5, 91
Ben West Library, 107
Bertram, James, 18, 60–63, 92, 95–97
Bevel, James, xix, 114, 127
Birmingham Board of Public Education, 115
Birmingham Commercial Club, 115
Birmingham Library Association, 115
Birmingham News, 124–25, 130–31
Birmingham Public Library (BPL), xi–xii, xv, 22, 46, *120*; African Americans and, 117–19; bid for new construction, 130–31; early years of, 116–17; end of segregation in, 127; growth of, 113; improvements made to, 124; integration of, 129, 139–41; library construction grants for, 115–16; quality of, 125; segregation in, as complicated, 131–32; student sit-ins at, 49
Blackmon, Charles, 68
Blair, Karen J., xiii–xiv, 16
Blanchard, T. Wayne, 71
Blue, Thomas, 43, 63, 99
Blue Triangle Chapter (Nashville), 99
Board of Education for Librarianship (BEL), 44, 59, 137
Bobinski, George S., xvi–xvii, 20, 25, 34n27; on Carnegie, A., 59; on southern public library development, 22–23
Bogle, Sarah, 43–45
Bontemps, Arna, 100
Booker T. Washington Branch (Birmingham), 119–20, 124, *126*
bookmobiles, 28, 103, *104*, 124
boosterism, 7
boosters, 23
BPL. *See* Birmingham Public Library
Broad River Group, 5–6
Brooks, Hallie, 74–75

Index

Brown, Ludie, 121
Brown, Virginia Pounds, 115
Brown v. Board of Education, xii, xvii, 32, 50, 70, 80, 125
Brown v. Louisiana, 54n45
Buchi Plumbing Company, 102–3
Burge, Flipper, 67

Cahill, Edwin, 70, 73–74, 139
CAP. *See* Central Atlanta Progress
capitalism, 2–3, 22
Carmichael, James V., xviii, 26, 34n40, 60, 64
Carnegie, Andrew, x, xvi–xvii, 1, 33n6, 56; Bobinski on, 59; business manager for, 57; CLN mentioned by, 94; funding by, 60, 87, 92–93, 137–38; racial customs and, 59; role of, 25; wealth of, 10–11, 20
Carnegie Corporation of New York (CCNY), xvii, 15, 18, 59, 138; CLA communication with, 60–61; complaints made to, 117–18; funding from, 97–98; grants from, 33n7, 62–63, 66; role of, 25
Carnegie grants, 18–19, 21; for CLA, 60–62; for public libraries, by number of buildings, 25; for public libraries, by number of communities, 26
Carnegie Libraries: Their History and Impact on American Public Library Development (Bobinski), xvi–xvii
Carnegie Library of Atlanta (CLA), xv, xviii, 57, 69, 81n3; advisory committee for, 63–64; CCNY communication with, 60–61; grants for, 60–62; renaming of, 81n3
Carnegie Library of Nashville (Tennessee), xv, 91–92, 96; funding for, 95
Carnegie Library School of Atlanta (CLSA), 59, 121–22
Carnegie Steel, 17, 33n6
Carr, David, 138
Cary, Alice, 63

CCNY. *See* Carnegie Corporation of New York
Central Atlanta Progress (CAP), 77
Chafe, William H., 88
Cha-Jua, Sundiata Keita, xi, 141
Chapman, Lila May, xv, 116, 121–23, 132
Chattanooga Railroad, 114
child labor, 3
The Children (Halberstam), 87
child workers, 3
Choate, Herbert, 67
citizenship, xiii
City Beautiful Movement, 23–24
Civilities and Civil Rights: Greensboro, North Carolina, and the Black Struggle for Freedom (Chafe), 88
civil rights activists, xi, 32
Civil Rights Movement, xi, xvi, xix, 48–50, 56, 127; books focusing on, 87; center of, 74; leaders of, 140; local levels of, 132
Civil War, ix, 1–2, 5, 16, 58
CLA. *See* Carnegie Library of Atlanta
Clawley, Paul, 86n95
Clemon, U. W., 128
Cleveland, Grover, 58
CLSA. *See* Carnegie Library School of Atlanta
Cobb, Robert L., 49
COFO. *See* Council of Federated Organizations
Cold War, 141
Colored Carnegie Library, Houston, 43
Columbia University, 65
community engagement: APL and, 66–68
Conner, Eugene "Bull," xvi, 127
control and regulation, 9
convict-lease labor, 6, 12n17
corruption, 3, 9
Cotton States and International Exposition, 7–8
Council of Federated Organizations (COFO), 54n49
Cresswell, Stephen, 48

Crisis, 71
Cronon, William, 4–5, 6
Crowell, Thomas Y., 16
culture: education and, 96; immigration, social control and, 21–24
Cunningham, Virginia, 16–17

Daniel, Lois, 100
Danton, Emily Miller, 46, 118, 122–23, 132
Danville Public Library, 47, 74
Darnell, Emma, 75
David Lipscomb University, 5
Davis, Donald G., Jr., 13n30, 25
democracy, xiii
desegregation efforts, x, xviii, 73, 125–26; for APL, 79–80; for NPL, 87–88
The Desegregation of Public Libraries in the Jim Crow South: Civil Rights and Local Activism (Wiegand, W., and Shirley), x
Dinkins, Charles, 102, 104, 110n61
Dixon, V. H., 103–4
Dobbs, John Wesley, 71, 73, 99
Doyle, Don, 5–7
Drew, Addine, 128
DuBois, W. E. B., 60, 67
Dudley, William L., 95
Dunbar, Paul Laurence, 16–17
Durham, Walter T., 12n13
Dye, Nancy S., 10

Eagan, Jacob, 120–21
education, xiv; culture and, 96; funding for, 59; progressivism, race relations and, 88
Edwards, Sandra, 128
Elyton Land Company, 5, 114
Emory University, 59
employment, xiv; by APL, 55; in libraries, 17, 42; race relations and, 55, 76
Engstfeld, Caroline, 116
Enoch Pratt Free Library, 38, 39
Enseley branch (Birmingham), 129
Ewing, Albert G., 104

Eyes on the Prize, 106

Faulkner, W. J., 100
Federal Emergency Housing Corporation, 67
Federation of Women's Clubs, 121
Ferguson, John, 75–76
Fisk University, 2, 5, 43–44, 91
Flagler, Thorne, 67
Ford, W. H., 100
Foreman, Clark, 44
Frankel, Noralee, 10
Freedom Rides, xvi
Freedom Summer, 54n49
Friends of the Library group, 73
funding: for African American branch libraries, 97; Anders on, 40–41; Barker seeking, 60–62; from CCNY, 97–98; for education, 59; for libraries, 31, 76
Futz, Michael, 45

GACHR. *See* Greater Atlanta Council on Human Resources
Gaston, M. L., 124
GEB. *See* General Education Board
gender: Progressive Era and, 10; race relations and, 10; southern public libraries, society and, 16–17
gender boundaries, xv
gender restrictions, 16
General Education Board (GEB), xvii, 40–41, 137–38
General Federation of Women's Clubs, 16
George Peabody University, 5
Georgia Road branch library (Birmingham), 127
Georgia State University, 66
Georgia Tech University, 67
Germany, Jeff, 130
Gleason, Eliza Atkins, xiii, 37, 45, 51
Glustrom, John, 69, 80
Goin' Someplace Special (McKissack), 142–43
Gordon, William, 69, 80

Grady, Henry, 2, 6–7
Graham, Patterson Toby, x, 24, 120–21
Grantham, Dewey W., 8–10
Great Depression, 27, 32, 42
Greater Atlanta Council on Human Resources (GACHR), 70, 73–74
Greenback-Labor Party, 9

Hadley, Marian M., 98–99, 118
Hadley Park branch library, 105
Hadley Park neighborhood, 104–5
Halberstam, David, 87, 94, 105
Hall, Jacquelyn Dowd, xi, 141
Hammond, Horace, Mrs., 124
Hampton Institute, 2, 43–44
Hampton Institute Library School, 44–45, 63
Hanes, Art, 128, 131
Hartsfield, William B., 70–73, 79, 84n70, 139
Harvey, Bruce G., 7–8
Hawkings, W. D., 100
Hayes, Carol H., 124
Hayes, Rutherford B., 1
Hendricks, Elias, 126–27
Hendricks, Lola, 129
Hendricks vs. City of Birmingham, 129
Herd, Mattie, 118–19
Hill, Rowland M., 105
Hofheinz, Roy M., xii
Holden, Ann, 46
Hooker, Mary K., 78–79
Hope, John, 67
Houston, Benjamin, xix, 88, 94, 105, 107, 139
Houston Colored Carnegie Library, 40
Houston Public Library (Texas), xii
Howard, Hunt, 90–91
Howard Library, 90–91
Howard Library Executive Committee, 91–92
Howard University, 2, 43
Howell, Clark, Sr., 67
Howell, Evan P., 59, 93–94
Howland, Max, 58

Howse, Hillary, 97–98
Hunter, Julie, 79
Huntsville Library Association, 35n44

Ideson, Julia, 43
If We Could Change the World: Young People and America's Long Struggle for Racial Equality (de Schweinitz), 142
immigrants, 3, 19, 21
immigration, social control, culture and, 21–24
industrialization, 2–3; influence of, 11; rejecting, 7–8
Ingram Park (Birmingham), 123
International Research Associates, 45, 50
Isaac, E. W. D., 104

Jackson, Irene Dobbs, 70–71, 99
Jackson, Maynard, 65, 70, 76–77
J. C. Napier Courts housing project, 99
Jefferson County Library System, 121, 135n31
Jim Crow era, xv, 65
Jim Crow practices, 3, 138
Johnson, Alvin S., 23
Johnson, Andrew, 1
Johnson, Joan Marie, xiii
Johnson, Mary Hannah, 91–93
Jones, Catherine, 128
Jones, Daisy, 121
Jones, E. Paul, 124
Jones, Robbie D., 97
Jones, Virginia Lacy, 74–75
Josselyn, Lloyd W., 116

Kelley, Walter M., 57–58, 60, 93–94
Keppel, Frederick, 43–44
Key, James L., 62, 67
King, Martin Luther, Jr., xvi, xix, 50; in Birmingham, 127–28; intellectual growth of, 65; "Letter from a Birmingham Jail" by, 114
Kirkland, James H., 22, 91

Knott, Cheryl, ix, xii–xiv, 64
Kruse, Kevin, xviii, 84n70; on national press, 72; on transition of power, 76–77

Lafayette, Bernard, 110n61
Lang, Clarence, xi, 141
leadership: African Americans in, 99; of APL, 51; of Wallace, A., 58; of women, 76–77
League of Women Voters, 68
"Letter from a Birmingham Jail" (King), 114
Lewis, John, xvi, 110n61
Lewis, W. David, 5
librarians, ix, 76; counties sued by, 86n95; economic hardship of, xviii
library management instruction for, 80n1
librarianship, xiv, 10; interest in, 43; women gaining power through, 64
library construction grants, 55, 82n22, 87, 143n3; for BPL, 115–16; for NPL, 92
Library Journal, 61, 122
library maintenance, 18–19
library patrons, 68–73
library segregation, 47, 59, 70–71, 79–80
library services, xv; for African Americans, xi, 26, 37, 46–47, 55–56, 100, 121; application for, 47–48; growth and development of, 60–66; as meager, 62–63; as valued, 68
library staff: integrating, 74–80; pay range for, 75; racial discrimination of, 78–79
library systems, x
Library Work with Negroes Roundtable, 26
light literature, 17
Lincoln, Andrew, 1
Link, William A., ix, 3
Linn-Henley Research Library, 117
Linn Park (Birmingham), 117

Lipscomb University, 91
Lockhart, Ophelia, 100, 103
Long, Don, 130, 132
Looby, Z. Alexander, 110n61
Lost Cause, xiii
Louisville Public Library, 42–43, 63, 118
Louisville Public Library Eastern Colored Branch, 43
Louisville Public Library Western Colored Branch, 43
Louisville Railroad, 114

magazines, 24
Malone, W. N., 115
Marshall, Mae Z., 63
Martin, Robert Sidney, 21
Mason, Ulysses G., 117
Mason-Dixon line, 48
McClain, William, 74
McClure, William, 79
McCrary, Mary Ellen, 91, 101, 105
McKenzie, Fayette Avery, 44
McKissack, Patricia, xix, 142–43
McPheeters, Annie L., xiv–xv, 48, 56, 141; groups organized by, 73; history of, 65–66
Mechanics Institute and Library Association, 89
Medical Department of Central Tennessee College, 91
Meharry Medical College, 5, 105
Meigs High School, 110n46
Memphis Public Library (MPL), 111n72
Memphis State University, 105
Mercantile Library Association, 89
Merrick, John, 20
Mickelson, Peter, 21
Milam, Carl, 42–43, 118
Miles College, 114, 128
Milner, John T., 114
Ministers Alliance, 102
Montgomery Bus Boycott, 106
Moore, Aaron McDuffie, 20
Morehead College, 2

Morgan, Francesca, xiv
Morgan, J. P., 17, 33n6
Morton, J. W., 95
Moss, Otis, 70
MPL. *See* Memphis Public Library
Murchison, Imogene, 129

NAACP. *See* National Association for the Advancement of Colored People
NACWC. *See* National Association of Colored Women's Clubs
Napier, James C., 94–97, 140
Nash, Diane, xvi, 110n61
Nashville Banner, 91, 105, 106
Nashville Electric Service, 103
Nashville Gas Light Company, 90
Nashville Globe, 98
Nashville Library Association, 89–90
Nashville Library Company, 89
Nashville Public Library (NPL), xi, xv, xix; bookmobile by, 103, *104*; establishment of, 90; integration of, 48, 101, 139–41; library construction grants for, 92; reports by, 102; segregation at, 88
Nashville Railroad, 114
The Nashville Way: Racial Etiquette and the Struggle for Social Justice in a Southern City (Houston), xix
National Association for the Advancement of Colored People (NAACP), 44, 47, 60, 102, 110n61; magazine for, 71; national level of, 113–14; segregation fought by, 50
National Association of Colored Women's Clubs (NACWC), 121
National Baptist Publishing Board, 108n23
National Baptist Training Union (NBTU), 104
National Sunday School Publishing Board, 110n61
National Youth Administration, 120
Nature's Metropolis (Cronon), 4–5
NBTU. *See* National Baptist Training Union

Negro Advisory Committee, 124
Negro Board of Trade (Nashville), 98
Negro Branch Library (Nashville), 98–102
Negro History Collection, 66
Negro Women's Voter League, 68, 75
New South Era, 1–2, 4, 6, 22, 122
New South Movement, 87
New South Vision, 7–8
newspapers, 24. *See also specific types*
New York Public Library (NYPL), 66
NPL. *See* Nashville Public Library
Nutting, James R., 60
NYPL. *See* New York Public Library

Oberlin College, 110n61
Office of Education, US, 2
Oliver, Herbert, 129
Origins of the New South (Woodward), 5
Osborne, Bessie, 43

Palmer, Charles Forrest, 67
The Paradox of Southern Progressivism (Link), ix
Parke, Thomas D., 116–19
Part of Our Lives: A People's History of the American Public Library (Wiegand, W.), 48
Peabody College, 91
Pergamon Press, 66
Pethel, Mary Ellen, 5, 10
philanthropy, x, 8–11, 37, 137
Phillips, John Herbert, 115, 117, 119
politics: progressive, 73; race relations, economic development and, 8–9; shifting of power within, 76–77
Pratt Mines, 115
Procter, H. H., 61
professionalization, 26
Progressive Era, ix, 1–2, 92; gender and, 10; refinement in, 142; reform efforts in, 10, 137; shift in attitudes during, 17; social classes in, 21
Progressive Party, 9
progressive reform, 19

progressivism, ix, 79, 88
The Promise of Cultural Institutions (Carr), 138
protests, 127–28
public education, 11, 41
public transportation, 24, 45
Public Works Administration (PWA), 67
public works projects, 22, 29–30
PWA. *See* Public Works Administration

race relations, 51; characterizing, 59; economic development, politics and, 8–9; employment and, 55, 76; gender and, 10; Houston on, 107; managing, 89; modern stance on, 72–73, 88; progressivism, education and, 88
racial discrimination: of banks, 77; of library staff, 78–79; opposition to, 48; restriction and, 88
racial segregation, 20; complications from, 51; consequences of, 57
racism, 3, 49
railroads, 3–4, 5, 114
Read, Florence, 67
reading, 51
reading rooms, 17, 47
Reconstruction, 1–2, 9, 12n13, 90
Red Mountain (Birmingham), 123
respectability, 142
Reynolds, Quintus, 74
A Right to Read: Segregation and Civil Rights in Alabama's Public Libraries (Graham), x
Robert Woodruff Library, 78
Rochelle, Carlton, 76
Rockefeller, John D., Sr., 40–41
Roger Williams University, 5
Rollins, Charlamae Hill, xiv, 16
Rose, Wickliffe, 43
Rosenwald, Julius S., 41
Rosenwald Fund, x–xi, xv, xvii, 40–45, 66, 137
Russell, James Michael, 4, 6, 8

Schwab, Charles, 33n6
de Schweinitz, Rebecca, 142
SCLC. *See* Southern Christian Leadership Conference
sectionalism, 4
segregation: African Americans fighting, 51; ALA stance on, 48; in BPL as complicated, 131–32; end of, in BPL, 127; institutionalizing, ix, xv, 51, 56, 80; moderate, 105–6; NAACP fighting, 50; at NPL, 88; practices in, 100; push for, 32; struggle with, xix. *See also* library segregation
SELA. *See* Southeastern Library Association
Settelmayer, John, 70
Shields, Mitchell. J., 76–77
Shuttlesworth, Fred, xix, 114, 127
Signal Mountain, 34n40
Simons, George I., 67
Sixteenth Street Baptist Church bombing, xvi
slavery, 7–8, 93
slaves, 5–6
Slossfield Community Center (Birmingham), 126–27
Sloss Furnaces, 115
SNCC. *See* Student Nonviolent Coordinating Committee
Sneed, Delia Foracre, 61
social classes, in Progressive Era, 21
social control, 11; immigration, culture and, 21–24; libraries as device for, 19, 21
social efficiency, 9
social justice, 9
Solid Block Woman's Club, 102
Southeastern Library Association (SELA), 26, 30–31, 34n40, 42
Southern Christian Leadership Conference (SCLC), xvi, 49, 113, 132
Southern Ladies, New Women: Race, Region, and Clubwomen in South Carolina (Johnson, J. M.), xiii
southern leaders, 7–8, 23

The Southern Negro and the Public Library (Gleason), xiii
southern public library development, ix, 11, 15; Anders on, 20, 25–28; Bobinski on, 22–23; forefront of, 55; Gleason on, 51; periods of, 25
Southern Regional Council (SRC), 46
Spelman College, 2, 67
Spruce Street Railway Company, 90
SRC. *See* Southern Regional Council
state library associations, 31
stereotypes, racist, 16
Stockell, Will, 89
Stone, Ronald C., Jr., 13n30, 25
Student Nonviolent Coordinating Committee (SNCC), xvi, 50
subscription library model, 89, 115
Supreme Court, US, xii, xvii

Talladega Public Library, 48
Tarbell, Ida, 22
Techwood housing project, 67
Tennessean, 105, 106
Tennessee General Assembly, 89
Tennessee Manufacturing Company, 90
Tennessee State University (TSU), 100
Tennessee Valley Authority (TVA), xvii, 15, 137–38; annual contractual commitments of, *30*; impact of, 27; public works projects by, 29–30
Tennessee Valley Library Council (TVLC), 30
Thornley, Fant, 128
Trevecca College for Christian Workers, 91
Truman, Harry, 102
TSU. *See* Tennessee State University
Tucker, Cynthia, 78
Turner, Mabel Thuston, 115
Tuskegee Institute, 2, 41, 94–95
TVA. *See* Tennessee Valley Authority
TVLC. *See* Tennessee Valley Library Council

UNC. *See* University of North Carolina

Union army, 5
University Homes Branch Library, 67–68, 75–76
University Homes housing project (Atlanta), 66–67
University Homes Tenant Association, 76
University of Chicago, 91
University of North Carolina (UNC), 44
University of Toulouse, 71
University of Washington, 78

Vanderbilt University, 5, 22, 91
Vann, David, 132
Van Slyck, Abigail A., 17–18
vertical integration plan, 47, 74
Victorian era, 17
violence, 74, 79–80
voting act, 50
voting rights, 9, 73

Walden, Austin, 73
Walker, Wyatt, xix, 128
Wallace, Anne, xv, 56, 62; Carnegie, A., and, 57–58; leadership of, 58
Ward, Mary Jamerson, 79
Warren, Robert Penn, 13n30
Washington, Booker T., 41, 58–59, 118
Watkins, Hattie L., 98–99
Watkins, Samuel, 90
Watkins Institute, 90, 107
We Build Together (reading list), xiv
West, Ben, 89, 105
West Hunter Branch Library (Atlanta), 56, 68, 80
White Flight: Atlanta and the Making of Modern Conservatism (Kruse), xviii
white privilege, 56
white supremacy, 88, 99–100
Wiegand, Shirley, x, 45
Wiegand, Wayne, x, 21, 45, 48
Wilson, Louis Round, 26, 35n42, 43–44
Wilson, William H., 23–24
Wilson Library Bulletin, 75–76
Winfrey, Oprah, 143

women: commitment of, 16–17; leadership of, 76–77; power for, gained through librarianship, 64; public sphere entered by, xiii; role of, 15, 137
women's clubs, xiii, 16, 32, 137
Woodward, C. Vann, 5
work relief programs, 27
Works Progress Administration (WPA), xvii, 15, 68, 138; libraries built by, in 1941, 28; sections within, 27–28
World War I, 33n7, 62
World War II, 27, 68
WPA. *See* Works Progress Administration

Yates, Ella Gaines, 76–79
YMCA. *See* Young Men's Christian Association
YMLAA. *See* Young Men's Library Association of Atlanta
Young, Andrew, xix, 127–28
Young, Whitney, 68, 70, 139
Young Men's Christian Association (YMCA), 89
Young Men's Library Association of Atlanta (YMLAA), 57
Young Women's Christian Association (YWCA), 99

Zinn, Howard, 70, 71, 139–40

About the Author

Dallas Hanbury currently works as county archivist at the Montgomery County Archives in Montgomery, Alabama, where he has worked since 2015. He holds a PhD in Public History from Middle Tennessee State University. His research centers on African American history, local government records, and institutional histories.

www.ingramcontent.com/pod-product-compliance
Lightning Source LLC
Chambersburg PA
CBHW061716300426
44115CB00014B/2714